Satire in the Elizabethan Era

This book argues that the satire of the late Elizabethan period goes far beyond generic rhetorical persuasion, but is instead intentionally engaged in a literary mission of transideological "perceptual translation." This reshaping of cultural orthodoxies is interpreted in this study as both authentic and "activistic" in the sense that satire represents a purpose-driven attempt to build a consensual community devoted to genuine socio-cultural change. The book includes explorations of specific ideologically stabilizing satires produced before the Bishops' Ban of 1599, as well as the attempt to return nihilistic English satire to a stabilizing theatrical form during the tumultuous end of the reign of Elizabeth I. Dr. Jones infuses carefully chosen, modern-day examples of satire alongside those of the Elizabethan Era, making it a thoughtful, vigorous read.

William R. Jones is an Associate Professor of English at Murray State University, USA. His scholarly work has been published in *Helios*, *The Huntington Library Quarterly*, and *Literature Compass*. His current project focuses on satire in American musical theater.

Routledge Studies in Renaissance Literature and Culture

For a full list of titles in this series, please visit www.routledge.com.

32 The Renaissance and the Postmodern
   A Study in Comparative Critical Values
   Thomas L. Martin and Duke Pesta

33 Enchantment and Dis-enchantment in Shakespeare and
   Early Modern Drama
   Wonder, the Sacred, and the Supernatural
   Edited by Nandini Das and Nick Davis

34 Twins in Early Modern English Drama and Shakespeare
   Daisy Murray

35 Gender, Speech, and Audience Reception
   in Early Modern England
   Katie Kalpin Smith

36 Women's Prophetic Writings in Seventeenth-Century Britain
   Carme Font

37 Mendacity and the Figure of the Liar in Seventeenth-Century
   French Comedy
   Emilia Wilton-Godberfforde

38 Forms of Hypocrisy in Early Modern England
   Edited by Lucia Nigri

39 John Bunyan's Imaginary Writings in Context
   Nancy Rosenfeld

40 Milton's Italy: Anglo-Italian Literature, Travel, and
   Connections in Seventeenth-Century England
   Catherine Martin

41 Satire in the Elizabethan Era
   An Activistic Art
   William R. Jones

Satire in the Elizabethan Era
An Activistic Art

William R. Jones

NEW YORK AND LONDON

First published 2018
by Routledge
711 Third Avenue, New York, NY 10017

and by Routledge
2 Park Square, Milton Park, Abingdon, Oxon OX14 4RN

Routledge is an imprint of the Taylor & Francis Group, an informa business

© 2018 Taylor & Francis

The right of William R. Jones to be identified as author of this work has been asserted by him in accordance with sections 77 and 78 of the Copyright, Designs and Patents Act 1988.

All rights reserved. No part of this book may be reprinted or reproduced or utilised in any form or by any electronic, mechanical, or other means, now known or hereafter invented, including photocopying and recording, or in any information storage or retrieval system, without permission in writing from the publishers.

Trademark notice: Product or corporate names may be trademarks or registered trademarks, and are used only for identification and explanation without intent to infringe.

Library of Congress Cataloging-in-Publication Data
CIP data has been applied for.

ISBN: 978-1-138-71022-1 (hbk)
ISBN: 978-1-351-18108-2 (ebk)

Typeset in Sabon
by codeMantra

This book is dedicated to Lis, Brynn, Patrick, Mom, Dad, Genie, and Les. I am eternally grateful for your unwavering support, infinite patience, and unconditional love.

"For thy sweet love remembered such wealth brings / That then I scorn to change my state with kings."

Contents

	Acknowledgments	ix
1	Satire, History, and Ideology	1
2	Satire and Empire: The Ideological Encoding of English Renaissance Imitative Satire	35
3	Satire Unleashed: The Rise of Juvenalianism and the Bishops' Ban of 1599	64
4	Anti-Feminist Satire and the Bishops' Ban	96
5	Shakespearean Satire: Redux	127
	Index	161

Acknowledgments

I am extremely grateful to the enormous number of people who have given their wisdom, guidance, support, kindness, and above all, their time to help bring this project to fruition. I am forever in your debt. Thanks also to my family not noted in the Dedication (Lisa, Max, and John, especially).

Thanks to my colleagues, the support staff, and the administration of Murray State University (Go Racers!). Because of Murray State's dedication to faculty research, this project was well supported through teaching assignments, travel funds, release time awards, sabbatical, and an array of research fellowships. Special thanks to the MSU Department of English and Philosophy, the Dean of the College of Humanities and Fine Arts, the Provost's Office, the President's Office, and the Committee on Institutional Studies and Research. I also extend my thanks to the staff at MSU's Waterfield Library.

I have received invaluable assistance from the staff at The Huntington Library (Pasadena, CA), where a great deal of the archival research for this project took place (along with many walks through the gardens). Thanks also to the staff at The British Library for their help and guidance. I also appreciate the professional support I have received from the publishing and editorial staff at Routledge.

I wish to thank the administrators and members of the Shakespeare Association of America. I was fortunate to lead a seminar on "Shakespeare and Modes of Satire" in 2012, and both before and since that time, I have participated in a range of seminars that have proved immeasurably helpful to the development of this book.

I have been fortunate over the years to learn from a group of exceptional scholars and educators from a number of prestigious institutions, and so I send my deep appreciation to all of them. From the University of California, Santa Cruz (Go Banana Slugs!), thanks to Drs. Margo Hendricks, Mary-Kay Gamel, Karen Bassi, Deanna Shemek, Carla Freccero, Jody Greene, and Harry Berger. UCSC also showed great trust in giving an inexperienced graduate student the opportunity and freedom to design and conduct courses on satire as he saw fit, which in hindsight proved very important to this project. Thanks also to

Drs. Roland Greene (Stanford University; Go Trees!), Joan Pong Linton (Indiana University; Go Hoosiers!), and Heather James (University of Southern California; Go Trojans!) for their support and advice over the years.

But most of all, my humblest thanks to Dr. Michael Warren, who for the past twenty years has given me more of his time, knowledge, counsel, guidance, and compassion than any educator should be expected to give. I have benefitted as much from our regular teatime chats as from any course I have taken or any book I have read. Thank you.

Tea soon, Michael?

1 Satire, History, and Ideology

> I like it that jokes can hurt. I like it that [North Korean leader] Kim Jong-un was wounded by a movie. [i.e. *The Interview*, Sony Pictures, 2014] If you're a satirist, that's winning.[1]
> —Bill Maher, Real Time with Bill Maher (HBO)

In 1964, United States Supreme Court Justice Potter Stewart famously remarked that although he was unable to define precisely the distinguishing characteristics of obscenity, "I know it when I see it," and this same intuitive response is often applied to the understanding of satire. At some point during a novel or a film, a play or a television program, a poem or a song, whether comic, tragic, romantic, etc., readers and auditors will be suddenly struck by an awareness that the work in question was merely a ruse, a host fiction employed by a parasite lying within, waiting to leap forth and skewer its unsuspecting victims. What, then, is it, precisely, that sets off the satire alarm bell? A consistent critical perspective and manifest targets are two potential factors that alert us to satire's presence, but when pressed to codify other defining features of 'Satire,' or to identify a specific tipping point that morphs a genre containing satiric elements into *a* Satire proper, readers and scholars often find themselves adrift in a sea of subjective judgments. Because of its antagonistic nature and concomitant need for self-protection, perhaps more than any other artistic genre—a problematic term, because while satire has qualities and antecedents that grant it the vaunted status of genre, it can, and often does, function more like a mode, a form, a tone, an attitude, or as Charles Knight describes it, a "frame of mind" shared between author and reader—satire regularly defies, subverts, and manipulates attempts to impose clarity and uniformity on its farraginous practices.[2] For literary scholars, the end result of such dissimulation is a history of eminently useful formalist, Historicist, Reader Response, and many other approaches to satiric literature that are nonetheless plagued with manifold exceptions, uncomfortable generalities, and interpretive dead ends.

2   Satire, History, and Ideology

Indeed, the chasm between theoretical approaches to satire and the practice of satire remains as broad and deep today as it has ever been, particularly with regard to satiric historicity, or the nature and degree of contact a particular form of satire has with the various material conditions of its historical moment. On the academic side of the expanse, scholars of satire have long acknowledged the need to account for the presence of historical forces in the interpretation of satiric literature, but more often than not, they have subsumed satire's overt historicity beneath the genre's more legitimizing formal features. The ephemeral nature of satire's unapologetic interest in topicality, of representing "particular events," and as a consequence, becoming "inescapably tied to those events but at an uneasy tension with them" (Knight 50), is certainly valuable to scholars. That engagement provides a tantalizing window into, or more precisely, a distorted mirror that reflects (a popular metaphor for the satirist's art) contemporary realities, those "things that men do, their desires, their fears, their rage, their pleasures, their joys, their fumbling around" as Juvenal writes (85–86).[3] However, as fascinating as topical referentiality is, it should come as no surprise that literary exegetes have tended to prefer the "universal" in satire over "dated" representations because an excessive focus on topicality in satiric literature threatens to anchor the work in question too firmly, too materially, in a precise temporal moment whose political and cultural specifics are largely unrecoverable, not to mention risking the devaluation of the aesthetic complexity of the work. It is certainly important for literary scholars to admit, for example, that John Dryden's Absalom and Achitophel represent, at one level, the Duke of Monmouth and the Earl of Shaftesbury, or that Jonathan Swift's King of Lilliput is, again, at one level, a parody of King George I. However, in early-twentieth-century Historicist criticism, such analogical parallels only served to diminish the role of history in the interpretation of satire by presenting such historical components as little more than an intriguing *Roman-à-clef* requiring more biographical than literary fortitude to unlock the 'true' identity of the satirist's target. Once the mask of satiric fictions and other self-protective distancing strategies were successfully removed, the critic's task, with regard to history at least, was deemed complete.

A related danger of an excessive focus on history in satire is the deterministic effect inherent in the Historicist approach, an effect which renders satire as primarily a knee-jerk response to historical change. For example, Oscar Campbell's 1938 Historicist study, *Comicall Satyre and Shakespeare's Troilus and Cressida*, relies on a unidirectional cause-and-effect relationship between historical forces and satire.[4] Campbell posits that the transition to formal verse satire in the 1590s was

> partly the result of conscious imitation of Latin satirists and partly a natural reaction to a changing social world... For in the final

analysis it was the disordered economic structure which stimulated writers of all sorts with zeal to reform the world in which they lived.

(15)

For the Historicist critic, satire is a purely retaliatory form whose shape is dictated by both social determinants and the author's bias with respect to such determinants; satire reacts, never initiates, and to understand the history is to understand the satire. There are echoes here of Juvenal's famous pronouncement that in a vicious, degraded society, "it is difficult *not* to write satire" (30), that the satirist is always responding like a moral watchdog, barking at the newest and greatest threats to society, an image which, to be fair, has some veracity behind it. However, the deterministic perspective renders satire less potent, which is clearly unsatisfactory as it negates the degree of artistic autonomy behind such factors as the choice of target, the timing of the attack, and the best methods for assault. And yet, it is important to remember that those artistically defined targets refer to real historical antecedents that demand, at some level, a historical focus. Thus scholars of satire find themselves in a catch-22: foreground the historicity of satiric literature, and you run the risk of being labeled a bad historian, your work "degenerat[ing] into discussion of an author's moral character and the economic and social conditions of the time," but if you ignore the history, you run the risk of being labeled an insufficiently rigorous scholar.[5]

This predicament was at the heart of the Historicist-formalist binary prevalent in early- to mid-twentieth-century satire scholarship. Dustin Griffin outlines the tendentious relationship between the Old Historicist Chicago School of satiric criticism dominant in the 1930s through the 1950s and the Yale Formalist School that evolved in order to address the Chicago School's perceived shortcomings:[6]

> The Yale formalists of the early 1960s now seem to have insisted too much on satire's transcendence of the particular... The older Chicago historicist claims about "discernible historical particulars," unable to account for a satire as canonical as Gulliver's fourth voyage, now seem based on a narrowly positivist view of historical "facts."
>
> (119)

The most notable early attempt to transcend, as Fredric Bogel describes it, this "preformalist investigation of satire, devoted to unearthing historical targets," was made by Maynard Mack, whose essay advanced rhetoric as the dominant mediating force in satiric exegesis:

> Inquiries into biographical and historical origins, or into effects on audiences and readers, can and should be supplemented, we are

beginning to insist, by a third kind of inquiry treating the work with some strictness as a rhetorical construction: as a "thing made," which, though it reaches backward to an author and forward to an audience, has its artistic integrity in between—in the realm of artifice and artifact.[7]

Mack does not wholly disavow the utility of satire's connection to historical incidents (its role as "artifact"), but his emphasis on "artifice" is intended to raise satire up to the realm of legitimate genre and out of the realm of untidy and unpleasant personal responses to supposed slights whose relevance was lost long ago.

Although satire has been subjected to a great deal of critical sophistication since the formalist period, the majority of critics continue to highlight rhetorical forms and strategies while downplaying history, leading to critical inertia. Robert Phiddian offers a number of reasons for this stagnation: "a simple and economical explanation is that the formalist satire boom of the 1950s and 1960s glutted the market. Theorists could see that satire had been 'done' and could feel no need to add to a mature body of scholarship."[8] Phiddian also argues that in addition to a plethora of formalist analyses, the animosity to authorial intent inherent in the influential literary theories of William Wimsatt and Monroe Beardsley, Jacques Derrida and Paul de Man, and Roland Barthes was particularly damaging to the study of satire because satire relies so heavily on the reader's perception of a "shaping intention" to assault a manifest, recognizable target:

> as satire is a mode or attitude rather than a genre or identifiable set of textual practices, the removal of recourse to arguments about a deliberate intent to persuade an audience (of the beastliness of Domitian's Rome, of Walpole's duplicity, of Thatcherism's brutality, etc.) makes it close to untheorisable.
> (Phiddian 48–9; 51)

A few mid-century theorists swam against the persistent tide of formalist studies represented by such studies as David Worcester's *The Art of Satire* (1940; reissued 1960) and Ronald Paulson's *The Fictions of Satire* (1967), both of which were bent on advancing an autonomous "rhetoric of satire" largely free from what Worcester derides as "historical survey."[9] For example, in 1963, Edward Rosenheim attempted to bring historicity back to the fore by insisting on the veracity of satire's referential imperative:

> All satire is not only an attack; it is an attack upon discernible, historically authentic particulars. The "dupes" or victims of punitive satire are not mere fictions. They, or the objects which they

represent, must be, or have been, plainly existent in the world of reality; they must, that is, possess genuine historical identity.

(Bogel 8)

Similarly, in 1983, R.B. Gill posited satire as akin to temporally specific "occasional literature": "confrontation with historical people in occasional literature enlivens it and gives it a biting edge" (Griffin 119). However, in the decades that followed Gill's work, Formalism continued to hold the high ground. For example, in 2001, Bogel argued for a brand of "intenser formalism" to account for the persistent historical references in satire, while Griffin rejected the utility of such an interpretive system as too prone to relegating "history and the world 'out there' to the formal order of satire" (119). However, Griffin's own work also tends to diminish the importance of historical referentiality in satire by advancing a rhetoric of "inquiry," "provocation," "display," and "play" (39). In addition, while Knight admits that satire "straddles the historical world of experience and the imaginative world of Ideas and insists on the presence of both," he advances his own rhetoric of satire, in this case, a performative one (45).

A number of alternative theoretical approaches to satire stepped outside the historical-formalist binary. Robert Elliott's *The Power of Satire: Magic, Ritual, Art* (1960), for example, provides an indispensable anthropological engagement with satire's origins in ancient magical ceremonies and apotropaic rituals, while Northrop Frye's *Anatomy of Criticism* (1957) posits satire as one of the archetypal pre-generic *mythoi*, specifically, a form of "militant irony" whose "moral norms are relatively clear, and it assumes standards against which the grotesque and absurd are measured" (223). In addition, Leon Guilhamet (1987) offers a compelling analysis of satire's intricate strategies for inhabiting and deforming other, more venerated genres for its own persuasive ends.[10] Such innovative approaches aside, the continued emphasis on the formalist perspective on satire is curious considering the impact of modern and postmodern cultural studies methodologies on the understanding of other literary genres. Hermeneutic systems such as Marxism, Feminism, Queer Theory, Colonial and Post-Colonial Studies, etc. have much to offer to an historically saturated genre like satire. However, instead of benefiting from more multifarious interpretive systems, satiric theory remains largely, as noted by Bogel, in an outdated stasis, "poised guiltily between a formalist analysis that seems incomplete and an historical analysis that seems retrograde and antiliterary" (8).

Despite such academic hand-wringing, striking events on the world stage continue to demonstrate, in no uncertain terms, the primacy of satire's historicity, and the pressing need for more assiduous scholarly attention to satire's most salient defining feature: its purposefully antiliterary synchronic dialogue with its immediate historical and cultural contexts, as well as the sociopolitical effect of that dialogue. In the second decade of the twenty-first century, for example, satire had a very visible presence in many military conflicts, but nowhere more dramatically than in the war-torn Middle East. For example, in 2011, as a response to the increasingly oppressive actions of Syrian president Bashar al-Assad's government, a group of ten Syrian artists known collectively as Masasit Mati began posting a satirical puppet show called "Top Goon: Diaries of a Little Dictator" on the Internet platform *YouTube*. The popular series revolves around "Beeshu," a diminutive finger-puppet parody of the Syrian president, who suffers from both a God-complex and feelings of persecution. Two of the more popular episodes of "Top Goon" parody the American television programs *American Idol* and *Who Wants to Be a Millionaire?*; in "Syrian Idol," Beeshu and other thinly veiled representations of members of the al-Assad regime compete for dominance, and in "Who Wants to Kill a Million?," Beeshu strives to supersede the notorious autocrats Hosni Mubarak of Egypt and Muammar Gaddafi of Libya. A public statement by Jameel, a pseudonym used by Masasit Mati's spokesperson, underlines the link between the defamatory images in the videos and Mati's political agenda: "[al-Assad] is a puppet; you can carry him in your hand, you can break him. You can actually deal with everything that is scary with laughter... It's peaceful, effective protest."[11] Jameel also reports that, thanks to the popularity of the series, Syrians have begun referring to al-Assad as Beeshu, an act which humbles the al-Assad regime's image of unassailable authority.

Other Middle Eastern satiric artists who have sought to diminish state-sanctioned images have not fared so well. In August 2011, the exiled Syrian political cartoonist Ali Ferzat, winner of the Sakharov peace prize, was severely beaten by a group of al-Assad loyalists who shattered his hands. Ferzat was well-known for employing the traditional satiric technique of using typological symbols to represent regnant vices in society, but by 2011, the scope of the regime's brutality motivated Ferzat to mock al-Assad in an identifiable form. One of Ferzat's most effective cartoons depicts, once again, a diminutive and readily recognizable al-Assad flexing his puny arms in front of a gigantic mirror that shows him the powerful image he both holds of himself and hopes to project to the world. When asked why he would take such a risk, Ferzat replied,

> I wanted to show people that they did not need to be scared anymore... I had a responsibility to do what I did. If I am not prepared to take risks, I have no right to call myself an artist. If there is no mission or message to my work, I might as well be a painter and decorator.[12]

Also in 2011, Egyptian satirist Bassem Youssef came to prominence during the early months of the Arab Spring protests after posting amateur videos on *YouTube* criticizing the worst excesses of Hosni Mubarak's government. After Mubarak was ousted in February 2011, Egypt was ruled by the military until June 2012, when Egyptians elected Mohamed Morsi to the presidency, a man with close ties to the Egyptian political organization known as the Muslim Brotherhood. During the post-revolutionary period of relative political openness, Youssef began a television series called *al Bernameg* ("The Show") modeled on the U.S. satirical news program, *The Daily Show*. During Morsi's brief term as president, Youssef's mockeries of the government were generally tolerated, but as Morsi's rule began to waver, *The Show* received increasingly severe accusations of insulting Islam, disrupting public order, and was eventually the subject of a state-sponsored investigation. When Morsi suspended the constitution and assumed all legislative power in November 2012, protestors began to call for Morsi's resignation, and on July 3, 2013, Morsi was removed by forces led by Field Marshal Abdel Fattah el-Sisi. Before being elected president in June 2014, el-Sisi's military forces conducted a violent campaign against pro-Morsi supporters, much to the dismay of many Egyptian civil rights organizations.

Youssef added his voice to the chorus of dissent by mercilessly mocking both the escalating violence and the country's new nationalistic, pro-military fervor. "Fascism in the name of religion will be replaced by fascism in the name of patriotism and national security," Youssef told his audience, and the reaction by the authorities came swiftly thereafter: in November 2013, the Egyptian television channel CBC refused to air an episode of *The Show*, citing the program's use of "phrases and innuendos that may lead to mocking national sentiment or symbols of the Egyptian state." Another public official rationalized the repression of Youssef's show by claiming that the satire "distorts the image of Egypt."[13] In April 2014, Youssef's satellite broadcasting company, MBC-Misr, announced that it would not air *The Show* during the run-up to the election in order to "avoid influencing Egyptian voters' opinion and public opinion."[14]

The tipping point came when Youssef dared to describe el-Sisi's takeover as a "coup" during a broadcast. Suddenly, el-Sisi's carefully cultivated image as the champion of Egyptian democracy, heroically expelling Morsi for his crimes against the constitution, was replaced with an image of the general as just another military-backed strongman, an image that reached over thirty million Egyptian viewers. Soon after, *The Show* was censored via a jammed broadcast signal. On the eve of el-Sisi's installation as president, Youssef decided not to continue to produce *The Show*, citing pressures on his employers from the el-Sisi government, a lawsuit from his original network, and the increased levels of censorship, not to mention fear for his safety and that of his family: "The present climate in Egypt is not suitable for a political satire program," Youssef told a news conference. After fleeing Egypt, Youssef accepted a fellowship at

Harvard's Kennedy School of Government to teach a course insightfully titled, "The Joke Is Mightier than the Sword."

2014–2015 also saw the rise of ISIS (Islamic State in Iraq and Syria), the Islamic militant organization bent on establishing a caliphate in the Middle East. Born out of the policies of the al-Assad government, sectarian tensions between Sunni and Shia factions, U.S. military incursions into Iraq after September 11, 2001, and a host of other factors, ISIS forces quickly came to dominate large portions of Syria and Iraq. Governments, resistance groups, and individuals fought against ISIS forces with conventional weapons, but also, intriguingly, with satire, which was disseminated across a variety of media platforms. Groups from Syria, Iraq, Palestine, and other affected regions created scathing lampoons and deeply parodic anti-ISIS satires intended to expose the hypocrisy of the organization, as well as to offer measures of comfort to a terrified populace. After moving to Jordan to ensure his safety, Iraqi comedian Ahmed Albasheer began hosting *The Albasheer Show*, an Iraqi version of (again) *The Daily Show*, which regularly satirized both ISIS and corrupt government officials in order, according to Albasheer, "to fight them [ISIS] with comedy... I believe that we are hoping to improve the situation in Iraq. The show is changing minds, especially among the youth."[15] The Iraqi government even went so far as to sponsor a television series called *State of Myths*, which mocked ISIS for its indiscriminate violence and simple-minded ideology. In a 2014 interview with National Public Radio, Dr. Marwan Kraidy, a professor of Arab media and politics, described a scene from *State of Myths* in which the leader of ISIS, Abu Bakr al-Baghdadi, emerges triumphant from a tiny bird's egg, after which he kills all of his fighters, and finally, himself. With equal measures of lampoon, parody, invective, irony, and diminution, this satire, according to Kraidy, is driven by specific artistic, political, and social intentions:

> We want our children to be less afraid. And in a way, this is how parody works, right? So you have the original. You have this very scary thing called ISIS. And what you do—you create a funny copy of it. And between the original and the copy, you have a gap, right? People see the two images. And within that gap, what you do is you explore the hypocrisies—the gap between what ISIS claims to be and what it is in fact or what people—the way people perceive it to be.[16]

Even the group's name was subjected to satiric diminution by opponents seeking solace, as the original Arabic version of the English acronym ISIS, when transliterated into English, is "DAESH," an acronym which closely resembles the derogatory Arabic word *Daes* ("one who crushes others underfoot"), which carries tyrannical overtones. As Arabic translator Alice Guthrie writes, "the insult picked up on by DAESH is not just that the name makes them sound little, silly, and powerless, but that it implies they are monsters, and that they are made-up."[17]

Such a purpose-driven artistic strategy is nothing new to the Middle East; Robert Elliott describes the long history of pre-Islamic poet-warriors who employed satire as a means to destroy an enemy's social image:

> The poet's chief function was to compose satire (*hijá*) against the tribal enemy. The satire was like a curse, it was thought always to be fatal… The *hijá* proper, which was extemporized verse, employed humor, ridicule, and sometimes obscenity, and was designed to attack the enemy's honor. The supreme obligation of life in pre-Islamic Arabia was to preserve one's honor unsullied; in attacking honor, therefore, ridicule attacked life itself.
>
> (15–16)

Although satire certainly has never killed anyone literally (although death is certainly a possibility for its practitioners), as the cited examples make clear, satire frequently goes far beyond fictionalized rhetorical persuasion. Satire was, and remains, a weapon, and an interventionist weapon at that. The methods cited above also demonstrate satire's unique capacity for *perceptual translation*; just as the Syrian satirists Ali Ferzat and the Masasit Mati group consider it the "mission" of the satiric art to bring measures of solace by denigrating the image of Bashar al-Assad and his regime, so those fighting against ISIS use the weapon of satire to 'kill' an image or an idea, in this case, the ideology of divinely sanctioned authority fostered by ISIS, by translating it to an alternative, less threatening image in order to change public perceptions, as well as actions. Kraidy discusses this capacity with reference to a Kurdish anti-ISIS music video posted on *YouTube*:

> And what that does—I think the reason that's very important is—so ISIS claims its own definition is heroic. They even claim to be sacred when they start speaking in the name of Islam. And what you do here—what anti-ISIS parodies do is they move the image from the domain of the heroic to the grotesque.

The power of satire to reorient ISIS' image of omnipotence, to change the nature of their ideological narrative through perceptual translation, and to re-render that ideology as false, self-interested, and shameful represents a real threat to powerful figures anxious to bolster a specific image of themselves. The acknowledgment of perceptual translation as a threat is evidenced by censorious authoritarian reactions such as the el-Sisi regime's attempt to silence Youssef in order to 'safeguard' "national sentiment[s] or symbols of the Egyptian state" against 'distortions' of that image, as well the regime's desire to quash dissenting perceptions under the guise of protecting "Egyptian voters' opinion and public opinion."

Any such overview of the dialogue between satire and (relatively) recent Middle East sociopolitics must include the debate over freedom of expression versus blasphemy/cultural insensitivity inherent in the publication of satiric cartoon representations of the Muslim prophet Muhammad. A necessarily reductive timeline will prove useful: in 2005, the Danish newspaper *Jyllands-Posten* published twelve cartoons critical of aspects of Islam. At least in part because some conservative branches of Islam consider representations of Muhammad a breach of prohibitions against idolatry, there was an immediate outcry by Danish Muslims, followed by protests across the Middle East. In early 2006, even as the editors of *Jyllands-Posten* were issuing an apology for the cartoons, newspapers in Germany, Italy, Spain, and most notably, France's satirical magazine *Charlie Hebdo* reprinted the cartoons. The reprints in *Charlie Hebdo* were presented to readers as a clear and uncompromising challenge to the protestors; the magazine's cover featured a cartoon of Muhammad despairing over extremism, stating, "*C'est dur d'être aimé par des cons*" (It's hard to be loved by idiots), and the cartoons themselves were accompanied by a large banner reading "*Pour la liberté d'expression!*" (For freedom of expression!). At nearly the same time, protestors attacked and burned the Danish embassy in Lebanon and the Danish and Norwegian embassies in Damascus, Syria; several people were killed in these incidents. In 2007, Muslim groups sued *Charlie Hebdo* for inciting racial hatred. In 2008, Osama bin Laden, founder of the radical group al-Qaeda, issued a video threatening the European Union over the reprinting of the cartoons, calling their publication part of a new crusade against Muslims. In 2011, the offices of *Charlie Hebdo* were attacked and burned, and the magazine responded with more satirical representations of Muhammad. In 2012, the magazine's website was hacked, another lawsuit was filed, and *Charlie Hebdo* cartoonists responded with biographical illustrations of the life of Muhammad, an act that, although not necessarily satirical, was still considered by some to be provocative, even blasphemous. Finally, in early 2015, armed gunmen attacked the offices of *Charlie Hebdo*, killing twelve people, including the magazine's editorial director, Stéphane Charbonnier.[18]

Although most American newspapers, magazines, and websites refused to reprint the Danish and French cartoons, citing policies concerning the publication of "hate speech or spectacles that offend, provoke or intimidate, or anything that desecrates religious symbols or angers people along religious or ethnic lines,"[19] Trey Parker and Matt Stone, the creators of the American animated television program *South Park*, which aired in the U.S. on Viacom's cable network channel, Comedy Central, created an episode in early 2006 that purposefully featured a cartoon image of Muhammad. Interestingly, *South Park* had already depicted Muhammad in a mid-2001 episode, which attracted little attention at the time. However, in the wake of events such as the *Charlie Hebdo* controversy, the embassy attacks, and an attack by protestors on a U.S. military base in Bagram, Afghanistan, Comedy Central executives forbade Parker and Stone to proceed with the 2006 episode. Ever defiant and hopeful to join the international debate over freedom of expression through satire, Parker and Stone ignored network demands and created a two-part episode in which Muhammad would appear. When the episode aired, instead of seeing an image of Muhammad, viewers saw only a black screen emblazoned with the words, "Comedy Central has refused to broadcast an image of Mohammed on their network." In a late-2006 interview at the National Film and Television School in London, Parker and Stone lamented this act of censorship, while struggling to articulate exactly how to cope with the range of mercurial factors that affect the production of satire, including corporate concerns over economic impacts, issues of personal safety, rapid changes in geopolitics, and the satirists' moral imperative to criticize those who would impinge on America's revered First Amendment free speech rights:

> We could do this [depicting Muhammad] in a smart way that will make a cool point, and when they wouldn't do it, that's when we got really disappointed, way less about Viacom and more about America... no one would have shown that in the United States... But just in the last six months, we've been through a lot.[20]

The "lot" referred to by Stone is other acts of censorship leveled against *South Park* in 2006, including prohibitions against an episode satirizing Catholics, and a threat to remove an episode satirizing Scientology due to concerns over potential litigation. An increase in religious sensitivity, economic and legal concerns, shifts in the political context, ongoing international violence, and a perceived threat to civil rights, all represent quite a minefield for a satirist in 2006 America to navigate. Years later, the 2001 and 2006 episodes were made unavailable on Comedy Central's website and on *Netflix* streaming service, and compilation DVDs contain only the censored versions.

The *South Park* controversies and other incidents described above raise a number of issues that reflect the pressing need to incorporate historical forces within theories of satire with greater sophistication. The fact that a very mildly satirical image of Muhammad produced before the terrorist attacks of September 11, 2001 caused no concern, but after this pivotal date, all images, no matter how vitriolic or benign, were deemed unacceptable by both Muslim protestors and the arbiters of American popular media, demonstrates the actively dialogic and socially engaged nature of satire, as well as the degree to which any analysis of satire must accommodate a range of historical forces, including economics, social norms and values, cultural developments, issues of race, and geopolitics, all of which are inextricably linked. For example, with regard to satirizing Islamic fundamentalism in America in late 2006, while it is certainly reductive to point to a single incident like the 2001 attacks on New York and Washington, D.C. as the sole catalyst for tension between Middle Eastern and American cultures, the event serves as a useful nexus point for scholars of early-twenty-first century satire as it embodies a host of historical factors frequently expressed in ideological terms, namely, the so-called 'Clash of Cultures' that satirists like Parker and Stone were compelled to negotiate.

At the same moment, Muslims around the world (and Muslim Americans in particular) were forced to cope with increasingly oppressive levels of scrutiny and prejudice. In an essay entitled, "Muslims in America, post-9/11," Professor Wahiba Abu-Ras argues that 9/11 traumatized Arab Americans "three-fold... the devastation of the attack itself, the backlash from individuals, and new government policies targeting this population, such as the Patriot Act." Psychological, economic, and political factors post-9/11 on both sides of the supposed cultural binary compelled the arbiters and creators of popular culture to walk an increasingly fine line between sensitivity to the concerns of all American consumers (Muslims included) and a desire for revenue-producing dramatizations of contemporary social conditions.[21] While for the satirists of the time, whose mandate is, as Ruben Quintero argues, both a moral vocation and a concern for the public interest, the problems were particularly keen: how does one engage the major social issues of a hypersensitive society while avoiding the economic, political, legal, or personal consequences of having one's critiques deemed either unpatriotic or racially divisive?[22] Certainly, American satirists could take the defiant approach of Bassem Youssef or Ali Ferzat and place their social mission over possible negative personal and professional consequences, but if they wanted their art to be seen, to be influential and profitable, American satirists had to (and, I would argue, have always had to) accommodate shifts in sociocultural conditions, to alter their satiric purposes to suit, or to defy (to greater and lesser degrees) cultural norms, even as they strove to translate those norms. The self-evident dialogism between satire and its material context makes a more sociologically sensitive critical approach to satire all the more imperative.

Finally, there was a curiously revealing incident in April 2011 involving satire in England, a country that often touts its diversity, cultural openness, and tolerant attitude towards social criticism. As millions watched the pomp and pageantry of the royal wedding of Prince William and Catherine Middleton, one group was denied access to the ceremony: as reported by the British newspaper *The Independent*, Clarence House (Prince William's office) "banned the use of footage of the ceremony in any drama, comedy, satirical, or similar entertainment program or content."[23] A few months later, Helen Lewis Hasteley, writing for London's *New Statesman*, bemoaned the fact that American satirical programs were permitted to use clips of activities in the U.S. Congress in a critical manner, while British satirical media was (and remains), according to a spokesperson from Britain's Channel Four, "prevented by parliamentary rules from broadcasting parliamentary proceedings in a comedic or satirical context." The spokesperson later added the following:

> Guidelines on the use of the pictures are less prescriptive. They do specify that no extracts from parliamentary proceedings may be used in comedy shows or other light entertainment, such as political satire. But broadcasters are allowed to include parliamentary items in magazine programmes containing musical or humourous features, provided the reports are kept separate.[24]

One is left to wonder why "light entertainment, such as political satire," would require such a sweeping act of censorship in a supposedly open and inclusive society. As Dustin Griffin points out, if satire is truly so "light," if it, in fact, "has little power to disturb the political order, then why have governments thought it important to control?" (153). Furthermore, as stated, satire (and satire scholarship) must accommodate many social forces in addition to political pressures: in a 2011 interview with British television comedian and satirist John Oliver, Hasteley suggests that the BBC is "too hemmed in by corporate and public pressure to do satire—as opposed to topical comedy." The difference between the genres, according to Hasteley, is that topical comedy is not driven by what Phiddian terms an intentional rhetorical, or put another way, by an authentically persuasive, social purpose (5); satire, Hasteley asserts, is

> a call to action, highlighting a wrong to be righted. There's a difference between a joke that says, in effect, "Isn't [Conservative Member of Parliament] Eric Pickles fat?" and one that says, "This person is a hypocrite," or "Our political system is broken."[25]

As in historically earlier efforts by British authorities to regulate the media, such as the 1599 ban on satire, the rationale for these acts of censorship is often left unspoken, but its message is deafeningly clear: potentially unflattering representations must be tightly controlled in order to prevent violations in cultural norms, to paraphrase Debora Shuger's ideas on early modern censorship. In other words, apparently the British government's decision to deny content to an increasingly decentralized media was based on a desire to avoid subversive mockery, thus protecting the iconic image of enduring social stability inherent in the hierarchical social structures that empower the governing class.[26]

For English society, which values notions of honor and reputation quite highly, regulation of ideological systems is crucial, both in 2011 and in the Elizabethan era. This desire is quite similar in theory, if not in practice or in degree of severity, to the repressive acts of the el-Sisi government conducted in the name of protecting and stabilizing nationalist ideologies, or the acts of the al-Assad regime undertaken to maintain the state's image of uncontestable dominance, or the acts of ISIS intended to silence those who could potentially undermine their own narrative of manifest destiny through satiric perceptual translation.

The motivation for such acts of censorship and others like it can be argued to be political, moral, or legal, but at its core, satire's most significant threat to systems of authority is ideological. Ideology is at the heart of the conflict between repressive political forces and the purpose-driven art of satire, which is "an *instrument* [my italics] to pinch the pranks of men," as Thomas Drant wrote in 1566, a surgeon's tool that cuts, sometimes neatly, sometimes radically, not just individuals, as the Old Historicist model would have it, but all forms of sanctioned activities that embody the worst aspects of a nation's orthodoxies.[27] However, the satirist does not see him or herself as a butcher; the overarching intention of the scourging satirist is a constructive one, a "public spirit prompting men of genius and virtue, to mend the world," as Jonathan Swift writes.[28] One of the satirists' typical rhetorical poses is to glory in this reformative social mission, proudly distinguishing themselves from 'artists' whose erudition serves only to delude rather than to improve the readership, as the remarks of the banned Elizabethan satirist John Marston make clear: "O what a tricksy learned nicking strain / Is this applauded senseless modern vein!"[29]

The close proximity of satire to its context, and the explicit nature of the satirist's socially reformative artistic mission, invite a comparison between satire and a homologous art form rarely discussed in satire criticism, namely, activist art. To begin, both modes are distinguished by what Nancy Love and Mark Mattern define as a public performative aesthetic:

> Most important, a performative aesthetic construes audiences as participants in artistic experiences and stresses the artist's engagement with a wider community. Unlike formal aesthetics that elevate art, in part, by making it an object of detached observation in designated spaces, a performative aesthetic explores how people enter into artistic experiences. In doing so, it challenges the assumption that art is somehow autonomous and embraces its role in processes of socioeconomic and political change.[30]

Certainly, activists can and do use satire to achieve their ends, but not exclusively, and as such, is it then reasonable to conclude that all satire *ipso facto* is necessarily activist? Perhaps not, and yet the examples of the purpose-driven nature of satiric historicity cited earlier suggest that describing satire not as activist, but as 'activistic' is both reasonable and useful to those seeking to understand the unique complexities of the form.

Although one might deem it excessively meticulous, the distinction between activist and activistic is key. If a Moralist, for example, can be defined as a serious purveyor of moral judgments, then terming someone 'moralistic' suggests an interest in making moral judgments without the same level of commitment. Thus for the activist, social change is produced by direct social intervention, while satire's form of intervention is more representational than tangible, more mediated than immediate. However, like the activist, satirists are activistic in that they are motivated by a genuine desire to use artistic perceptual translations of realistic figures to provoke changes in the way the reader perceives and relates to society.[31] Furthermore, at the core of both forms is a performative aesthetic often manifest through the voice of a disenchanted, disenfranchised cynic who publicly challenges not just the excesses of society, but also the languor of readers who indulge in those excesses, just as Sir Philip Sidney argues in his 1595 work, *The Defence of Poesy*: "Or the Satiric... who sportingly never leaveth till he make a man laugh at folly, and at length ashamed, to laugh at himself, which he cannot avoid without avoiding the folly" (229). In *The Arte of English Poesie* (1589), George Puttenham also links satire's reformative agenda to public performance, arguing that the mode was derived from theatrical sermons performed by primitive poet-priests disguised as Satyrs, whose care for humanity moved them "by good admonitions to reform the evil of their life, and to bring the bad to amendment" (30–31).[32]

Many modern scholars of satire have identified similar performative components in satiric discourse: Alvin Kernan, for example, argues for the utility of translating the messy historical and biographical elements of satire into a comprehensive formalist system akin to the terms of dramatic performance, namely, "scene, character, and plot" (7). Robert Elliott contends that satire originated in the performance of the Greek Phallic Fertility Rituals, in which singers would abuse individuals whose vices threaten public abundance and peace (5). Ronald Paulson posits a host of performative personae through which satirists may dramatize themselves as a separate speaker, thus distancing the authors from their criticisms through meta-satire, or as Elliott terms it, "the satirist satirized" (98). Similarly, Charles Knight posits the performative aspect of both dramatic and poetic verse forms as largely a defensive strategy: "by placing the message in the mouth of a character, the satirist shields himself from both its unpleasantness and from the unpleasant fact that he is writing it, thereby retaining the message without taking responsibility for it" (156). However, as Knight admits, any scholarly attempt to shift responsibility for attack from author to the rhetoric of a fictive mediating performer runs the risk of denying the veracity and relevance of the consciously selected and targeted historical particulars at the heart of the satire:

> If we exculpate the poet by inventing a mediating figure or mask, what prevents us from performing a similar exercise on the satiric target? Although satiric attack is often entertaining, there seems little point in a literary construct (the persona) attacking a fictional victim he has constructed.
>
> (157)

In other words, the performer persona may be a construct, but is simultaneously connected to an author whose animosity for an identifiable target and reformative agenda are real. Thus, at some level, satire reflects an authentic and intentional socio-moral agenda that can never be fully independent of the author.

Despite the dizzying range of techniques intended to obscure direct responsibility for their intentional assaults (irony, dialogue, allegorical personification, parody, humor, sarcasm, hyperbole, diminution, generic housing fictions, etc.), the performances of both activist art and satire are, as argued, purpose-driven, their practitioners responsible for their critiques, and fully invested in the world they criticize. Viewers, auditors, and readers are aware of the fact that a self-appointed moralist has consciously selected a target he or she has rendered both recognizable (at various levels of critical distance depending on the desired accessibility/exclusivity of the attack) and pernicious with the intent to use perceptual translation not merely to persuade the auditor or reader, but to truly degrade the authority of the target as motivation to personal action. In short, the chosen persona may be malleable, but what does not change is the reader's understanding of an intention to attack that is necessarily linked to an authorial choice and a social agenda that is more authentic than philosophical, yet not exclusively one or the other. Gulliver is not Swift, nor is Candide Voltaire, but Gulliver's and Candide's mutual disgust at human arrogance is also Swift's and Voltaire's because they *consciously choose to assault it*, they desire the reader to at least acknowledge it, and thus, both seek to question, revise, and to some degree, undermine the foundations of Enlightenment ideology. Satirists and activists have no need to invent a "fictional victim" in whom they have no investment; their desire to affect some level of social change requires them merely to select the most egregious dissimulators and expose them, as John Dryden makes clear: "the very name of Satire is formidable to those persons who would appear to the world what they are not in themselves" (67). Patricia Spacks agrees, arguing that more than any system or "pattern of plot, scene, or character," satire's defining feature is its activistic intentionality: "satire has traditionally had a public function, and its public orientation remains... [the satirist] creates a kind of emotion which moves us toward the desire to change."[33]

Satire and activist art have much more in common than authentic, reformative public agendas. Both forms also covet their outsider status and their lowly position on the hierarchy of genres (although both forms have become more mainstream of late), which aid their ability to challenge the hierarchy of culture by critiquing established forms from a position of relative obscurity. Furthermore, one of the activist's most potent weapons against orthodox institutions is parody, a technique that the satirist also frequently employs to sharpen the contemporary relevance of the work. In fact, Northrop Frye contends that the satiric structure as a whole is best understood as a parody of the *mythos* of Romance, or "the application of romantic mythical forms to a more realistic content that fits them in unexpected ways" (223); Ronald Paulson and Leon Guilhamet both independently define the satiric structure as parody of established genres, which are then molded to suit the author's social agenda; and Linda Hutcheon describes parody as a process of 'transcontextualization' through which the decoder analyzes the deviation from the norm and acts on the pertinent "counter-expectation" created by the ironic structure.[34]

Beyond the use of parody, both the satirist and the activist also strive to create consensual communities in the public sphere through 'rhetorics of difference' (Bogel 42) that espouse an 'us-versus-them' ideology, or as Knight describes it, that foster a sense of "satiric nationalism" (50). Satirists, like activists, traditionally place themselves, literally and figuratively, at the community's public spaces and enumerate, in recognizable terms, the vices that they see: "Surely I'm allowed to fill a roomy notebook while standing at the crossroads, when an accessary to fraud is carried past on as many as six necks already" (Juvenal 1.63–66). As Swift points out, auditors forced to look into the mirror of their society often rest smugly in their belief that they "do generally discover everyone's face but their own," which helps create the kind of 'enlightened' proponents of change that both the satirist and the activist desire.[35] Similarly, although both art forms can and do remake themselves to suit particular audiences, satire and activist art often project a more populist than esoteric aesthetic in their quest for relevance; with the current multiplicity of media platforms, it is increasingly easy to disseminate a satirically activistic story, song, or image to a massive audience just seconds before or after an event will occur or has occurred.

On the other hand, activist art can be (and should be) distinguished from satire by, among other things, the former's focus on actions that advance the very specific concerns of marginalized communities, while satire can and often does present an entire *lanx satura*, or overflowing dish, of wrongs to be righted, delivered by what Kernan terms the

18   *Satire, History, and Ideology*

"conservative revolutionary" persona, a speaker who calls for social upheaval only in order to return to "the good old ways" (41). However, at their cores, both forms are linked by an antagonistic ideological stance against an unjust aspect(s) of the status quo, delivered by colloquial, even vulgar perceptual revisions: for example, the street artist Banksy's 2015 art exhibit (in Weston super-Mare, U.K.) entitled "Dismaland Bemusement Park," a sprawling parodic version of Disneyland featuring satiric critiques of such contemporary social issues as commercialism, immigration, and media culture, this last issue portrayed most strikingly in the form of Cinderella's carriage overturned in ways reminiscent of the 1997 death of Diana Spencer, the Princess of Wales; or the 2010 *YouTube* video "NiqaBitch Shakes Paris" ("*Niqabitch Secoue Paris*"), in which two women are shown walking the streets dressed in Islamic Niqabs (long black head veils) and (in an ironic juxtaposition) mini-shorts, explaining on their website that their satiric intent was to challenge both the hypocrisy and the constitutionality of the French government's ban on wearing veils in public spaces.[36] Such activistic satiric performances function, as argued by Angelique Haugerud, much like the Shakespearean Fool, showing those in power their 'true' grotesque image, despite the dangers involved, in order to elicit actual moral and social change:

> [contemporary satiric parodists] The Billionaires, Yes Men, Jon Stewart, and Stephen Colbert all hold a mirror up to society. We have seen them use irony and satire to destabilize—to open to scrutiny and critique—conventional political and media narratives. Billionaire Ivan Tital (Ken Mayer) says, "Like Lear's fool jester, we use humor to present otherwise unpalatable, unspeakable ideas in an accessible, digestible way."[37]

Haugerud's argument for the ability of ironic social performances to disrupt the authorities' narratives, or "branding messages," and to "destabilize dominant corporate and discursive frames by exposing contradictory meanings" (191) is just another expression of satire's strategy of image translation performed with the activistic goal of inspiring the public to address the observable and shameful ills referenced in the work.

Yet, Satire's investment in representing recognizable social referents comes with a cost: satires are often dismissed as obscure because their subjects/targets are too 'dated,' including the one's featured in this book, which will no doubt become, in a very short time, peculiar to a specific generation and geography. Furthermore, the temporal specificity of satiric historicity seems to stand in opposition to what is generally accepted as satire's uniquely inclusive chronotopic structure. Although localized in a temporal moment relevant to both satirist and auditor, satire is surprisingly free to manipulate the boundaries of time and location. Yet even if the satiric reference is to an event or person in the distant past or from an unfamiliar culture, if the attack is to be effective, the reader must recognize the ongoing relevance of the target and/or a related contemporary corollary. For example, Juvenal claims contemporary localization, standing at the crossroads of modern Rome, while simultaneously reaching back into the past for examples of vices perpetrated by the dead, many of whom belong to the time of the infamous Roman Emperor Domitian: "Then I'll see what I can get away with saying against the people whose ashes are covered by the Flaminian and the Latin roads" (1.170–171). Juvenal's critiques of Domitian-era excesses, although likely decades old when he wrote them, remain effective because they are either still memorable or because they resonate with the excesses of Juvenal's own time: "Therefore," writes John Dryden, "wheresoever Juvenal mentions Nero, he means Domitian, whom he dares not attack in his own person, but scourges him by proxy" (91).

Similarly, exposing the crimes of the present with an eye towards the past does not preclude the possibility of anticipating the continuation of those same historical particulars in the future. In Bakhtinian terms, this dialogic chronotope is best reflected in the fanciful satires of François Rabelais: the time-space relationship is both "profoundly spatial and concrete," while also "unified in an unmediated way": "life is one, and it is all thoroughly historicized" (*DI* 208–209). Exposing the particular vices of the present creates "unexpected matrices" and "linguistic connections" between the past, present and future, all of which fall under the satirists' intentional purpose to reimagine and reform (*DI* 169).[38]

However, satire's inclusive chronotopic structure does not diminish the primacy of the synchronic element of satiric historicity; in fact, it underlines such primacy. The power of satiric referentiality derives from its comparative connection to the auditor's here-and-now. The past and the future serve as palimpsests through which the satirist can use perceptual translation to call for change in corrupt systems of contemporary authority, and because the call is genuine rather than purely rhetorical, it is also dangerous. As the Roman poet Horace wrote of the origins of satire, when the form existed as a comic tradition that Horace calls "Fescennine license," a verse exchange of "rustic taunts" enjoyed during fertility festivals, the effect was only one of "delightful sport"; however, when the old jests grew cruel, fearlessly biting the "respected houses," the Roman law of the Twelve Tables was enforced, in part, to prohibit such abusive, defamatory songs (*"malo carmine"*; *Epistles* 2.1.144–153).[39] Jesting is delightful play, warmly embraced and easily excused, but satire involves risk, it intends to wound and enjoys doing so, and as such, it is much the more dangerous form. No one is offended by a simple joke or by the tales of Aeneas or Achilles, claims Juvenal, but blaze like Lucilius, the progenitor of Roman verse satire, choose to make war against the powerful and the orthodox, and incur the wrath of those who can recognize their guilt even at a distance: "So turn all this over in your mind before the trumpets sound. Once you've got your helmet on, it's too late for second thoughts about fighting" (Juvenal 1.168–170).

What makes activistic satire worth the risks is the significant effects the art can exert on ideological perception, as demonstrated earlier, effects which Knight argues are the purpose of satire, and which often culminate in real change: "change in behavior may well result from change in perception" (5). To be fair, it would be foolish, for example, to posit that John McCain and his running mate, Sarah Palin, lost the 2008 U.S. presidential election because of the scathing satiric cartoon image of McCain's age, irascibility, and his wife's supposed drug use as depicted on the cover of *Vanity Fair*, nor is it probable that their campaign failed due to Tina Fey's initially devastating lampooning imitations of Palin's political naivety on the American television program, *Saturday Night Live*. On the other hand, such representations have the power to affect public opinion and, potentially, individual actions, by offering an alternative version of the ideological narrative or image sanctioned by those in authority. In fact, a 2008 study by Jody Baumgartner showed that political attacks *do have* a measurable negative effect on voter's perceptions, as well as a concomitant positive effect on political participation.[40]

Perceptual translations will assuredly be labeled as "biased," "propaganda," "libel," and even, in some cases, "treason" by authoritarian social forces under assault, but one must remember that satire is an activistic weapon that is just as available to authorities as it is to iconoclasts; as Hayden White puts it, "Satire can be used—and here I move into the area of ideological implications—for either Conservative or Liberal purposes, depending on whether the object satirized is an established or an emerging social force."[41] Turning to an example from the late Elizabethan period, John Weever's 1601 work, *The Whipping of the Satyre*[42] is an ideologically conservative attack on the poets John Marston, Everard Guilpin, and Ben Jonson, the first two authors having been singled out in the 1599 Bishops' prohibition against the publication of satire and unlicensed histories and plays: "If not, dare you usurp an office then, / Without the license of her majesty / To punish all her Subjects with the pen," rages Weever, "'tis petty treason all" (583–587). Ideology is at the heart of Weever's objections: the banned satirists are both recognizable historical figures, and they symbolize a larger social problem, namely, the transgression of culturally and politically sacrosanct notions of hierarchical class boundaries, the arrogant usurpation of the Queen's role as supreme moral and legal authority, and most importantly, the degradation of the image of national sovereignty that should be held uppermost in the minds of England's subjects:

Or if ye would not for your country's sake,
(Whose love should be the supreme of your breast)

> Yet it behou'd [behooved] a Christian care to take
> Of your own selves as sinful as the rest.
>
> (949–952)

The best way for satire to mend a sinful country, Weever contends, is not to indulge in a style dripping with "poisoned malice," but to adopt a decorous style, the intent of which is to heal with "gentlest speech" (492; 488). But why would Weever set out to destroy the image of satirists already degraded by the Bishops' ban and burn order issued two years earlier? The most compelling answer is to be found in the intentional imperative housed in Weever's work itself, an imperative that guides the ideological agenda at the heart of all satiric discourse, from Weever's time to our own.

Satire, Ideology, and the Intentional Imperative

On the surface, Weever's translation of the image of the Bishops' ban from one of authoritarian repression to a just and holy foiling of an insidious plot against the ideological stability of the English nation is less propagandistic and more an effort to use satire's activistic ability to create a nationalistic consensus, which would certainly be to his social and economic advantage. As Knight argues, a brand of nationalistic satire like Weever's

> looks at a nation from the critical or sympathetic position of a member of that nation… The satirist may exercise a role as the voice of social responsibility, speaking on behalf of a communal consensus and excoriating those who have made themselves enemies of the people.
>
> (52)

Thus Weever presents an image of the banned satirists as traitorous apostates whose political, religious, and artistic crimes must be exposed for the good of England:

> for had ye gone forward with approbation, as ye began with presumption, ye would shortly have proved as mischievous to the inhabitants of England as Tyrone [Irish rebel leader Hugh O'Neill, the Earl of Tyrone] hath been to the frontiers of Ireland.
>
> ("To the Vainglorious" 13–16)

The effect is not merely nationalistic, but also centripetal, a sociolinguistic concept developed by Mikhail Bakhtin: Weever's satiric agenda is to support the centralization of authority in traditional institutions, as opposed to what he sees as the ideologically centrifugal power of

Marston's satiric mode, which disrupts authority in favor of more individualistic, unauthorized perceptions of society: "My soul is vexed," writes Marston, "Who'll cool my rage? Who'll stay my itching fist / But I will plague and torture whom I list" (SV 1.2.9–10). Debora Shuger also notes the centripetal-centrifugal binary in Weever's response to Marston's mode:

> Weever's "Whipping of the Satyre" hinges on the contrast between "those that speak in love and charity" and those who "mock, deride, mis-call, / Revile, scoff, flout, defame and slander" (623–626). By opposing defamation to charity, these passages underscore the theological premises of Tudor-Stuart civility—and of Tudor-Stuart censorship. The legal and cultural rules regulating language cannot be understood apart from the normative model of Christian community they presupposed.
>
> (142)

Central to all effective satire is a direct or implied statement of intent that informs the style and goals of the work. Fortunately, in Weever's case, the author gives a clear statement of intent in order to prevent misinterpretation, a statement which the reader then ascribes, generally correctly, to authorial assent. For Weever, the axiom "*Vis unita fortior*" (Unified strength is stronger) encapsulates his intent to use his satire to diminish the divisive influence of the banned satirists and their mode in favor of strengthening the community based on traditional ideological systems ("Vainglorious"; my trans.; 173).

This kind of antiliterary, purpose-driven structure is what makes satire both unique and troubling to literary scholars. Whereas great art supposedly avoids partiality, satire is an inherently ideological act determined in part by the nature of its target and the purpose of the assault. Satirists align themselves in opposition to something, often an institution or an individual "Adversarius" who speaks on behalf of that institution, and thus ultimately, the *idea(s)* that the Adversarius propagates is the true target of perceptual change, not the individual.[43] So, regardless of the author's 'true feelings,' the fact of an intentional critical stance against an ideology, sanctioned or otherwise, implies an oppositional ideology in the satire, which contributes to the blurring of speaker and author. Furthermore, because the author who chooses to attack an ideology must also accept the very real risk, as Juvenal warns us, of being "set ablaze on that pine torch where men stand" (1.155–156), the decision to attack should be viewed as activistic, that is, as socially engaged, authentically reformative, and ideologically explicit. If the intention to attack is not clear, and if the target is not manifest at some level to at least some particular audience, and if there does not seem to be some ideologically

Satire, History, and Ideology 23

Figure 1.1 Image used with permission of BustedTees.com

activistic purpose driving the intentional attack, then the work cannot be clearly said to be either an effective satire, or a satire at all.

An analysis of a somewhat recent (yet increasingly ephemeral) satirical graphic image may help to clarify some of the contentions made above (see Figure 1.1). Depicted in a nationally specific red, white, and blue color scheme, the figure displays the seemingly oblique phrase "Invisible Obama" over the year "2012," the numbers disrupted in the middle by a drawing of a rather unique stool, and ends with the line, "A Chair We Can Believe In." A "shaping intention" to attack is initially perceived via the potentially derogatory reference to "Invisible [President] Obama," while the incongruous nature of the phrase suggests the possibility of an ironic subtext in need of decoding. The date of "2012" localizes the attack in a particular temporal moment, in this case, a campaign season that decoders will have to struggle more and more to recall with the relentless progression of time, and houses the ironic message within the aesthetic framework of a campaign poster, complete with the eye-catching slogan, "A Chair We Can Believe In." The drawing of the chair revises the original obliquity of "Invisible Obama" through an extratextual reference to a notorious historical event featuring the very chair depicted in the image: in the summer of 2012, organizers for the Republican National Committee invited actor and director Clint Eastwood to speak at the Republican National Convention in support of Mitt Romney's candidacy for president. Unfortunately for the committee members, the speech did not go as planned: Eastwood spoke for nearly seven minutes to an 'invisible' "Mr. Obama" seated in a chair to Eastwood's left, asking and answering questions in a rather bizarre 'dialogue.' Remarkably soon after Eastwood's performance, parodic and satiric versions of the incident began to crop up across a range of media platforms, including the "Invisible Obama" image, which was printed on T-shirts and sold online.

As an inevitably dated piece of activistic satire, the "Invisible Obama" image both succeeds (in part) and fails (overall) due to obscurity in the inextricably linked matters of perceived intent, the nature of the target, and the consequential ideological alignment. As mentioned, there are three essential components of *a* satire proper: a clear intention to criticize, a recognizable target, and a conscious participation in *poesis*, a sense of the work's carefully constructed schema, an aesthetic that helps distinguish the form from polemical ranting.[44] As stated, the surface level cryptic language and image of a chair alert the reader to the potential for irony, and in the process of decoding that irony, the decoder searches for the kind of militant targeting noted by Northrop Frye that will signal the work as a satire. Furthermore, the nature of the decoded target will help to determine the ideological agenda informing the work, and hence the decoder's acceptance of or rejection of that consensual community, depending on their own sociopolitical biases. The author of the Invisible Obama image seems to intend to mock, but the enigmatic nature of the target weakens both the perception of an intention and the resulting ideological effect: is the intent to change the perception of President Obama as so ineffective and inconsequential ("invisible") that he can be reduced to an inanimate object like a chair (a reading that does not rely on excessive ironic decoding), or is the intent to deride the Republicans (a more ironic reading) for foolishly agreeing to align themselves with an actor who believes in the political efficacy of speaking to an invisible figure in an empty chair?

In the absence of more definitive markers of intent, especially the degree of irony intended, the Invisible Obama satire is so ambiguous as to be constrained by the viewer's individual perspective. One could argue that such vagueness of target and ideology might itself be intentional, as it both protects against libel and provides a distinct economic advantage, considering that the image was conceived as a commodity. However, as activistic satire, the image fails to create an appeal to a specific enlightened community of the ideological danger inherent in a particular historical incident, as well as failing to create a clear perceptual translation that could motivate the expulsion of the dysfunctional ideological force.

The kinds of aforementioned difficulties inherent in creating an effective ironic utterance within a satiric attack are described in Linda Hutcheon's *Irony's Edge* as a decidedly "risky business" that, any point, can suffer such breakdowns of communication between ironist and interpreter due to misjudgments of intent, discrepancies produced by differences in discursive communities, and the often confusing "transideological nature" of ironic/satiric discourse.[45] According to Hutcheon, irony, like satire, is a socially determined act that, at its core, focuses on a specific "target," and yet ultimately, the ideological agenda driving the targeted ironic (and satiric) speech act is available to any and all parties: "irony can be provocative when its politics are conservative or authoritarian as easily as when its politics are oppositional and subversive: it depends on who is using/attributing it and at whose expense it is seen to be" (15). What is required to make the ideological alignment of the work clear is agreement on the ironist's intention that results from the extremely complex act of deciphering the markers of verbal, situational, or graphic irony (11).

However, as Hutcheon demonstrates, such social agreement rarely comes easily. The interpreter brings into the interpretive act his or her own set of community-derived biases or "participation framework[s]" that affect whether or not they "get" or "make possible" the intended ironic/satiric statement: "they may not care at all; they may simply misunderstand (i.e. interpret differently) because they are operating within a different discursive context" (95). Interpreters might become confused due to a lack of topical awareness, or misread the irony as direct attack, or create their own ironic reading that the ironist never intended. All of these potential stumbling blocks lie in the path of the Invisible Obama satiric utterance, just as they do for many examples of satire, and such blocks only increase as time passes. However, if the possibility of mis-, re-, or non-interpretation make irony a risky business, such potential miscommunications are much riskier for satire as a potentially slanderous mode that relies on the recognizability of its targets to achieve its activistic goals. For all its distancing, self-protective strategies, satire cannot risk a misinterpretation of its intentional attack; if the purpose and ideological orientation are not clear, the satire fails, the reformative impulse dies, and the rogues prevail.

Directions for the Study of Satire and Their Applicability to the Late Elizabethan Age

As I have attempted to demonstrate, while the study of satire, generally speaking, has seen the polarizing binary between history and rhetoric apparently 'resolved' in favor of the latter to the detriment of the former, the practice of satire demands greater attention to its activistic impulse for ideological change propelled by the interplay between the rhetorical techniques and historical referents that populate its pages. What is required, then, in the study of satire is not a return to Old Historicism, but as Phiddian accurately contends, "we need a theory that crosses disciplinary boundaries to allow an understanding of the wider social and cultural *effects* of satire" (54; my emphasis). Such a multidisciplinary theory should contain four interrelated foci intended to synthesize the overt historicity of satire with the mode's obvious rhetorical complexity without sacrificing either one:

One: acceptance of satiric historicity as authentic (i.e. extra-rhetorical) and activistic, which must include attention to authorial intention and the consequent ideological effects.

26 *Satire, History, and Ideology*

Two: unapologetic sensitivity to the specific conditions of satire's dialogue with its context, as evident in the individual works.

Three: deployment of the sociolinguistic systems proposed by Mikhail Bakhtin—including heteroglossia, menippea, and carnival—in order to better understand how satiric rhetoric supports, augments, and/or mollifies its activistic agenda.

Four: incorporation of neglected cultural studies perspectives pertinent to satire's sociopolitical dialogism, such as Feminism and Marxism, for example.

The necessity of suggestion One has been made evident in the preceding pages. As for suggestion Two, there is much to be gained by examining satire with the kind of sociological consciousness practiced by, as one example, the philosopher Pierre Bourdieu. In the preface to *The Rules of Art*, Bourdieu asks the resistant reader to consider the utility of viewing works of art through a sociological lens, even at the risk of violating the sacrosanct ineffability of the literary aesthetic.[46] The sociologist, Bourdieu claims, in defiance of "literary hagiography," rejects New Criticism's insistence on textual autonomy in favor of the "free associations made possible by a liberated and liberating usage of historical references" in order to uncover "systems of intelligible relations capable of making sense of sentient data" (xviii). The overarching goal, writes Bourdieu, is to integrate the "social world *in which* [not *by which*] it [a work of literature] was produced and which it brings to light" (47; my emphases), a decidedly dialogic rather than deterministic focus well-suited (and generally missing from) the current state of satire criticism, and early modern satire criticism in particular. Some of the mediating influences Bourdieu cites in *The Rules of Art* that affect the way an artist's work negotiates the contextual "field of power" (50) include tangible market forces (bourgeois economics, publication requirements, censorship, etc.) and less tangible sociocultural forces, such as "tastes," "values," and "lifestyle" (49–50), all of which Bourdieu refers to as systems of "structural subordination"; however, with a form as protean as satire, the phrase "dialogic exchange" is more appropriate than "structural subordination" as satire has a long history of developing means to subvert or flout those "forms of domination" whose very purpose is to monitor and suppress the satiric agenda (448–449).

In *The Field of Cultural Production*, Bourdieu expands on what is lost when New Critical formalist principles deny the web of historical influences refracted by a work of art such as satire.[47] Formalism, argues Bourdieu, as an effort to delimit the social conditions visible in a particular work of literature, refuses to acknowledge that it is itself the product of historical forces that have allowed for the idea of autonomous art, which reduces the efficacy of its epistemological system (189).

Alternatively, the goal of a sociological approach is more synthetic, embracing both synchronic and diachronic forces:

> The science of cultural works has as its object the correspondence between two homologous structures, the structure of the works (i.e. of genre, forms and themes) and the structure of the literary field, a field of forces that is unavoidably a field of struggle. The impetus for change in cultural works—language, art, literature, science, etc.—resides in the struggles that take place in the corresponding fields of production. These struggles, whose goal is the preservation or transformation of the established power relationships in the field of production, obviously have as their effect the preservation or transformation of the structure of the field of works, which are the tools and stakes in these struggles.
>
> (183)

As demonstrated earlier, satire, more than any other art form, will inevitably struggle publicly with its fields of production (economic, political, religious, cultural, educational, etc.) as it strives to achieve its transformative ends. However, as seen in the examples from Weever's work, satirists need not necessarily be antagonistic to the dominant field of forces acting upon them; in fact, within a single work, an author might act to preserve some dominant fields by opposing other, less dominant fields, and in openly intertextual works, satirists can haggle over exactly which forces (and their proponents) represent the greatest threats.

This kind of a struggle is readily apparent in late Elizabethan satire, especially in the works of the satirists banned in 1599. To borrow Bourdieu's terms once again, the shared social capital of the banned satirists, especially Marston, Guilpin, Joseph Hall, and Thomas Middleton, resides largely in their common bond as youthful law students in London's Inns of Court, an institution which brings with it degrees of social legitimacy and authority, not to mention a system of well-placed patrons and supporters. The shared cultural capital of the banned satirists also comes through their advanced humanist education and participation in a milieu that supports the production of stylistically innovative and socially engaged cultural forms (e.g. epigrams, dramas, and most importantly, satire). However, the Bishops' ban on satiric production represents an acknowledgment from the dominant political field of an ideological transgression by those whose novel portrayals of current events are too neoteric to be tolerated.

As for suggestion Three, the sociolinguistic theories of Mikhail Bakhtin are the most potentially influential (and the most underutilized) ideas for the study of satire in recent scholarship. Whereas Bourdieu's sociological emphasis provides potential insights into satire's fraught

28 Satire, History, and Ideology

negotiations with the ideological fields of power it actively seeks to reimagine, Bakhtin's sociolinguistic emphasis augments sociology by viewing the art of language itself as a "living utterance" that has "taken meaning and shape in a particular historical moment in a socially specific environment... woven by socio-ideological consciousness around the given object of an utterance" (276). In *The Dialogic Imagination*, Bakhtin opens with the supposition that, "Form and content in discourse are one, once we understand that verbal discourse is a social phenomenon" (259), and as a social phenomenon, language is invested in a struggle between closed, unitary, normative systems that seek to "centralize the verbal-ideological world" and the more realistic forces of dialogic heteroglossia, or multi-voiced intra- and extra-cultural perspectives that naturally tend to open or decentralize verbal-ideologies (270). Historically, the novel, claims Bakhtin, was "shaped by the current of decentralizing, centrifugal forces," as opposed to poetry, and Epic poetry in particular, whose task was a centripetal "cultural, national and political centralization of the verbal-ideological world in the higher official socio-ideological levels"; however, Bakhtin makes an exception for satiric poetry, which he views as a naturally novelized, heteroglossic, and dialogized "low genre" (273; 287).

In "Epic and Novel," Bakhtin elucidates the verbal-ideological schism between monoglossic and monologic Epic poetry and its mirror image, the polyglot "parodic travestying discourse" (63) of the "serio-comical genres," which includes "Roman satire (Lucilius, Horace, Persius, Juvenal), the extensive literature of the 'Symposia' and finally Menippean satire (as a genre) and dialogues of the Lucianic type" (21–22). In serio-comical satires, "contemporary reality serves as their subject" (22), a subject which is brought into a direct, familiar, evolving, and even crude zone of contact with the reader's cultural ethos, as opposed to the valorized, distanced, closed verbal-ideology of Epic:

> The destruction of epic distance and the transferal of the image of an individual from the distanced plane to the zone of contact with the inconclusive events of the present (and consequently of the future) result in a radical restructuring of the image of the individual in the novel—and consequently in all literature... Its first and essential step was the comic familiarization of the image of man. Laughter destroyed epic distance; it began to investigate man freely and familiarly, to turn him inside out, expose the disparity between his surface and his center.
>
> (35)

Ultimately, the purpose of travestying literature, which includes "satyr-drama, improvised comedy, satire, [and] plotless dialogue," is the kind of activistic, corrective re-rendering of sanctioned ideological images seen in the contemporary examples from the Middle East, America, and England cited earlier. Chapter 3 employs Bakhtin's theories as a guide for understanding how the banned satirists disrupted "straightforward genres, languages, styles, voices" with the intent to "force men to experience beneath these categories a different and contradictory reality that is otherwise not captured in them," much to the dismay of Queen Elizabeth's censors (59).

In addition to the influence of heteroglot language on the ideological effect of satiric historicity, other aspects of Bakhtin's theories that are useful to the study of satire (and to this current study) include Carnival, *menippea*, and the intrinsic intentionality of language. In *Rabelais and His World*, Bakhtin expands upon the relative liberty and semantic openness at the heart of parodic, populist Carnival rituals, including Roman Saturnalia and medieval Feast of Fools celebrations, during which society allows "a temporary suspension of the entire official system with all its prohibitions and hierarchical barriers" (89). For a proscribed period, Carnival rituals display an alternative, debased, and debasing (to the point of the Grotesque) perceptual translation of mankind and his world, which is given temporary dominion over sanctioned ideologies, much like the fourth drama of the ancient Greek Satyr Play offered a parodic version of the tragic elements presented in the plays that preceded it (88). The effects of Carnival freedom are of great interest to Shakespeare in *Troilus and Cressida* in particular (see Chapter 5).

In *Problems of Dostoevsky's Poetics*, Bakhtin links this process of carnivalization to a number of serio-comical genres, but especially to menippean satire. Named for the cynic dialogues of the third-century B.C.E. Greek satirist Menippus of Gadara, menippean satire, in Bakhtin's view, is composed of a specific set of characteristics, including a strong comic element, topicality, poly-vocality and poly-tonality, the use of inserted genres, a focus on moral-psychological investigation, scenes of scandal and slum naturalism, and a freedom of plot invention that can include elements of the fantastic, the grotesque, and the otherworldly. This final characteristic is, for Bakhtin, the most important as it helps the menippean genre to function "not as an embodiment of truth, but as a mode for searching after truth, provoking it, and most important, testing it" (114). Often, the sociocultural 'truths' that menippean satire critiques and reshapes are embodied by individuals, whom Bakhtin calls "ideologists," who function not as themselves, but as "the *image of an idea*," as seen, for example, in the dialogues of Socrates (111–112). Thus, the importance of identifying historical particulars in the study of Elizabethan satire lies not in the Old Historicist method of decoding a target's 'true identity,' but in the menippean interest in using individuals to dissect established and emerging ideological conditions, sometimes with the intent to support them, and sometimes with the intent to dismantle them. Anne Lake Prescott argues persuasively that the menippean genre was of great interest to early modern English humanist imitative poets bent on examining ideological certainties, including John Barclay (*The Ship of Fools*), Thomas More (*Utopia*), Erasmus of Rotterdam (*The Praise of Folly*), and Robert Burton (*Anatomy of Melancholy*).[48] So, too, the anti-feminist satires noted in the Bishops' ban display unique menippean characteristics (see Chapter 4).

Finally, to apply Bakhtin's theories requires the acceptance of intentionality in the interpretation of a dialogized form such as satire. Because heteroglossia is a socially determined dialogizing force, it is impossible to "ignore the impulse that reaches out beyond [the words]," an impulse containing its own intentional worldview:

> All words have the "taste" of a profession, a genre, a tendency, a party, a particular work, a particular person, a generation, an age group, the day and hour. Each word tastes of the context and contexts in which it has lived its socially charged life; all words and forms are populated by intentions.
>
> (*DI* 292–293)

Intentionality is part of a "double-voiced discourse" in the sense that it "is *another's speech in another's language*, serving to express authorial intention, but in a refracted way" (324). Weever's odd neologism "Tyroneing," for example, creates an extra-textual link between the banned satirists and the idea of treason against the English state, and thus the refracted authorial intention is an alignment between Weever's satiric ideology and that of Elizabeth's authorities. In the earlier English verse satires of Sir Thomas Wyatt, the invocation of the Roman satirist Horace conveys a similar intention to align Wyatt's satiric ideology with England's aspirations to sovereign authority as descended from the artistic and political grandeur of Augustan Rome (see Chapter 2).

In the chapters that follow, the multivalent dialogic epistemology of satire described above will be applied primarily to the verse satires of the late Elizabethan age, a topic that has been largely neglected since Alvin Kernan's influential study, *The Cankered Muse* (1959). However, whereas Kernan's work is more encyclopedic than the current study in the sheer number of works scrutinized through its formalist lens, this study chooses to focus primarily on the satiric works named in the Bishops' 1599 prohibition, with some latitude given for precursors to the banned satires, as well as those dramatic satires which escaped the Bishops' notice, especially the dramas of Ben Jonson and William Shakespeare. By using the Bishops' act of censorship as a nexus for better understanding how certain satires translated the conventions and orthodoxies of the time, some failing to negotiate the fields of power they sought to reimagine with others succeeding, it is the hope that this purposefully limited analysis may be extended more generally to the manifold examples of satire from the early modern period and beyond.

In addition to applying dialogic and sociological methods to the verse satires noted in the Bishops' ban, the long-overdue perspectives of Feminist and Marxist criticism will be brought to bear on certain examples of satire in the period. As recommended in the fourth suggestion for updates to the epistemology of satire, as a dialogically activistic form of literature, the banned verse works frequently engage with underrepresented and oppressed social groups, women especially, in a variety of ways and with a variety of ideological agendas (few of them empowering), thus making the need for employing a range of cultural studies perspectives all the more vital.

The full range of historical particulars under critique at the end of Elizabeth's reign are without a doubt unrecoverable; however, the current stagnation in the study of English satire requires a liberating effort to explore seriously "the systems of intelligible relations" and ideological associations made possible by the use of those intentional historical references that remain manifest in the satire of the period, even if those references are to less specific aspects of social history, the "tastes" and "values" which the satirists replicate and/or revise. We may never know, for example, the true identity of Marston's "Crispus," who shifts from "Jew, then Turke, then seeming Christian, / Then Atheist, Papist, and straight Puritan… So that some guilt may grease his greedy fist" (*SV* 1.3.153–156), nor should we necessarily try to discover that identity; what is more intriguing is the gesture towards religious counterfeits within London society at the time, as well as the role that the image of rampant religious hypocrisy plays within Marston's overall assault on "the lewdness of Britania," which he warns will be delivered with unabashed ferocity (*SV*, Proemium, 1).

Just as Ali Ferzat did centuries later, Marston and his fellow banned Juvenalians chose to advance the flag of radical iconoclasm despite the obvious dangers, while satirists like Weever chose to sound a prudent retreat. Still, both Weever and Marston, and all the satirists before and after them, had to *choose* exactly how to engage their specific enemy, where they should position themselves among the fields of power, the best weapons for the job, the most appropriate targets to gather in their sights, and exactly what attacking those targets says about both themselves and their relationship to the ideas that their society holds dear.

Notes

1 Maher, Bill. "Real Time with Bill Maher: Self-Censorship vs. Free Speech (HBO)" *YouTube*, uploaded by Real Time, 16 Jan. 2015, www.youtube.com/watch?v=ipu0ifyC-Xc.

2 See Knight, Charles A. *The Literature of Satire*. Cambridge University Press, 2004, p. 1

3 Translations of Juvenal are modified from the Loeb edition of *Juvenal and Persius*. Edited and translated by Susanna Morton Braund, Harvard University Press, 2004.

4 Campbell, Oscar J. *Comicall Satyre and Shakespeare's Troilus and Cressida*. 1938. Huntington Library Publications, 1970.
5 Kernan, Alvin. *The Cankered Muse: Satire of the English Renaissance*. Yale University Press, 1959. See p. 2.
6 See Griffin, Dustin. *Satire: A Critical Reintroduction*. University Press of Kentucky, 1994.
7 Bogel, Fredric V. *The Difference Satire Makes: Rhetoric and Reading from Jonson to Byron*. Cornell University Press, 2001. See p. 5. Mack, Maynard. "The Muse of Satire." *The Yale Review*, vol. 41, no. 1, 1951, pp. 80–92. See p. 82.
8 See Phiddian, Robert. "Satire and the Limits of Literary Theories." *Critical Quarterly*, vol. 55, no. 3, 2013, pp. 44–58. See p. 47.
9 See Paulson, Ronald. *The Fictions of Satire*. The Johns Hopkins Press, 1967. See also Worcester, David. *The Art of Satire*. Russell and Russell, 1960, p. 9.
10 See Elliott, Robert C. *The Power of Satire: Magic, Ritual, Art*. Princeton University Press, 1960; Frye, Northrop. *Anatomy of Criticism: Four Essays*. Princeton University Press, 1957; Guilhamet, Leon. *Satire and the Transformation of Genre*. University of Pennsylvania Press, 1987.
11 Hume, Tim. "Syrian Artists Fight Assad Regime with Satire." *CNN*, uploaded by CNN, 27 Aug. 2012, www.cnn.com/2012/08/27/world/meast/syria-uprising-art-defiance/index.html.
12 Stelfox, Dave. "Ali Ferzat, Cartoonist in Exile." *The Guardian*, uploaded by The Guardian, 19 Aug. 2013, www.theguardian.com/world/2013/aug/19/ali-ferzat-cartoonist-exile-syria.
13 See Kingsley, Patrick. "Egyptian TV Station Suspends Satirist Bassem Youssef's Show." *The Guardian*, uploaded by The Guardian, 1 Nov. 2013, www.theguardian.com/world/2013/nov/02/egyptian-tv-bassem-youssef-cbc-suspends. Also, Kingsley, Patrick. "Egyptian Satirist Bassem Youssef Winds Up TV Show Due to Safety Fears." *The Guardian*, uploaded by The Guardian, 2 June 2014, www.theguardian.com/media/2014/jun/02/bassem-youssef-closes-egyptian-satire-tv-show-over-safety-fears. Quote concerning "distor[ting] the image of Egypt" in documentary, *Tickling Giants* (film viewed at www.ticklinggiants.com on 18 June 2017; time stamp not available).
14 Hofsommer, Molly. "Satirist Bassem Youssef Pulled from Air until after Egyptian Elections." *Human Rights First*, uploaded on 25 April 2014, www.humanrightsfirst.org/blog/satirist-bassem-youssef-pulled-air-until-after-egyptian-elections.
15 "Daily Show in Iraq: Ahmed Albasheer Fights ISIS with Comedy." *YouTube*, uploaded by AJ+, 1 July 2015, www.youtube.com/watch?v=JYYyezKmURw.
16 Kraidy, Arwan. Interview by Audie Cornish. "Anti-ISIS Satire Lampoons Militant Group's Hypocrisy." *NPR: All Things Considered*, uploaded by NPR, 10 Nov. 2014, www.npr.org/2014/11/10/363101475/anti-isis-satire-lampoons-militant-groups-hypocrisy.
17 Guthrie, Alice. "Decoding Daesh: Why Is the New Name for ISIS so Hard to Understand?" *Free Word*, uploaded by The Arts Council England, 19 February 2015, www.freewordcentre.com/explore/daesh-isis-media-alice-guthrie.
18 Foreign Staff. "Prophet Mohammed Cartoons Controversy: Timeline." *The Telegraph*, uploaded by The Telegraph, 4 May 2015, www.telegraph.co.uk/news/worldnews/europe/france/11341599/Prophet-Muhammad-cartoons-controversy-timeline.html.
19 Farhi, Paul. "News Organizations Wrestle with Whether to Publish Charlie Hebdo Cartoons after Attack." *The Washington Post*, uploaded by The

Washington Post, 7 Jan. 2015, www.washingtonpost.com/lifestyle/style/news-organizations-wrestle-with-whether-to-publish-charlie-hebdo-cartoons-after-attack/2015/01/07/841e9c8c-96bc-11e4-8005-1924ede3e54a_story.html?utm_term=.a54d8bda0d8e.
20 "South Park Creators Trey Parker and Matt Stone Discussing the Prophet Mohammed Episode." *YouTube*, uploaded by PolitiscRfun [SIC], 11 Nov. 2010, www.youtube.com/watch?v=_2ix3mIvBlA. See also Mallory Simon and Manav Tanneeru. "Security Brief: Radical Islamic Website Takes on 'South Park.'" *CNN*, CNN Blog posting, 19 April 2010, http://news.blogs.cnn.com/2010/04/19/security-brief-radical-islamic-web-site-takes-on-south-park/.
21 See Clay, Rebecca A. "Muslims in America, post 9/11." *American Psychological Association Online Journal*, vol. 42, no. 8, 2011, www.apa.org/monitor/2011/09/muslims.aspx. For another interesting perspective on this issue, see Pless, Deborah. "From *24* to *Homeland*: The Shift in America's Perception of Terrorism." *Representing 9/11: Trauma, Ideology, and Nationalism in Literature, Film, and Television*, edited by Paul Petrovic, Rowan and Littlefield, 2015. See pp. 119–129.
22 Quintero, Ruben. "Introduction." *A Companion to Satire: Ancient and Modern*, edited by Ruben Quintero, Blackwell Publishing, 2007. See p. 3.
23 Malkin, Bonnie. "Royal Wedding: Clarence House Blocks Satirical Coverage by Australian Comedians." *The Telegraph*, uploaded by The Telegraph, 28 April, 2011, www.telegraph.co.uk/news/uknews/royal-wedding/8479247/Royal-wedding-Clarence-House-blocks-satirical-coverage-by-Australian-comedians.html.
24 Hasteley, Helen Lewis. "Why Our Parliament Is Literally beyond Satire." *New Statesman*, uploaded by New Statesman Blog post, 27 July 2011, www.newstatesman.com/blogs/helen-lewis-hasteley/2011/07/commons-shows-stewart.
25 Hasteley, Helen Lewis. "How Healthy Is British Satire?" *New Statesman*, uploaded by New Statesman Blog post, 21 July 2011, www.newstatesman.com/blogs/helen-lewis-hasteley/2011/07/john-oliver-daily-satire.
26 I am deeply indebted to Professor Michael Warren for this phrasing. See also Shuger, Debora. *Censorship and Cultural Sensibility: The Regulation of Language in Tudor-Stuart England*. The University of Pennsylvania Press, 2013.
27 Drant, Thomas. *Horace: His Arte of Poetrie, Pistles, and Satyrs Englyshed*. Edited by Peter Medine, New Scholars' Facsimiles and Reprints, 1972.
28 Swift, Jonathan. "A Vindication of Mr. Gay and *The Beggar's Opera*." *The Intelligencer III. The Prose Works of Jonathan Swift*, vol. 9, edited by Temple Scott, George Bell and Sons, 1902. EBook, archive.org/details/proseworksjonat00jacogoog. See p. 318.
29 Marston, John. "The Scourge of Villanie." *The Poems of John Marston*, edited by Arnold Davenport, Liverpool University Press, 1961. See poem 9, lines 44–45.
30 Love, Nancy S. and Mattern, Mark. *Doing Democracy: Activist Art and Cultural Politics*. State University of New Your Press, 2013. Ebook uploaded by Project Muse, muse.jhu.edu/book/27401, p. 7.
31 I am (again) indebted to Professor Michael Warren for his invaluable assistance in clarifying the term "activistic."
32 See Sidney, Sir Philip. *Sir Philip Sidney*. Edited by Katherine Duncan-Jones, Oxford University Press, 1989. Puttenham, George. *The Arte of English Poesie*. Edited by Gladys D. Willcock and Alice Walker, Cambridge University

Press, 1936. See also editor Peter Medine's introduction to Casaubon, Isaac. *De Satyrica Graecorum Poesi & Romanorum Satira (1605)*. Scholars' Facsimile and Reprints, 1973.
33 See Dryden, John. "A Discourse Concerning the Original and Progress of Satire" (1693). *Essays of John Dryden*, edited by W. P. Ker, Oxford University Press, 1900. Print. See also Spacks, Patricia. "Some Reflections on Satire." *Satire: Modern Essays in Criticism*, edited by Ronald Paulson, Prentice Hall, 1971, p. 363.
34 Hutcheon, Linda. *A Theory of Parody: The Teachings of Twentieth-Century Art Forms*. University of Illinois Press, 1985. See p. 35.
35 Swift, Jonathan. "Preface of the Author to the Battel Fought Last Friday between the Ancient and Modern Books in St. James's Library." *The Writings of Jonathan Swift*, edited by Robert Greenberg and William Piper, W. W. Norton and Company, 1973. See p. 375.
36 Moors, Annelies. "NiqaBitch and Princess Hijab: Niqab Activism, Satire and Street Art." *Feminist Review*, no. 98, 2011, pp. 128–135. JSTOR, www.jstor.org/stable/41288864. See p. 129.
37 Haugerud, Angelique. *No Billionaire Left Behind: Satirical Activism in America*. Stanford University Press, 2013, p. 189.
38 See Mikhail M. Bakhtin's following works: *The Dialogic Imagination: Four Essays*. Edited by Michael Holquist, Translated by Caryl Emerson and Michael Holquist, University of Texas Press, 1981; *Problems of Dostoevsky's Poetics*. Edited and Translated by Caryl Emerson, University of Minnesota Press, 1984; *Rabelais and His World*. Translated by Helene Iswolsky, Indiana University Press, 1984. The works will be cited in text as *DI*, *PD*, and *RW*, respectively.
39 Quotations from Horace are adapted from the translation by H. R. Fairclough in the Loeb edition of *Horace: Satires, Epistles, Ars Poetica*. Harvard University Press, 1926.
40 Baumgartner, Jody C. "Polls and Elections: Editorial Cartoons 2.0: The Effects of Digital Political Satire on Presidential Candidate Evaluations." *Presidential Studies Quarterly*, vol. 38, no. 4, 2008, pp. 735–758. JSTOR, www.jstor.org/stable/41219713.
41 White, Hayden. *Metahistory: The Historical Imagination in Nineteenth-Century Europe*. The Johns Hopkins University Press, 1973. See p. 67.
42 See Weever, John. *The Whipping of the Satyre*. *The Whipper Pamphlets*. Edited by Arnold Davenport, University Press of Liverpool, 1951.
43 Randolph, Mary Claire. "The Structural Design of the Formal Verse Satire." *Philological Quarterly*, vol. 21, no. 4, 1942, pp. 368–384.
44 See Jones, William R. "'People Have to Watch What They Say': What Horace, Juvenal, and 9/11 Can Tell Us about Satire and History." *Helios*, vol. 36, no. 1, 2009, pp. 27–53. See p. 30.
45 Hutcheon, Linda. *Irony's Edge: The Theory and Politics of Irony*. Routledge, 1994, p. 9.
46 Bourdieu, Pierre. *The Rules of Art: Genesis and Structure of the Literary Field*. Stanford University Press, 1996.
47 Bourdieu, Pierre. *The Field of Cultural Production: Essays on Art and Literature*. Edited by Randal Johnson, Columbia University Press, 1993.
48 Prescott, Anne Lake. "Menippean Donne." *The Oxford Handbook of John Donne*, edited by Jeanne Shami et al., Oxford University Press, 2011. See pp. 158–179.

2 Satire and Empire
The Ideological Encoding of English Renaissance Imitative Satire

As Dante the errant pilgrim is led into Limbo in Canto IV of the *Inferno*, he encounters an anomalous region of fiery light capable of overcoming the eternal "hemisphere of darkness" that surrounds it (68–69). Dante asks his guide, the Roman poet Virgil, to identify the group of "honorable people" (72) whose obvious merits have granted them this small amount of comfort unavailable to the other damned souls; their venerated names ("*nominanza*") on Earth, Virgil informs him, has moved heaven to offer them a measure of solace, although salvation remains out of their reach, leaving the group "neither sad nor joyful" (76–84).[1] The term "*nominanza*" (named-ness) is an example of Bakhtinian socially charged intentionality, implying that the historical names of these virtuous pagans have evolved over time into desirable titles of honor, and the relative grace afforded to their revered spirits speaks to the salutary function of these ancients in the Pilgrim's contemporary world.

The "four great shades" (83) approach Virgil and the pilgrim, forming a "beautiful school" of privileged authors and their texts, with Dante and the *Commedia* as the newest members. Virgil then introduces the rest of the company: "He is Homer, sovereign poet; next is Horace the satirist ("*Orazio satiro*"); Ovid is the third, and finally Lucan" (88–90). It should come as little surprise that the authors of such epics as *The Illiad* and *The Odyssey*, *The Aeneid*, *The Metamorphoses*, and *The Pharsalia*, works of high esteem in western culture, would receive a special dispensation from the torments of Hell; in fact, their exemption underlines Dante's acceptance of the hermeneutic congruity between aspects of 'pagan' and Christian ideologies, with imperial Rome as a privileged nexus: "Their [the epics'] truth status means that the Latin epic poems can be read as directly linked to, and significant for, Christian salvation history, as *scriptura paganorum*."[2] What *is* seemingly anomalous is the moral equivalence of satire and epic in the Limbo of the Virtuous Pagans.

Just as the word "*nominanza*" carries with it an intentionality connoting highly sanctioned levels of social and cultural capital, the word "*satiro*," in Dante's case, embodies a surprisingly positive ideological valence and refracted centripetal intentionality. Whereas Robert Durling (1996) translates "*Orazio satiro*" literally as "Horace, the satirist," as does Allen Mandelbaum (1980), John Sinclair (1939) proffers the phrase "Horace, the moralist" as the more appropriate translation, as does Edward Moore (1896); the difference need not be troubling. By the time the historical figure of Horace reached Dante in the early fourteenth century, Horace had been thoroughly appropriated as a proto-Christian moralist, and his satires encoded as tools intended to produce a "*politicum hominem*" (man of the state)—*politicus* implying both prudent civility and the responsibilities of productive citizenship—through the effective dialogue of controlled poetics, a socially centripetal agenda, and an ideology buttressed by strong imperial associations. Thus the characterization of Horace as "*satiro*" (the moral satirist) is no mere "intertextual allusion"; it signals Dante's advancement of Horace, and Horatianist satire in particular, as poetically and ideologically equivalent to the more venerated literary traditions.[3]

Suzanne Reynolds' work on the sources and implications of "*Orazio satiro*" supports the implications of the phrase as not merely a synthesis between the Christian and classical worlds, but a purpose-driven intention to combine evolving conceptions of satiric poetry with positive moral values and a program of social image stabilization.[4] Dante's phrase, argues Reynolds, creates "a model of literature that is primarily functional," in other words, a model of satiric poetics driven by centripetal moral and political agendas (138). Angela Wheeler agrees that despite some anxiety from early Christian thinkers, such as St. Jerome, concerning the wisdom of employing pagan authors within a Christian context, the appropriated and adulterated poetics of Horace, hereafter termed "Horatianism," provided the early modern period with socially beneficial "precepts, *sententiae*, and pungent phrases" that harmonized with centralizing socioreligious agendas.[5] Thus Dante's entire "beautiful school" is unified not just by their proto-Christian *ethoi*, but by their ability to legitimize Italy's imperial past, its contentious present, and aspiring future.

On the surface, satire's activistic power to invoke and translate the recognizable historical particulars of the auditors' lives for the author's particular purposes would seem to be at odds with the closed and distanced structure of classical epics such as *The Illiad* and *The Aeneid*. As mentioned in Chapter 1, Mikhail Bakhtin characterizes the epic genre as it came to Dante as a highly valorized, self-sufficient, monoglossic, and monologic construct constituted by three essential features that are counterpoised to the novelistic nature of satire: an "absolute past" as subject, a "national tradition" as source, and a separation between the epic world and contemporary reality (*EN* 13). While point three in particular makes the presence of an historicized genre like satire among high epics seem aberrant, Dante clearly recognizes Horatianism's ability to represent a morally and politically complete and valorized national tradition as its primary, and most valuable, characteristic (one consonant with epic), and his comic, often indirect, engagements with contemporary particulars as secondary, which helps to explain Horace's own resistance to declaring his works as "satires."[6]

As Thomas Habinek argues, wittingly or not, Horace's nationalistic mode provided Dante's era and others with "a blueprint for an imperial literature" that justifies—or "whitewashes," in Ellen Oliensis' view—the inception of the empire by claiming its ascendency as a form of divine providence that will extend into the future.[7] Similarly, Heather James invokes the practice of synthesizing Rome's political past with contemporary political aspirations as the *"translatio imperii"* (translation of empire), an ideological project whereby privileged literary models of "poetic and nationalistic ambition" (8), particularly Virgil, Ovid, and Horace, are used to facilitate the "transfer of authority from Troy, to imperial Rome, and eventually, to London (Troynovant [New Troy])."[8] Satire, in short, was demarcated as both a legitimate and a legitimizing cultural force.

Is it correct, then, to deride Horatianism as mere imperial propaganda, and to deride Horace himself as a "naturally servile" apologist for the imperial project of his patron Maecenas and the emperor, as John Dryden claims? (87) Kirk Freudenburg and Ellen Oliensis, respectively, have cast reasonable doubt on the long-standing depiction of Horace as a sycophantic mouthpiece for the Empire, Augustus's "well-mannered court-slave," as Dryden depicts him,[9] and yet, the rapid assimilation of horatian satire into the humanist ethos of the late Middle Ages and the Renaissance suggests that scholars, poetic imitators, and authorities recognized the inherent benefits of what William Anderson terms the "constructive, humane" ideology of horatian poetics, the "sweet and useful" (*"utile dulci"*) poetics of public life whose centralizing intentionality harmonizes with the established sociopolitical fields.[10] Charles Martindale describes this recognition as such:

> Horace's skillful accommodation of himself to the existing order (though, in his case, used to support a "revolutionary" leader) is usually seen as a "conservative" stance, and certainly has been popular with writers who would see themselves as having a conservative disposition.
>
> (21)

In essence, poets and scholars of the Middle Ages and the early Renaissance appropriated Horace as a highly privileged satiric model effectively closed to all interpretations but the unitary imperialistic ideology.[11]

Horatianism, thus described, came to the Elizabethan era as a fully developed and sanctioned mode of satire with clearly defined poetic and political parameters that were both acceptable to authorities and conformable to what Alvin Kernan calls the preexisting "native strain" of medieval English satire that tended to target the social and religious events of its time to ensure "the fundamental ideals of Christianity and the stable, hierarchical social structure which we think of as characteristic of the Middle Ages" (Kernan 41–42). That is not to say that the entirety of English satire before the age of Elizabeth was rigidly conservative; however, those early modern English verse satirists who chose to imitate Horace (or modes like it), poets like Sir Thomas Wyatt, Thomas Drant, Joseph Hall, and John Weever, were signaling a specific intentionality and corresponding ideological alignment, even when their satires lacked direct statements of intention. Horatianism itself implied a commitment to the purpose of "satiric nationalism,"[12] that is, a conscious desire to reimagine or to translate those historical particulars that would impede or destabilize the socially centripetal ideology of the *translatio imperii* so useful to the governing classes. In essence, Horatianism was a politically indispensable constituent of what Richard Helgerson describes as "the whole cultural system by which [England's] own identity and their own consciousness was constituted" (3), a cultural product buoyed by (among other things) a history of critical commentaries on classical sources, educational treatises, and poetic theories and imitations.

As part of a centuries-old tradition, English Horatianism held an exalted place in that part of the literary field dedicated to consolidating and reinforcing England's "corporate identity" (5), as Claire McEachern aptly describes it, which no doubt rendered the antagonistic counter-discourse of radical Juvenalianism that arose in the late 1590s all the more shocking and politically intolerable.[13] In the politically contentious aftermath of the Bishops' ban (1599), the desire to reinvigorate those cultural products devoted to supporting the image of an exceptional and unified body politic was even more crucial. Earlier in the century, foundational English imitators such as Wyatt and Drant were drawn by Horatianism's cultural capital as the best choice for creating their own national poetic tradition. These satirists strove to produce the kinds of continentally inspired cultural materials that would contribute to the idea of English sovereign nationhood, while also using those same materials as a justification for a break with older systems of authority, just as Henry VIII had done politically with the Act in Restraint of Appeals (1533), which declared England an "Empire" based on "diverse sundry old authentic histories and chronicles."[14] "In claiming control over the temporal affairs of the realm," McEachern writes, "the crown sought to appropriate the local power of the papacy... [the Act of Appeals] is an announcement based as much in a competitive, mimetic resemblance to foreign authority as in a rejection of it" (1–2).

Bruce McLeod calls this new ideology of English corporate identity in the early-sixteenth-century "Imperial Britain," which McLeod likens to a culturally based "informing spirit" that legitimizes the emerging national identity of England by assimilating narratives of an imperial past, and Horatianism was just this kind of informing spirit.[15] McEachern, too, argues that what animates English producers of culture such as Wyatt, Drant, Spenser, Hall, and others are appropriated images of "union... a similar syncretism on the part of a specific ideological configuration in late Elizabethan England" that validates the integrity of the English corporate body politic through and against external systems of authority (4). Indeed, the ideology of English imperial syncretism is often reflected in bodily terms, or more specifically, as a legitimate masculine force under threat from a feminized or feminizing external force. In post-Reformation England, this external corrupting power is often an allegorized expression of anti-Catholic anxieties, as in, for example, the satiric figure of the Amazon queen Radigund in Book Five of Edmund Spenser's *The Faerie Queene* and, to some degree, within the satires of Wyatt and Drant.[16]

Certainly, there were Tudor-era satires that ran counter to the tradition of politically centripetal Horatianism; however, it was not until the Juvenalian vogue of the late sixteenth century that one sees the clearest indications in the texts (and in the sociopolitical reactions to them) that a transgression against the privileged satiric tradition had occurred. The Juvenalians' rejection of Horatianism, coupled with their advancement of a new satiric style with new targets, a new form of perceptual translation, and a correspondingly new ideological alignment, was marked as intolerable by Elizabeth's arbiters of culture, or in other words, as antithetical to the stable conveyance of the image of Imperial Britain.[17]

Horace in the Fields of Power

The apotheosis of Horatianism may be best understood, in terms outlined in Pierre Bourdieu's *The Field of Cultural Production*, as the product of a nearly unanimous ratification of a subcategory in the literary field deemed congruent with the concerns of the dominant fields of power. For Bourdieu, a "field" is defined as "an autonomous universe endowed with specific principles of evaluation of practices and works."[18] The literary field thus develops its own evaluative methodology and rankings, which then, like all forms of cultural production, must negotiate a unique position for its preferred forms among the more dominant social fields of power (demographic, political, economic, religious, etc.). This negotiation is not an abstraction; in Bourdieu's formulation, this positioning is indicative of a very real struggle in which artists strive for capital within both their own field and within a multi-dimensional sociopolitical power structure that exerts an influence on the art, a dialectical struggle which is "refracted" in the literary products themselves (163–164). Consequently, the estimation of authorial and textual cultural capital is both internally and externally determined, and both should be considered when interpreting a work of literature; however, in the case of satire, accounting for the external influences is particularly important because so much of what defines satire is the nature of its critical engagements, or in Bourdieu's terms, its "relationships," with those very influences (165–166).

Therefore, to speak of Horatianism's high cultural capital in the medieval and early modern periods is to speak of a mediated relationship in which there is very little antagonism between the established valuation of this mode of satire and the requirements of the dominant fields of production which the satire inhabits. Horace's satire, as John Dryden implies, became a privileged mode in the literary field in part because it struck a dialogic accord with the dominant ethos of its historical moment: Horace was, states Dryden, "a mild admonisher, a court satirist, fit for the gentle time of Augustus, and more fit, for the reasons which I have already given," that is, the ability of Horace's satiric style to successfully navigate the potentially violent responses to sociocultural criticism in Rome's new imperial order (91).

Clearly, with regard to Dante's *Orazio satiro*, this relationship between Horatianism and the dominant fraction is presented as a convivial one, but to go further, the preeminence of Horace's works (the *Satires* and *Odes* in particular) within many medieval and early modern cultural and political fields refracts the authorities' endorsement of those politically centripetal cultural materials they find most useful. This endorsement in turn affected the capital associated with Horatianism in the literary field, while also endorsing the mode as a stabilizing social force, as opposed to the more generically typical iconoclastic impulse of Horace's predecessor, Lucilius, and his successor, Juvenal. The early modern satirists who chose to adopt Horace as a model are thus licensed to translate images of established social forces into their satires with relative impunity because to use this highly valuated mode signals the imitators' sanction of those very same power structures that provide both material and ratification for their genial critiques. Furthermore, horatian satire, like the more exalted genres, offers its practitioners the opportunity for gains in personal and social capital, as well as plausible deniability should its salutary intentions be misinterpreted.

Horace himself provides the perfect example of this form of ideologically centripetal satiric poetics. In *Satire* 1.9, Horace carefully deploys an ironic and palliative version of early imperial Roman society. More than just a humorous tale of Horace the poet's uncomfortable exchange with a verbose, aspiring sycophant desperate to join the inner circle of Horace, his patron Maecenas, and by extension, the emperor himself, the poem parodies an epic battle scene, the irony of which intentionally targets not the humble and dithering Horace, but his adversary and those like him who are unworthy of a place in the new status quo.

Ostensibly speaking of himself, Horace says pointedly to the sycophant, "each has his own place" ("*est locus uni cuique suus,*" 50), the word "*locus*" connoting the insurmountable difference in rank between Horace and the aspiring pest. The poem also provides a comic version of the Roman system of patronage, as well as a "chuckle rather than a grimace at the violent factionalism and rapid rise of the class of *novi homines* (new men) that occurred during and after the civil wars"; the final image of the poem consists of the victory of the newly established order by way of the banishment of the emerging power (the sycophant is whisked off to court by his accuser), and ultimately, the preservation of "Maecenas' world intact."[19]

In Bakhtinian terms, while the presence of heteroglossia in *Satire* 1.9 in the form of a dialogue between the spokesman for the dominant social force ("Horace") and the voice of the emerging social force (the Sycophant) should open up the verbal-ideological world to the fact of a linguistically and politically unstable present, the dominance of restrained, monoglossic speech, the choice of the "new man" as the central target, and the preponderance of Horace's perspective (the auditor is privileged to hear what Horace says to *and* what he thinks of his adversary) privilege the centripetal ideology of masculine aristocratic elitism in a way more characteristic of epic than of Lucilian satire.[20] Because of Horace's efforts to render his satiric style ideologically and linguistically neutral, or 'impotent,' as Horace himself describes it ("*sine nervis,*" *Satire* 2.1.2), or put another way, as a result of his intention to fill his works with ironic strategies that seek to soften or "neutralize the text's explicit utterances"[21] in ways that support the dominant social fields, over the centuries, generations of interpolators construed the core of Horatianism's satiric intentionality as a synergy between the mode and consolidating national identity, or in Dryden's terms, using Horace as a "minister of state in Satire" (87).

For the particularly precarious English Reformation and post-Reformation periods, when English isolation from and scrutiny by Catholic powers on the continent was most acute, the need for synergizing cultural products seems as vital as it was during the early years of the Roman empire. Both eras saw new political orders striving to create empowering national corporate identities in the face extreme internal and external dissent, violent repression, economic and social insecurity, and a host of other potentially destabilizing factors too numerous to enumerate here. In essence, both historical periods are linked by incubate empires in crisis, struggling to fortify their national images and hierarchical structures against oppositional forces, and justifying the means by which they gained their imperial statuses. With this in mind, the popularity of a centripetal informing spirit like Horatianism becomes understandable.

Horatianism and Humanism: Continental Constructions of Horace

As indicated earlier, it was Horace himself who began the process of aligning his mode of satire with the concerns of the governing social systems by distinguishing his satires from those of Lucilius, the Roman progenitor of verse satire whose invective style Horace damns with faint praise as too much like a muddy stream running over the banks of poetic and social decorum (*"ultra perfectum," Satires* 1.10.50; 69–70). Instead, Horace posits the didactic utility of stylistic "brevity" (*"brevitate"*) and "humor" (*"ridiculum"*) over excessive verbiage and personal ferocity (*"acri," Satires* 1.10.9–14). These are the main components of the horatian ideologically efficacious "middle way,"[22] a process of juxtaposing negative and positive moral *exempla* (*laus et vituperatio*, praise and blame) in order to teach individual and social virtues, a technique which Horace claims he learned from his "best of fathers" (1.4.121–126). Horace purposefully conflates the purpose of satire with the paternalistic ideologies of family and nation: the practitioner of satire must act as the *pater patriae* (father of the country) would have him act, as the *"custodis"* (protector) of a fragmented society, a moral guardian whose teachings are meant to vilify only those individuals who threaten the continuance of the "life," "reputation," and "customs handed down from our forefathers" (1.4.116–120) necessary for the stabilization of the new political order. For Kirk Freudenburg, the horatian project involves staging (and, I would argue, resolving) the ideological "crisis in Roman identity" and the supposed loss of individual freedom concomitant with the transition from Republic to Empire (*Satires of Rome* 4), a project equally attractive to those wishing to establish a strong English identity during the tumultuous early decades of the Tudor dynasty.

A mere forty-two years after Horace's death, the Roman satirist Persius writes admiringly of Horace's ability to manipulate public opinion ("expertly hanging the public from his shaken-out nose," *Satire* 1.118), while sixty years or so later, Juvenal sneers at Horace as free to give the Bacchic cry *"euhoe"* only because he and his style were favored. Furthermore, Juvenal laments the state of the schoolteacher whose well-worn editions of Horace and Virgil are blackened with the lamp soot,[23] suggesting that, in a single century, Horace's works had been granted the cultural capital of canonicity. Centuries later, medieval and early modern scholars, translators, and imitators continued to strengthen, and to be strengthened by, the alignment between the horatian literary field and the desires of the dominant fields of power to legitimate their own imperial images.

Much of this alignment came by way of the wealth of scholarly commentary produced for editions of Horace's poetry throughout the medieval and Renaissance periods. Once again, Suzanne Reynolds[24] provides a very useful sample of critical commentaries culled from editions of Horace's poetry dating from the ninth through the twelfth centuries, most of which echo Horace's own language in his *Ars Poetica* that the horatian mode is both "sweet" and "useful" in producing public benefits, a decorous form of satire that improves rather than shames the citizenry (Reynolds 152.17). The alternative models, including Juvenal, are implied to be more consistently negative, even iconoclastic, asserting the uniqueness of their style, as Colin Burrow argues, not by offering constructive lessons, but by conjuring a bleak vision of a decadent society in irredeemable decline.[25]

Although appended to Horace's *Epistles*, another medieval commentary also links individual morality to social capital in a way that is characteristic of early modern Horatianism. The commentator states,

> Horace's subject matter here is honesty with usefulness, around which he intends to do each thing... Horace's end is to produce a political man ["*politicum hominem*"], that is, to shape such a citizen who can do good for the country.
>
> (Reynolds 148.7)

Here, once again, is the union between satiric stylistics, intentionality, and the consequent ideological effect: Horatianism focuses more on human potential and less on human depravity with the goal of creating the kind of citizen who will actively work for the good of the *patria*. As Horace himself states in *Satires* 2.1.34–41, the socially minded satirist never draws dagger or pen to assault the good, but only to protect the integrity of one's country.

Perhaps nowhere else do the literary, cultural, and political fields interact more obviously than in the educational philosophies of the early European Renaissance. Early humanist thinkers such as Erasmus, Philip Melancthon, and Juan Luis Vives purposefully tailor their imitative curricula to foreground the Augustan poets as part of their rhetorical, moral, and ideological agendas. For the aspiring humanist poet, the touchstone of national authority was Augustan Rome, which was less of a historical reality than another informing spirit of authoritarian but benign political power, social order, and artistic grandeur. As William Woodward writes,

> The Roman world was, it is not unfair to say, presented as the ideal... Hence, to Erasmus, antiquity was not a subject of liberal study alone, but partook of the nature of a working ideal social order, to be adjusted to modern conditions, chief among which was the supremacy of the Christian faith.[26]

44 *Satire and Empire*

Thus for humanist educators, to replicate the poetry of the Augustans was as much an ideological as a rhetorical exercise whereby a new and improved (i.e. Christianized) imperial poetics could be created in support of contemporary national ambitions; Horace, unsurprisingly, was one of the most popular choices for imitation.

In *De Ratione Studii* (1511), Erasmus exhorts educators to offer Virgil, Horace, Cicero, and Julius Caesar as "sound models of style but [also] instructive by reason of their subject matter"[27]; however, Erasmus finds little imitative value in the ancient Cynics (a group which must include Juvenal) and others who are quick to make private shames public with little regard for the social consequences (De Copia 315). Erasmus reiterates this point in his epistles to Thomas More (1510) and Martin Dorp (1514) in defense of his satire, *The Praise of Folly* (1511). Here, Erasmus claims stylistic kinship with Horace in that he intends his work to be a "pleasant" assault on "laughable follies," rather than indulging in an imitation of Juvenal's more prurient interests.[28] In *De Tradendis Disciplinis* (1531), Erasmus' pupil, Vives, gives Horace special cultural capital by linking him to his esteemed master, and vice versa, while also endorsing the ideological dichotomy between Horace and Juvenal: Juvenal and his satires are depicted as mutually problematic on rhetorical and moral levels, while Horace and his *sermones* are deliberately uncoupled from the derogatory sense of satire as *carmina infamiam* (defamatory verses).[29]

Scholarly editions and educational theses no doubt asserted strong influences on conceptions of imperial Horatianism, and yet, poets such as Dante and his equally prominent successor, Francesco Petrarca (Petrarch), exerted perhaps the greatest influence on the image of horatian satire as an ideologically compliant mode. Petrarch's group of socially centripetal classical models modifies Dante's appropriations slightly (he ousts Lucan, for example, because Lucan committed suicide), and yet, Horace is once again featured prominently as the epitome of poets focused on producing an ethical mode of satire worthy of modern imitators. In his *Familiarum Rerum Libri* (Books on Familiar Subjects), Petrarch writes fictive letters to Virgil, Horace, and Homer, praising them all as models who benefit the citizens, and whose example can bring stability and grace to Petrarch's world of fragmented and bellicose city-states. In his "Epistle to Horace" (circa 1350), Petrarch commends Horace as "the king of lyric songs" for the Italian world, an eminently "sweet" model whose example always improves the imitator, as opposed to provoking the passions, as in Juvenalian imitation.[30] For Petrarch, Horatianism is an admirably flexible, socially didactic mode capable of inspiring the faithful one moment and biting the vicious the next. From the Bakhtinian point of view, the Christian intentionality behind Petrarch's linguistic designations of Horace as faithful ("*fido*"), sedulous ("*sedulus*"), and virtuous ("*virtutuem*") should not be overlooked; the imitator who chooses to follow the example of Horace, in Petrarch's view, is committed to more than following classical moral and rhetorical boundaries, but to a political project of producing not just the beneficial citizen, but the beneficial Christian citizen.

Horatianism in English Renaissance Scholarship

In *Horace Made New*, Colin Burrow claims that "preconceived notions and clichés" for what it meant to write in a 'horatian' style "were in short supply before the seventeenth century" (27), and therefore a grammarian, translator, and imitator such as Thomas Drant, whose popular English version of Horace's satires was published in 1566, had "no distracting notion of 'Horatianism'" to restrict him from creating whatever kind of horatian model he thought fit (28). As demonstrated, such a contention is not supported by philological evidence. The mode was readily available to English Renaissance educators and poetic imitators, who were likely drawn to it as a personally and socially beneficial model of critical discourse sanctioned by virtue of its complementarity with the established fields of power. Thus, Drant was not free to create his own English Horace, however, the literary field of Horatianism gave him a thoroughly codified poetic and ideological system through which he could advance his own legitimizing agenda for himself and for the English nation.[31]

Drant's original and revised editions of Horace's works (1566 and 1567), the only complete English translations available well into the seventeenth century and a strong influence on later Tudor authors such as William Webbe, Sir Philip Sidney, Edmund Spenser, and Gabriel Harvey (Medine xiii), demonstrate a thorough awareness and endorsement of the continental tradition of Horatianism as the most appropriate for the evolving genre of English imitative verse satire, even as Protestant England continued to strive to consolidate its relatively new imperial corporate self-image. For Drant, the horatian mode provides a "medicinable moral," as stated in the title of the 1566 edition, to a nation struggling to cure the illness of political and social instability. In his introductory comments, Drant claims that he is adapting, rather than strictly translating, Horace in order to accord with the English cultural ethos of the time, molding Horace's stabilizing notions of poetic and social restraint to the restrictions of traditional English "idioms" and "notions of taste."

As for his adherence to Horace's centripetal activistic purpose, Drant claims he has "much altered [Horace's] words, but not his sentence: or at least (I daresay) not his purpose," which is to act as a "zealous controller of sin" for the reader's moral benefit. Drant intends to downplay Horace's "obscurity" ("his private carping at this or that man") in favor of references that better suit his new "English livery," yet maintaining the original's centripetal function: in the post-civil war era, Horace was most useful, according to Drant, in cutting down any "religion" that "pretensed" the doctrine of destabilizing "forwardness," a function quite appealing to aspiring national poets in Drant's own time, when opposition to the revivified Anglican order under the recently crowned Queen Elizabeth came in many forms, including strident puritan radicals, moderate integrationists, and English Catholic recusants.[32]

Drant opens his translations of Horace's works with a verse definition of satire that holds a preeminent status as "the earliest separate, formal definition of satire in English literature," one that both reflects continental constructions of Horace and makes Horatianism's stabilizing agenda clear for an English readership.[33] Satire is defined as a "carping" instrument intended "to pinch the pranks of men" (1–2), a form that uses risible "taunting girds and gleeks and gibes" to uplift ("vere") the lewd (9), that "strains," but never breaks "courtesy" (10), that blames vice while remaining "friendly to the good" (16), all for the improvement of the populace: "To teach the worldlings wit, whose witched brains are dull" (21). Finally, Drant ranks the four major imitative models of classical Roman satire:

> Lusill [Lucilius], I wean, was parent of this nipping rhyme:
> Pert huddling Horace brave in Satyres grace.
> Thy praised pamphlet (Persie) [Persius] well detected crime,
> Sir Juvenal deserves the latter place.

Drant agrees with Quintilian in granting Horace the preeminent position, while Juvenal is rejected without justification. By implication, it is possible that Drant is suggesting that Juvenalian satire contains none of the elements (social didacticism, poetic and ideological restraint, etc.) that he attaches most prominently to Horace.

Although some humanist academics like Julius Caesar Scaliger (1561) objected that Juvenal's style did not signal the end of "pleasing satire" in the style of Horace,[34] Drant's "Englished'" adaptation of continental Horatianism exerts an influence on late sixteenth-century English scholars and educators alike. For example, in his 1589 work, *The Arte of English Poesie*, George Puttenham endorses the established image of the "noble poet Horace" as synonymous with Augustan authority: "Horace, the most delicate of all the Roman *Lyrics*, was thought meet and by many letters of great instance, provoked to be secretary of state to Augustus th' Emperor, which nevertheless he refused for his unhealthfulness sake" (17). In *The Defence of Poesy* (w. circa 1595), Sir Philip Sidney makes a claim similar to Drant's that Horatianism's value lies in its power to circumscribe the passions (or to produce a "well-balanced spirit") through the shameful public display of one's own viciousness (229).[35]

English educational scholars such as Thomas Elyot followed the lead of the Continental humanists in recommending Augustan imperial poets as models for the creation of the moral citizen. In *The Book Named the Governour* (1531), Elyot advances Horace as the preeminent model for inspiring "eloquence, civil policy, and exhortation to virtue,"[36] sound concepts, as Woodward notes, for training the sons of the "governing classes" in an historical moment "marked by a revolution in political organization and administration" (271). Other English humanist educators such as Roger Ascham put a greater emphasis on the moral rather than the political benefits of horatian imitation, and yet he also recognized Horatianism as preferable to those imitative models that foster social dissent. In *The Schoolmaster* (1570), Ascham finds nothing more profitable for either "a learned preacher or Civil Gentleman" than imitating Homer, Virgil, and Horace; however, Ascham is wary of the social consequences of imitating the 'ill words' of Greek and Latin "Stoics" such as Juvenal: "when apt and good words begin to be neglected... then also began ill deeds to spring, strange manners to oppress good orders, new and fond opinions to strive with old and true doctrine" (137).[37]

Horatianism in the English Satires of Thomas Drant and Sir Thomas Wyatt

Overall, Drant translates Horace rather faithfully; however, the most striking example of Drant's endorsement of Horatianism occurs in *Satire* 1.5 where Drant abandons translation completely and undertakes a "wholly altered" satire that dialogizes horatian principles with a decidedly English historical context. Whereas the source poem represents Horace's journey to Brundisium as part of a royal embassy to Marc Antony, Drant rejects the subject matter as "not worthy of my pain," perhaps due to Drant's appraisal that the source's tale of "babbling sophisters" lacks any kind of contemporary relevance. Retaining the most useful elements of Horatianism (the autobiographical speaker, the moralizing tone, the dialogue structure, and the centripetal imperative), Drant uses the activistic element of satire to reimagine and decry a contemporary historical particular that potentially threatened the authority, if not the very existence, of both the young Protestant Church and the English nation as a whole: the seditious influence of Catholic forces in England.

Neel Mukherjee argues that Drant's *Satire* 1.5 purposefully gestures to the "vestiarian controversy" of the 1560s, in which repatriated Marian exiles (English Protestants who fled to Europe during the reign of the English Catholic Mary I) began a Puritan separatist movement based on objections to the openly Catholic nature of the Anglican vestments and ceremonies. This controversy and others like it prompted Queen Elizabeth to reassert the 1559 Act of Uniformity, a legal edict which made the use of the Protestant *Book of Common Prayer* compulsory, repealed nearly all of Queen Mary's anti-Protestant laws, and codified a liturgy deemed inclusive of the various Protestant factions, including Catholic-leaning Bishops and Members of Parliament (2–3). Mukherjee makes special note of Elizabeth's 1565 letter to Archbishop Parker in which she warns him to guard against all nonconformists who delight in "singularities" and "manifest disorder," eventually ordering the Archbishop to repress "all such diversities" in order to establish "uniformity through our whole realm and dominions" (3).[38]

Drant's objection to foreign influence on English national affairs is indeed historically specific, as Mukherjee claims, yet it is also ideologically inclusive; for Drant, the target is more than just wrangling over vestments, but the imagined ability of duplicitous Catholics and Catholic sympathizers to endanger the corporate identity of the new empire by subverting notions of uniformity. Horatianism serves Drant as the perfect medium both to motivate action against foreign influences and to endorse repressive policies enacted to ensure the stability and coherence of the empire of England. Writing in the English common meter, Drant's persona of the "translator" (i.e. himself), allows the reader to eavesdrop on a conversation between the Catholic conspirators Pertinax and Commodus, two "popish daws" who swear themselves "best Protestants" while actually working to undermine the corporate unity of the nation.

As ideologists, Commodus, as his typological name suggests, is defined as a parasite residing in England not out of devotion, but only "for commodity," an idolater whose disingenuous "show of godly zeal" hides his true desire to "deface" the moral purity of the Anglican Church. His compatriot, Pertinax, an "imp of popish line," is an unabashed Catholic beholden to "Louvain," a name charged with religious and political intentionality as both a Flemish stronghold of anti-Reformation resistance and a university infamous among scholars as "a place of resort for those who could not accommodate themselves to the changes in religious allegiance required of them if they remained in England."[39]

Commodus goes into great detail about how he works for the papist cause by seeming to decry it, which entices vain and gullible Anglican ministers to "win me, if they could." After allowing himself to be 'converted,' Commodus spreads dissent amongst the ecclesiastical authorities either by advocating radical puritanical positions ("Me thinks this church, this English church, / Is clogged at this day / With ceremonies, more than needs"), or alternatively, by tempting the Bishops with brazenly Catholic forms of idolatry ("That ministers, (why would they not?) / Might go even like the rest. / In suits of silk, in chains of gold, / Appareled with the best").

At the time, "non-conformism and separatism become inseparable from papism," posits Mukherjee, "the demonization is so complete that purging can now proceed with total justification, indeed, with total faith and crusading zeal" (12), and indeed, Drant emphasizes the need to purge the empire of protestant England of papist provocateurs when

Commodus informs Pertinax that his influence over the English church and state has made him a kind of parody of the English ruling classes, able to bestow honor and title not by virtue of inherent nobility, but for personal gain: "I now can dub a Protestant, / And eke disdub again: / And make a Papist graduate, / If he will quit my pain" [i.e. give money]. Drant's satire ends with the return of the moralizing voice of the Translator, who zealously damns English recusants as "enemies unto God," but then quickly asserts his faith in the power of "Truth," embodied by the Protestant English church and crown, to bring justice to those who would use flattery and bribes to divide the nation with the goal of returning it to subservience under Rome: "Since God and our liege Sovereign / Bulwarks to truth do stand: / We fear not Commodus his craft, / Nor Pertinax his hand." As Freundenburg argued of Horace, Drant's *Satire* 1.5 demonstrates an activistic desire to stage, reimagine, and resolve the destabilizing threats to the post-Reformation English state, which, as Claire McEachern argues, relies on the perception of that state and its people as inseparably coherent (12).

Decades before Drant's decision to 'English' Horace, Sir Thomas Wyatt (b. 1503-d. 1542) created the first truly original English imitative satires by adapting classical and continental models to suit his chosen set of English historical particulars. Wyatt was a key figure in the rapid political and economic expansionism of the early sixteenth century, and as a result, his foundational role in planting, as Reed Dasenbrock describes it, "the seeds of the English Renaissance" is indisputable.[40] During his diplomatic embassies to France, Venice, and Rome in the late 1520s on behalf of the court of Henry VIII, Wyatt was exposed to humanist philosophy and cultural practices, resulting in some of the first English imitations of the poetry of Petrarch, Serafino, and other Italian humanists. However, Wyatt had an equally seminal role in employing continental discourses such as Petrarchism and Horatianism as a means to legitimize himself and Imperial Britain against the influence of more powerful colonizing forces on the continent, as suggested by Roland Greene and Jeffrey Knapp, respectively.[41] Greene notes Wyatt's tendency to engage such social and political issues as imperialism and colonialism within his seemingly private lyrics (249; 255), while Knapp argues for Wyatt's lyrics (the satires included) as both lamenting and celebrating England's "apartness," the realization that England had been cast out from the other empires of the world, but also that it "had also positively realized a destiny—perhaps faith—separate from and superior to that world": "For it is by his submission to England's disappointing limits that Wyatt apparently hopes to begin translating himself into a Brutus and his aparted home into a limitless empire" (54; 56–57).

Before examining the significance of Horatianism within Wyatt's satires, the issue of classification is central to understanding Wyatt's unique brand of satiric imitation. Written sometime between 1536 and 1541 and distributed in manuscript to an aristocratic readership,[42] the three satires, variously numbered and titled, but referred to here as "Mine Own John Poyntz," "My Mother's Maids," and "A Spending Hand," were published fifteen years after Wyatt's death in Richard Tottel's *Songs and Sonnets* (1557).[43] Catherine Bates notes the difficulty of classifying these so called "songs" and "lyrics": "modern editorial opinion remains divided over the genre of the poems, variously calling them 'satires,' 'epistolary satires,' 'so-called satires,' 'verse epistles,' or, perhaps most judiciously, nothing at all."[44]

However, in 1815–1816, editor G. F. Nott established the three poems as satires based on their imitative relationships to earlier sources (349–356): "Mine Own John Poyntz" is an imitation of Luigi Alamanni's tenth satire ("*A Thommaso Sertini*"), which in turn is based largely, as Anthony Miller has argued, on Juvenal's third satire, which recounts the manifold reasons for Umbricius' flight from dissolute Rome to the peaceful countryside. Although of possible Juvenalian origin, Claude Burrow notes the overtly horatian character of "Poyntz" ("Wyatt read and imitated the epistolary satires of Luigi Alamanni, who read Ariosto, and through him, Horace," 35), particularly the conversational tone, the morality of rural retirement, and the judicious restraint when dealing with themes of politics. Such restraint was possibly due, according to Burrow, to the passage of the Treasons Act in 1534, which prohibited descriptions of Henry as a "tyrant" or "usurper."[45] "My Mother's Maids," the Aesopian tale of the Town Mouse and the Country Mouse, is a direct imitation of Horace's *Satire* 2.6, while "A Spending Hand," a debate between an honest version of the courtier Sir Francis Bryan and a licentious version of Wyatt himself, imitates the debate in Horace's Satire 2.5 between Ulysses and the ghost of Tiresias. Bates is comfortable calling the trilogy "Epistolary Satires," all fully conversant with "the didactic tradition of neo-classical, humanist poetics which places a high cultural value on the ability of poetry to teach, improve, reform, instruct, and correct" (244).

Like Drant after him, Wyatt's decision to adopt and to adapt horatian satire to the particular historical, linguistic, and poetic concerns of his time, largely to the exclusion of Juvenal, implies both a recognition of the preeminence of the horatian tradition, as well as an implicit satiric intentionality to use the mode's activisitic potential to translate the image of the English nation from one of ineffectual weakness to one of imperial sovereignty. However, exactly how Wyatt structured his horatian satire so as to foster a nationalistic ideology is a question best approached in dialogue with a host of mediating factors, all of which assert their influence on Wyatt's satiric agenda.

Modern scholars have done a remarkable job enumerating some of the latent and patent mediating forces refracted in Wyatt's three epistolary satires, most of which center on avoiding or attacking the various vicissitudes of life at the court of Henry VIII. To cite just a few examples, as mentioned, Burrow points to the Treason Act as the motivator behind the "indirect speech, allusive speech" characteristic of all three satires; the consequence, according to Burrow, is a "moral unlocatedness" that finds freedom neither at court nor in domestic exile, which Wyatt experienced firsthand in 1536 after his release from prison (40; 48).[46] Similarly, Christopher Hobson rejects Stephen Greenblatt's contention that Wyatt is engaged in crafty self-fashioning, arguing instead that Wyatt is authentically compelled by the authoritarian nature of the Henrician court to employ double- and triple-voiced "concealment" in order to present a cynical world view in which "truth and personal integrity are not to be relied on."[47]

What links these viewpoints is the vision of Wyatt and his satires as employing the conventional "conservative revolutionary" satiric persona and ideology proposed by Alvin Kernan,[48] which renders an image of Wyatt as a rebel bent on diminishing the image of Henry's court as revenge for Wyatt's imprisonment. However, when one broadens the scope of mediating factors to include the ideological as well as the historical, not to mention the centripetal informing spirit of Horatianism, then it is perhaps more accurate to describe Wyatt's activistic purpose as closer to that of the *revolutionary conservative.* The distinction is a subtle matter of perspective, but an important one, as it hinges on the identification of intentionality. A conservative revolutionary, in Kernan's view, attacks contemporary orthodoxies in order to "return to the time-tested virtues" and the "good old ways" (41), which one certainly sees in Juvenal, and which accurately describes Wyatt's apparent advancement of the ethics of private retirement over unethical public service at court. Alternatively, the revolutionary conservative satirist seeks to use its sometimes disquieting perceptions of social orthodoxies to support rather than to undermine the ideology of the dominant field by selectively deploying its attacks against those invasive elements which threaten to destabilize it, which is an apt description of Horatianism as it came down to Wyatt, and which is visible in the works of Horace, Drant, John Weever, Joseph Hall, and others. In short, Wyatt's employment of Horace implies a satiric intention not to dismantle the current court system or to brand Henry a tyrant, as a revolutionary might do, but to strengthen the centripetal image of Imperial Britain imperiled by invasive forces that would disrupt its corporate integrity, as a conservative might do.

While the primary mediating factor in the determination of Wyatt's conservative intentionality is his preferred satiric model, the epistle genre offers a similarly unifying imperative. Steven Shelburne argues that the private nature of the horatian epistle form promotes the virtues of amity and social, political, and moral unity that acts as the "perfect foil to the Machiavellian reality of courtly dissimulation" that not only threatens to divide friends, but "threatens the larger social structure."[49] In essence, the epistle form implies an intent to build a consensual community of sovereign Englishness in defiance of those divisive forces that threaten the stability of the dominant political field. Roger Ascham expresses just this kind of desire for national consensus when he decries the power of continental culture to "mar men's manner in England" in a manner reminiscent of Wyatt's attacks on the potentially disruptive power of the vices at court: "for religion, papistry, or worse... for policy, a factious heart, a discoursing head, a mind to meddle in all men's matters... for manners, variety of vanities and change of filthy living."[50]

In the political field, Wyatt's conception of a unified Imperial Britain, argues Joel Davis,[51] was heavily influenced by resistance to the possible ascendancy of the Holy Roman Empire under the rule of Charles V. Davis contends that the thorny issue of maintaining amity between England and the various powers opposed to each other and, historically, to England as well, was a key concern to Wyatt during his time as Henry's ambassador on the continent: "Thus Wyatt spent much of the end of his career at the court of Charles V, whence he reported to Henry VIII on the state of the constantly shifting relationship between Francis I and Charles" (495). Despite proffering pledges of eternal friendship between England, France, and the Holy Roman Empire, Wyatt and his king lived in almost perpetual fear of a Europe unified under Charles' rule ready and, more importantly, financially able to invade England and return it to allegiance to Catholic Europe (508). Wyatt, in other words, was keenly aware of his nation's vulnerability, its "apartness" from other empires, and had a strong investment in strengthening the image of its sovereignty. Therefore, it is conceivable that this anxiety of external influence would find expression through the centripetal horatian satires produced by one of Henry VIII's most reliable ambassadors, a soldier and humanist whose extensive contacts with foreign powers left him suspicious and weary of the "internecine conflicts and failed spiritual and political leadership" on the continent.[52]

Like Horace's *Satire* 1.9, the epistle form of "Mine Own John Poyntz" allows the reader to eavesdrop on a 'private' account of the shifts in the evolving political order. Again, like Horace's satire, the poem presents a closed, monologic version of the contemporary courtier system, with Wyatt somewhat humorously denouncing the threats to the new status quo. The tacit approval of the poem prior to the reign of Mary I suggests the poem's (and the author's) general rapport with the dominant fields, despite the presence of such potential violations of the Treasons Act as, "I am not he that can allow the state / Of high Caesar and damn Cato to die" (37–38) and the disavowal of "tyranny" as "the right of a Prince's reign" (74–75). Satire's inclusive chronotope is useful here as Wyatt's historically analogical language of empire ("Caesar"), republicanism ("Cato"), and "tyranny" is less a revolutionary challenge and more an ironic warning to the noble readership: the emerging empire of England must not repeat the excesses of its failed Roman imperial predecessor.

The implied didactic image is of the English court as the moderate body it *should be* rather than the domain of vice it *could become*. With a kind of autobiographical nod to the conflicts Wyatt himself witnessed abroad, the readers are exposed to a range of images of excessive Machiavellian dissimulation they should avoid in order to protect the sovereignty of the new empire: "as drunkenness good fellowship to call; / The friendly foe with his double face / Say he is gentle and courteous therewithal; / And say the Favell [Flattery] hath a goodly grace" (64–67).

As the virtuous alternative to the influence of continental duplicity at the English court, Wyatt asks Poyntz, and the reading nobles, to join him in "Kent and Christendom" (100), a place which, as Burrow argues, has a special "ethical significance" (34) in the poem, in that it both embodies the Stoic virtues of the natural world and of study ("to hunt and to hawk / And in foul weather at my book to sit" 80–81) and also symbolizes the religious tensions at the heart of Reformation theology as a place of both free will and an ephemeral respite from obligations to a higher power: "No man doth mark where so I ride or go; / In lusty leas at liberty I walk, / And of these news I feel nor weal nor woe, / Save that a clog doth hang yet at my heel" (83–86). But when dialogized with its historical context, the invocation of Kent brings to bear a very specific sociolinguistic intentionality of imperial 'Englishness' whose historical roots in Celtic history support an ideology of English sovereignty and resistance to the encroachments of foreign authority at the heart of the poem.

As a location, Kent has distinct nationalistic significations that might be lost on the modern reader. For example, in his 1586 history of *Britannia*, William Camden notes that it was the "Kentish Britains" who first repelled the Romans under Julius Caesar in 55 B.C.E., and later fought nobly to maintain their "liberties and customs" against the Norman French in 1066: "for it saith that this County was never conquered, as the residue of England was, but by concluding of a peace subjected themselves to the dominion of the conqueror." Similarly, in his 1612 work, *Poly-Olbion*, Michael Drayton augments the political autonomy of Kent with religious preeminence as the kingdom where Christianity gained its first foothold on the site of what would become Canterbury Cathedral: "Good Ethelbert of Kent, th' first Christ'ned English King, / To preach the faith of Christ" (73–74). The lionization of English Kent even finds its way into the plays of Shakespeare: in addition to the depiction of the "honest-hearted" Earl of Kent in *King Lear* (1.4.19), Lord Say (2 *Henry VI*) cites Julius Caesar's praise of the Kentish people: "Kent, in the Commentaries Caesar writ, / Is term'd the civil'st place of all this isle: / Sweet is the country, because full of riches; / The people liberal, valiant, active, wealthy" (4.7.59–63).[53]

Susan Brigden casts doubt on the nationalistic implications of Kent, positing that 'Christian Kent' was an oxymoron at the time based on the proverb "in Kent *or* Christendom," King Elthelbert having been converted to Christianity, while the people of Kent remained pagan; the result, according to Brigden, is Wyatt's "Kent *and* Christendom" (my emphasis), which she reads as an ironic lament over England's injudicious separation from continental Catholicism in the wake of the Reformation. However, as Alastair Fowler argues, Wyatt's intentional alteration of the proverb from an ideology of difference to one of inclusion grants Kent a nationalistic significance amenable to the context of Reformation history and English sovereignty, as well as the horatian imperial impulse: "In short, Wyatt means that Protestant Kent is preeminently *in* Christendom."[54] For Wyatt, who had decidedly "Protestant" rather than Catholic sympathies (Muir 132), a return to "the good old ways" does not entail a return to Catholic Christianity, but the coherent preservation of a holy, sovereign Englishness.

Even Wyatt's word choices suggest the nationalistic emphasis of the poem, with Kent, again, at the center: "for all his humanist learning, Wyatt deliberately held to stark Anglo-Saxon folk words—even Kentish dialect words—and to a natural, colloquial English." Deeply suspicious of the "aureate diction of ambassadors" (Brigden 502) that he was forced to navigate as part of his emissary duties, Wyatt offers Kent as the conservative antithesis to the encroaching licentiousness of Italian culture and politics that threaten to divide the English body politic. Furthermore, while the poem is generally faithful to its Italian source, in a number of significant places (especially the addition of the Kent reference), Wyatt dialogizes the continental original with "Anglicize[d] references" to suit his stabilizing agenda (Muir 252). The result is an ironic coopting of authority from England's political and cultural rivals that invokes the practices of the dominant power only to render them inferior by comparison.

Wyatt is no revolutionary. He does not seek to destroy Henry, nor is his retreat to a county of sovereign Englishness a capitulation to the increasingly influential continental conventions at the court. Instead, Wyatt's activistic goal is to provide ironic images of the potential effects of ethical lapses in behavior typical of Machiavellianism, or more generally, typical of Catholic dissimulation, in order to bolster the concept of national sovereignty. Such an ambivalent view of Europe is not uncommon in Henrician England; as Jason Gleckman points out, while the bright side of Italian humanism is erudition and historical awareness, the dark side is "the nagging association of rhetoricians with flatters" of the type derided in "Mine Own John Poyntz," the duplicitous Machiavels whose manipulations of truth threaten to divide the state they purport to represent.[55]

To rectify such threats, Wyatt provides a very horatian litany of negative exempla the noble readership must heed in order to safeguard the reputations of themselves and their Protestant empire. In stark contrast to the ethics of English Kent, the list of immoral things Wyatt insists he "cannot" do ironically promotes an image of an empire free of the internecine divisions common in European politics: "I cannot frame my tune to feign, / To cloak the truth for praise without desert"; "I cannot honor them that sets their part / With Venus and Bacchus all their life long"; "I cannot wrest the law to fill the coffer / With innocent blood to feed myself fat"; "I am not he such eloquence to boast, / To make the crow singing as the swan" (19–20, 22–23, 34–35, 43–44).

In order to drive this point home, the satire ends with a list of moral excesses characteristic of the established continental empires that could find their way into the emerging force of the Henrician court (89–99). Wyatt deems rustic Kent superior to the vicious alternative of service in France, where the focus is never on truth, but on the private appetites: "I am not now in France to judge the wine, / With saffry sauce the delicates to feel." Nor is Wyatt unfortunate enough to be in Spain where the focus is on appearances only: "Nor yet in Spain where one must him incline / Rather than to be, outwardly to seem." Nor is he in Flanders, where drunkenness prevails: "Nor Flanders, cheer letteth not my sight to deem / Of black and white, nor taketh my wit away / With beastliness, they beast do so esteem." Here, Wyatt alters "Germany" in Alamanni's original to "Flanders," effectively altering the intentionality of the line from a scathing glance at the center of Protestant Lutheranism to a rejection of the stronghold of Catholic resistance invoked decades later in Drant's *Satire* 1.5. What makes the Englishman happiest of all is his separation from Rome, "where Christ is given in prey / For money, poison, and treason... A common practice used night and day." Such condemnatory extra-national references compel the reader to revisit their counterparts earlier in the poem, a reflexive reading which reinscribes these vices as external rather than internal political dangers; for example, in the lines "I cannot crouch nor kneel to do such wrong / To worship them like God on earth alone / That are like wolves these silly lambs among," although early Anglicanism was not yet abhorrent to words such as "saint," the association between Catholics and prowling wolves was a much more prevalent commonplace (25–27).

One final intriguing aspect of Wyatt's horatian satires is the fact that the trilogy appeared *twice* in very different historical contexts that would have exerted their own unique mediating pressures on the meaning and activistic agendas of the satires. As stated, satire's chronotopic structure is surprisingly fluid, able to create unexpected historical matrices and surprising linguistic connections between the past, present, and future, and yet, the activistic force of satire rests in its thorough historicization, its grounding in the auditor's here-and-now in which new and useful corollary meanings often arise. As mentioned, the epistolary satires were written and revised initially for distribution among a group who shared, by and large, a common set of community-derived participation frameworks (Protestant, male, aristocrat, similar education levels, etc.). However, when the satires were published in Richard Tottel's *Miscellany* in 1557, fifteen years after Wyatt's death, the discursive context of the satires had changed considerably.

First, the public audience for the *Miscellany* was much more socially diverse than Wyatt's original courtier readership. Because deciphering satire is a socially determined act, the fact of a wider bias of experiences across religious, class, education, age, and gender lines means that the process of deciphering Wyatt's manifold targets, the intentionality towards those targets, and the resulting ideological alignment would have become a far more individualized process.

But more importantly, the political and social conditions of the satires' original context had changed drastically in the intervening fifteen years so as to create new ideological valences somewhat independent of their original intentions. In short, in the years following Wyatt's death, England's worst sociocultural anxieties had come to fruition; England, it seemed, had lost the very sovereignty Wyatt's satires had worked to protect. For example, in October 1553, Mary Tudor, daughter of Henry VIII and the Catholic queen Catherine of Aragon, was crowned in Westminster Abbey, and by the end of the year, Mary's First Statute of Repeals had undone much of Edward VI's legislations of Protestant uniformity. By early 1554, Mary had announced her decision to accept the marriage proposal of Philip of Spain, son of Charles V, bonding England to Catholic Europe; Lady Jane Grey, the Protestant *de facto* queen who held power for a mere nine days after the death of Edward VI, had been executed. Even more significantly, Sir Thomas Wyatt's own son, Thomas Wyatt the Younger, was captured and executed in April 1554 after a failed attempt to overthrow Mary. By the end of November, Parliament had rescinded Archbishop Pole's attainder, and soon after, he declared the country Catholic once more. The years that followed were marked by darkly portentous and violent events, including the persecution of hundreds of English Protestants.[56]

When Wyatt the Elder's horatian satires appeared posthumously for a mass audience in the summer of 1557, it is quite plausible, although admittedly speculative, to assume that both Catholic and Protestant readers refracted the satires' original historical gestures through the intervening historical events, most notably, the failure of Wyatt's own son to prevent Mary's accession and the consequent return of England to Catholic control, creating unique dialogic relationships and ideological alignments. The fact that the satires of Wyatt, the Protestant ambassador for Henry VIII and father of a treasonous rebel, were allowed by the Marian government to be included in the *Miscellany* at all is a bit surprising, except when one takes into account that their centripetal horatian imperialism could be accommodated to the circumstances of the restored Catholic regime.

For example, for the Catholic authorities, there would be more value in taking "Poyntz" at face value rather than ironically, as the vices cited in the satire were tied historically to the Protestant court of Henry VIII, absolving and legitimizing the morality of the new order over that of Henry and his son, Edward VI. In particular, the apparently treasonous statements in the poem ("I am not he that can allow the state / Of high Caesar and damn Cato to die"; "and tyranny / To be the right of a prince's reign," 37–41, 74–75) are now more readily conversant with Henry's unilateral actions against Rome, thus offering the Catholic authorities their own centripetal utility. In other words, time and circumstance transmute the Catholic power from invasive cultural threat to imperial Britain into providential victors over the irreligious forces of Henry, Edward, Lady Grey, and Wyatt's own son.

The only direct evidence of displeasure from the Marian authorities appears in the revision of two of Wyatt's lines: "Nor I am not where Christ is given in prey / For money, poison and treason at Rome" was altered in the *Miscellany* to "Nor am I not where *truth* is given in prey / For money, poison, and treason—*of some*" (my emphases). In the original, the direct assault against the impiety of the Papacy reinforces the nativist ideology of a sovereign imperial Britain, while the alterations demanded by the new Catholic regime generalize the attack so as to render the centrifugal potential of the original lines inert; left intact, these lines could influence the earlier depictions of court vice in a manner threatening to the image of the new regime. However, the revision, clumsy as it is, succeeds in maintaining the general moral didacticism of the horatian original, while also reinforcing the legitimacy of Catholic England. It is interesting to note that the lines could have been completely excised, or the poem rejected from inclusion in the *Miscellany*, but apparently, the Marian authorities had more to gain by changing the lines than by either removing them or censoring the entire poem.

Epilogue: "Native English Satire"

In adopting such a specific focus, this chapter overlooks an huge body of medieval and early modern English satire that complicate the perception of the period as dominated by a single, ideologically conservative imitative satiric ideology; I speak of the wealth of vernacular "native English" satires described so thoroughly by Alvin Kernan, John Peter, and others.[57] Influential satirists and their works from the period include William Langland's *Piers Plowman*; Geoffrey Chaucer's *The Canterbury Tales*; Alexander Barclay's English version of Sebastian Brant's *Das Narrenschiff* (*The Ship of Fools*); Erasmus' *Praise of Folly*; Sir Thomas More's *Utopia*; John Skelton's poems and morality play; Edmund Spenser's *Mother Hubberd's Tale*,[58] and many more. Kernan unifies the works of Langland, Chaucer, and Skelton under the umbrella of the "plowman tradition" (47), a satiric persona developed in the fourteenth century who speaks from the perspective of the lower class in order to shame all levels of society into acting in accord with Christian dictates. For John Peter, the most prevalent native tradition is the Complaint genre and all its subgenres, including confession, dream vision, "diatribes, the lamentations, the verse homilies, the moral poems and fables, 'Mirror' and *Timor mortis* [Fear of death] poems," all of which are dedicated to moral correction (8–10).

Peter is correct when he argues that the Tudor era was deeply invested in the idea of finding common ground between the homiletic Christian didacticism of native satire and the ever-increasing examples of neoclassical imitative satire that accompanied the rapid expansion of humanist thought and commercial, political, and cultural change in the period. Horatianism in the Tudor era had much in common with the aforementioned examples of Native satire: the humble persona, the homiletic didacticism, the use of irony and allegory, the public versus private orientation, the compatibility with Christian hermeneutics, and the conservative alignment with the established fields of power. However, while the Horace-Juvenal binary at the time was more ideological than rhetorical, the Renaissance English satirist who chose Juvenal as a model, as opposed to choosing Horace or an example from the native strain, makes a powerful statement of an adversarial intentionality in direct defiance of the conservative traditions of both native English satire and English Horatianism.

Notes

1 The text and translations of the *Inferno* are taken from Charles S. Singleton's edition of *The Divine Comedy*, vol. 1, Princeton University Press, 1970.
2 Brownlee, Kevin. "Dante and the Classical Poets." *The Cambridge Companion to Dante*, edited by Rachel Jacoff, Cambridge University Press, 1993. See pp. 100–119. Quote is from p. 101.
3 See McLaughlin, M. L. "Humanism and Italian Literature." *The Cambridge Companion to Renaissance Humanism*, edited by Jill Kraye, Cambridge University Press, 1996. See pp. 224–245. Quote is from p. 240.
4 Reynolds, Suzanne. "*Orazio satiro* (*Inferno* IV, 89): Dante, the Roman Satirists, and the Medieval Theory of Satire." *The Italianist: Journal of the Department of Italian Studies, University of Reading*, vol. 15, no. 2, 1995, pp. 128–144.
5 See Friis-Jensen, Karsten. "The Reception of Horace in the Middle Ages." *The Cambridge Companion to Horace*, edited by Stephen Harrison, Cambridge University Press, 2007, pp. 291–303. Also, Wheeler, Angela J. *English Verse Satire from Donne to Dryden: Imitation of Classical Models*, Carl Winter Universitätsverlag, 1992. See p. 21. See also Burrow, Colin. "Horace at Home and Abroad: Wyatt and Sixteenth-Century Horatianism." *Horace Made New: Horatian Influences on British Writing from the Renaissance to the Twentieth Century*, edited by Charles Martindale et al., Cambridge University Press, 1993.

6 Horace refers to his poems variously, and somewhat defensively, as both "*satura*," i.e. "satire," and "*sermones*," i.e. little conversations. See, for example, Horace *Satires* 1.4.41 ("*sermoni*") and 2.1.1 ("*satura*").
7 Habinek, Thomas. *The Politics of Latin Literature*, Princeton University Press, 1998, p. 102; Oliensis, Ellen. *Horace and the Rhetoric of Authority*, Cambridge University Press, 1998, p. 125.
8 James, Heather. *Shakespeare's Troy: Drama, Politics, and the Translation of Empire*, Cambridge University Press, 1997. See pp. 8 and 1.
9 See John Dryden's "A Discourse Concerning the Original and Progress of Satire," p. 87. See also Freudenburg, Kirk. *Satires of Rome: Threatening Poses from Lucilius to Juvenal*, Cambridge University Press, 2001; see also Ellen Oliensis (note 7). Freudenburg argues that Horace's consistent employment of irony makes his relationship to authority difficult to categorize, and similarly, Oliensis argues that the range of *personae* adopted by the character "Horace" has a very similar effect with regard to figures of authority. Charles Martindale notes the depiction of Horace as a servile courtier as occurring as far back as Suetonius. See Martindale, Charles. "Introduction," *Horace Made New: Horatian Influences on British Writing from the Renaissance to the Twentieth Century* (note 5), p. 12.
10 Anderson, William. *Essays on Roman Satire*, Princeton University Press, 1982, see p. 39. The quote from Horace is taken from the *Ars Poetica*, l. 343: "*omne tulit punctum qui miscuit utile dulci*" (He who has blended sweetness and usefulness carries every vote).
11 All Latin quotes from this epistle are taken from Francesco Petrarca. *Opere*, vol. 1, G. C. Sansoni S. P. A., 1975, pp. 1268–1272. The translations are mine. For an English translation of this epistle, see Mario E. Cosenza, *Petrarch's Letters to Classical Authors*, University of Chicago Press, 1910, pp. 125–135.
12 The term is Charles Knight's. See Chapter 1.
13 Claire McEachern, *The Poetics of English Nationhood 1590–1612*, Cambridge University Press, 1996, pp. 1–23.
14 Tanner, Joseph Robson. "Act in Restraint of Appeals, 1533. *Tudor Constitutional Documents A.D. 1485–1603 with an historical commentary*. Cambridge University Press, 1930, Ebook, archive.org/details/cu31924030504322. See p. 41.
15 McLeod, Bruce. *The Geography of Empire in English Literature 1580–1745*, Cambridge University Press, 1999. See p. 1.
16 See Carroll, Clare. "The Construction of Gender and the Cultural and Political Other in the Faerie Queene 5 and A View of the Present State of Ireland: the Critics, the Context, and the Case of Radigund." *Criticism*, vol. 32, no. 2, 1990, pp. 163–185; Suzuki, Mihoko. "Scapegoating Radigund." *Critical Essays on Edmund Spenser*, edited by Mihoko Suzuki, Simon and Schuster, 1995, pp. 183–198.
17 Thanks to Catherine Collins and David Douglass, who framed my 2009 argument as the government's desire to maintain "stable conveyances of meaning" during times of political and ideological crises. See Collins and Douglass, "Representation and Resemblance in the Case of the Danish Cartoons." *Controversial Images: Media Representations on the Edge*, edited by Feona Attwood et al., Palgrave-Macmillan, 2013, pp. 36–51. See p. 48.
18 Bourdieu, Pierre. "Field of Power, Literary Field, and Habitus." *The Field of Cultural Production*, edited by Randal Johnson, Columbia University Press, 1993. pp. 161–175.
19 See Jones, William. "'People Have to Watch What They Say': What Horace, Juvenal, and 9/11 Can Tell Us about Satire and History." (Chapter 1, note 44)

60 *Satire and Empire*

     For a reading of Horace's Satire 1.9 as epic parody, see Anderson, pp. 84–102. The quote concerning the preservation of Maecenas' world is from Anderson, p. 82.

20 For more on how Roman satire uses "play" to construct male aristocratic identity, see Habinek, Thomas. "Satire as Aristocratic Play." *The Cambridge Companion to Roman Satire*, edited by Kirk Freudenburg, Cambridge University Press, 2005.

21 Kirk Freudenburg argues for the sexual connotations of the phrase *"sine nervis"* as "limp" or "impotent." See Freudenberg, Kirk. "Horace's Satiric Program and the Language of Contemporary Theory in Satires 2.1." *The American Journal of Philology*, vol. 111, no. 2, 1990, pp. 187–203. See also Hajdu, Péter. "The Betrayal of the Satirical Text." *Neohelicon*, vol. 40, 2013, pp. 47–57. See p. 50.

22 Horace's concept of *"medioctitatem,"* the decorous middle way, can be found in his *Odes*, 2.10.5–6: *"auream quisquis mediocritatem/ diligit"* (He who values the golden mean).

23 Juvenal Satire 7.62 & 226–227; translations are Braund's.

24 Suzanne Reynolds, "Dante and the Medieval Theory of Satire: a Collection of Texts," *The Italianist: Journal of the Department of Italian Studies, University of Reading*, vol. 15, no. 2, 1995, pp. 145–157. Reynolds provides neither dates nor translations; therefore, I am forced to be historically general. The translations are original, but with the inestimable assistance of Professor Mary Kay Gamel (UCSC).

25 Burrow, Colin. "Roman Satire in the Sixteenth Century." *The Cambridge Companion to Roman Satire*, edited by Kirk Freudenburg, Cambridge University Press, 2005, pp. 243–260. See p. 244.

26 Woodward, William H. *Studies in Education during the Age of the Renaissance 1400–1600*, Russell and Russell, 1965. See p. 111.

27 Erasmus, Desiderius. *"De Ratione Studii." Desiderius Erasmus Concerning the Aim and Method of Education*, translated by William H. Woodward, Cambridge University Press, 1904, p. 164.

28 Erasmus, *Collected Works of Erasmus: De Copia and De Ratione Studii*. Edited by Craig R. Thompson, vol. 24, University of Toronto Press, 1978, pp. 315 and 669; Erasmus, "Prefatory Letter to Thomas More" and "Letter to Martin Dorp." *The Praise of Folly*, translated by Clarence H. Miller, 2nd edition, Yale University Press, 2003, pp. 5 and 156.

29 Vives, Juan Luis. *Vives: On Education. A Translation of the De Tradendis Disciplinis of Juan Luis Vives*. Edited and Translated by Foster Watson, Cambridge University Press, 1913. Quotes are from pp. 160 and 159, respectively. See Vives' chapter on "Imitation" for lists of beneficial classical authors.

30 See *"Ad Horatium Flaccum Lyricum Poetam,"* Familiarum Rerum Libri, Book 24, Epistle 10 (note 11).

31 An humanist educator like Drant may have been influenced by the judgments of the classical oratory instructor Quintilian (circa 80 C.E.), who grants Horace preeminence in the curricula over the more unpredictable, libertine style of Lucilius and, by extension, Juvenal. See Quintilian, *Institutio Oratoria*. Loeb Classical Library, vol. 4, Books X–XII, translated by H. E. Butler, Harvard University Press, 1922, Book X, paragraph 94.

32 The full title of Drant's 1566 edition is "A Medicinable Moral, that is, the Two Books of Horace his Satyres, Englished according to the Prescription of Saint Jerome, [along with] The Wailings of the Prophet Jeremiah, done into English Verse. Also Epigrams." A Year later, Drant published a new

edition entitled, "Horace his Arte of Poetry, 'Pistles, and Satyrs Englished." I have modernized some spellings. The text of Drant's 1566 epistle "To the Reader" was transcribed from the original text held at The Huntington Library in Pasadena, CA. Call number 61580.
33. Randolph, Mary C. "Thomas Drant's Definition of Satire, 1566." *Notes and Queries*, vol. 180, 1941, pp. 416–418. The 1566 "*Priscus Grammaticus de Satyra*" and the two books of Horace's satires are reproduced in the 1567 edition with slight variations, but the "wailings" of St. Jerome and the Epigrams are omitted from the 1567 edition. For the authority of Drant's edition of Horace in the sixteenth century, see Drant, Thomas. *Horace His Arte of Poetrie, Pistles, and Satyres Englished (1567)*. Edited by Peter E. Medine, Scholars' Facsimiles and Reprints, 1972, pp. vii and xiii. The facsimile is unlineated, therefore, I have not provided line numbers.
34. Scaliger, Julius Caesar. *Select Translations from Scaliger's Poetics*. Translated by Frederick M. Padelford, Henry Holt, 1905, p. 43.
35. Sidney is quoting from Horace's Epistles 1.9.30: "*est Ulubris, animus sit e non deficit aequus.*" ([The contentment you seek is here], it is at Ulubrae [a marshy, unpleasant town], if your well-balanced mind does not forsake you). See Puttenham, George. *The Arte of English Poesie*. Edited by Gladys D. Willcock and Alice Walker, Cambridge University Press, 1936. Sidney, Sir Philip. "The Defence of Poesy." *Sir Philip Sidney*, edited by Katherine Duncan-Jones, Oxford University Press, 1989.
36. Elyot, Sir Thomas. *The Book Named The Governour* (1531). Edited by Henry H. S. Croft, vol. 1, Burt Franklin Press, 1967, pp. 67–68.
37. Ascham, Roger. *The Schoolmaster*. Edited by John E. B. Mayor, AMS Press, 1967. See p. 168.
38. In addition to Elizabeth's Act of Uniformity, similar political expressions of protectionism can be found in the sociopolitical fields, specifically, the legal accusation of *Praemunire*, a plaintiff's assertion of a foreign (usually papal) jurisdiction in English civil matters, which Elizabeth deployed frequently against Roman Catholics. As in Drant's time, the xenophobic accusation of *Praemunire* was also a central feature in Wyatt's time, as it was used to divest Cardinal Thomas Wolsey in 1529. Other examples include the near-continuous promulgation of the state-sanctioned Ideology of Order delivered through sermons and edicts. See the "Exhortation Concerning Good Order and Obedience" (1559) and *The Homily against Disobedience and Willful Rebellion* (1570).
39. Evans, G. R. *The Roots of the Reformation: Tradition, Emergence, and Rupture*. InterVarsity Press, 2012. Ebook, books.google.com/books/about/The_Roots_of_the_Reformation.html?id=GJCyKGGK0b0C&printsec=frontcover&source=kp_read_button#v=onepage&q&f=false. See p. 266. See also Clegg, Cyndia. *Press Censorship in Elizabethan England*, Cambridge University Press, 1997.
40. See Dasenbrock, Reed Way. *Imitating the Italians: Wyatt, Spenser, Synge, Pound, Joyce*, John Hopkins University Press, 1991.
41. Greene, Roland. "The Colonial Wyatt: Contexts and Openings." *Rethinking the Henrician Era: Essays on Early Tudor Texts and Contexts*, edited by Peter C. Herman, University of Illinois Press, 1994, pp. 240–266; Knapp, Jeffrey. *An Empire Nowhere: England, America, and Literature from Utopia to the Tempest*, University of California Press, 1992.
42. R. A. Rebholz shows that "Mine Own John Poyntz exists in five manuscript states (Parker, Egerton, Devonshire, Arundel, Hill, and Cambridge); "My Mother's Maids" exists in three manuscripts (Egerton, Arundel, and

Devonshire); "A Spending Hand" exists in two manuscripts (Egerton and Arundel). All three satires appear in the editions of *Tottel's Miscellany* published between 1557 and 1587.
43 See *Collected Poems of Sir Thomas Wyatt*. Edited by Kenneth Muir and Patricia Thomson, Liverpool University Press, 1969. All quotes from Wyatt's poems are taken from this edition; some spellings have been modernized. Muir and Thomson describe Wyatt's three epistolary satires as composed sometime between 1536 (eds. Rollins, Baldi, and Mason) and 1541 (G. F. Nott). See Hyder Edward Rollins, *Tottel's Miscellany*, 2 vols, Harvard University Press, 1965.
44 Catherine Bates, "'A Mild Admonisher': Sir Thomas Wyatt and Sixteenth-Century Satire." *The Huntington Library Quarterly*, vol. 56, 1993, pp. 243–258. The quote is from p. 243.
45 See Miller, Anthony. "Wyatt's 'Myne Owne John Poyntz' and Juvenal." *Notes and Queries*, vol. 38, 1991, p. 22. See also Burrow (note 5), pp. 35–37.
46 See Muir, Kenneth. *Life and Letters of Sir Thomas Wyatt*, Liverpool University Press, 1963, pp. 20–23. Wyatt was accused of consorting with Anne Boleyn.
47 Greenblatt, Stephen. *Renaissance Self-Fashioning*, pp. 129–130. Hobson, Christopher Z. "Country Mouse and Towny Mouse: Truth in Wyatt." *Texas Studies in Literature and Language*, vol. 39, no. 3, 1997, pp. 230–258. Quote is on p. 232.
48 See Kernan's *The Cankered Muse*, p. 41.
49 Shelburne, Steven. "The Epistolary Ethos of Formal Satire." *Texas Studies in Literature and Language*, vol. 36, no. 2, 1994, pp. 135–165. Quote is on p. 152.
50 See *The English Renaissance: An Anthology of Sources and Documents*. Edited by Kate Aughterson, Routledge, 1998, pp. 234–235.
51 Davis, Joel B. "'Thus I restles rest in Spayne': Engaging Empire in the Poetry of Sir Thomas Wyatt and Garcilaso de la Vega." *Studies in Philology*, vol. 107, no. 4, 2010, pp. 493–519.
52 See Brigden, Susan and Woolfson, Jonathan. "Thomas Wyatt in Italy." *Renaissance Quarterly*, vol. 58, no. 2, 2005, pp. 464–511. Quote is on p. 465. Brigden and Woolfson offer an intricately detailed portrait of Wyatt's political experiences as Henry's emissary to the continent.
53 For Camden's *Britannia*, see archived Ebook, archive.org/details/gri_britanniaora 02camd. Accessed 16 Nov. 2015. Quote drawn from Kent section. See also Drayton, Michael. "Poly-Olbion: A Chronological Description of Great Britain (1612)." *The Complete Works of Michael Drayton*, ed. Richard Hooper, vol. 2, *Polyolbion*, John Russell Smith, 1876, Google Books, archive.org/details/completeworksofm01 dray. All quotes from Shakespeare are taken from *The Riverside Shakespeare*, 2nd ed., edited by G. Blakemore Evans et al., Houghton Mifflin, 1997.
54 My emphasis. See Fowler, Alastair. "Hunting for Thomas Wyatt. *Times Literary Supplement*, uploaded by The Times Literary Supplement, 30 January 2013, www.the-tls.co.uk/articles/public/hunting-for-thomas-wyatt/ Web. 23 November 2015. Here, Fowler reviews a book by Brigden, Susan. *Thomas Wyatt: The Heart's Forest*, Faber and Faber, 2012. For Brigden's comments on Kent, see pp. 263–264. See also Rebholz, p. 445 (note 42).
55 Gleckman, Jason. "Wyatt's Epistolary Satires: Parody and the Limitations of Rhetorical Humanism." *Texas Studies in Literature and Language*, vol. 43, 2001, pp. 29–45, p. 32.

56 Historical information taken from Tittler, Robert and Richards, Judith. *The Reign of Mary I*, Third ed., Routledge, 2013, Ebook, books.google.com/books?id=gFUSB AAAQBAJ&printsec=frontcover&dq=The+Reign+of+Mary+I,&hl=en&sa=X&ved=0ahUKEwjP1efut4TVAhVE4YMKHdd-NCWgQ6AEIJjAA#v=onepage&q=The%20Reign%20of%20Mary%20I%2C&f=false. Quotes are from pp. 40–42.
57 Peter, John. *Complaint and Satire in Early English Literature*, Clarendon Press, 1956.
58 Rachel Hile describes Spenserian Satire as purposefully "indirect" and "allusive," requiring extensive decoding to uncover the meaning behind the targets. *Spenserian Satire: A Tradition of Indirection*. Manchester University Press, 2017.

3 Satire Unleashed

The Rise of Juvenalianism and the Bishops' Ban of 1599[1]

> In the time of panic and fear, satire is very difficult to swallow, very difficult to digest.
> —Egyptian satirist Bassem Youssef from *Tickling Giants*[2]

The Bishops' ban represents, as Debora Shuger notes, "the single most sweeping act of censorship during the entire period from 1558 to 1641," and one of the most ambiguous (76).[3]

Precisely why the Bishops issued the document on June 1st, 1599 is unclear, however, their desire to silence the satiric perspective is by no means a novel impulse. Despite its customary pose as an insignificant literary form, satire frequently demonstrates its transhistorical ability to disturb its sociopolitical context, as evidenced by the frequent censorious reactions of authorities tasked with regulating forms of representation. Although regrettably ubiquitous, censorship is useful to literary scholars in that it provides a unique interpretive nexus for the competing ideologies of art and sociopolitical power: "the proclamations thus allow us to *know* what authors, as well as authorities, recognized as impermissible—as violating the fundamental cultural and legal norms regulating language" (Shuger 76).

When authorities distinguish a text publicly as incompatible with a particular set of norms or values, as the Bishops' ban does, their policing efforts signal what Annabel Patterson describes as a violation of the "hermeneutics of censorship," a political indicator of a transgression in the unwritten code of what are and are not acceptable forms of social representation.[4] Pierre Bourdieu also acknowledges this dialectical relationship between artistic producers of culture and those social conditions that attempt to impose form on products through the intermediary force of censorship. Satire, in the case of the Bishops' ban, represents one among several "specialized languages," including histories, plays, epigrams, and erotic narratives, that failed to find (and in some cases, rejected) a compromise between the "expressive interest" of the satiric mode and the "structure of the field in which the discourse is produced and circulates."[5] In response, authoritarian systems use censorship to attempt to impose formal "norms of official propriety" on uncompromising discourses that foreground their "shocking outspokenness" (138); "by imposing form," Bourdieu writes, "the censorship exercised by the structure of the field determines the form... and, necessarily, the content, which is inseparable from its appropriate expression, and therefore literally unthinkable outside of the known forms and recognized norms" (139). The effect of this dialectic between the arbiters of the social field and the aspiring producers of culture is not as deterministic as Bourdieu's formulation suggests. However, for many of the satires named in the 1599 ban, the principal transgression is not, precisely speaking, their failure to negotiate the accredited forms and ideological norms, but their decision to reject the restrictions of their fields, and in specific texts, their outspoken reimagining of those stabilizing literary and social orthodoxies at the heart of Elizabethan ideological conceptions. In essence, with a few notable exceptions, many of the banned satirists dared to reimagine the English nation in ways the authorities considered both unthinkable and intolerable.

The Bishops' ban must have been a significant notice to the Stationers Company of their failure to regulate a range of forms of social representation coming from London's printers, who would now be subjected to intense oversight.[6] Issued by John Whitgift, the Archbishop of Canterbury, whose duties included the licensing of printed materials, the order prohibits the further publication not only of satires and epigrams, but as mentioned, unlicensed histories and plays as well. In addition, the Ban includes a list of particularly offensive satires to be recalled and burned, a command that was carried out in Stationers' Hall on June 4, 1599. The ban offers no clear explanatory language for its targeted prohibitions; apparently, the Bishops believed there was no need to tell the Stationers *why* satire (and the named satires in particular) would no longer be tolerated, the prohibition itself was deemed sufficient, and the nature of the transgression was taken as either understood or unworthy of documentation.

As Richard McCabe posits, the only aspect of the ban that is inarguable is that satire, rather than indecency or libel, was the Bishops' overriding concern, and especially the group of "new formal verse writings [that] head the Bishops' list."[7] All attempts to explain why the Bishops suddenly decided to eradicate satires that their own office had licensed for publication not long before must involve some degree of speculation; however, as suggested by Bourdieu, instead of seeking causes for the ban, more benefit may come from considering the document in dialogue with the increasingly mercurial sociopolitical and literary fields that contributed to the order's appearance. When viewed in this context, the ban appears not as an attempt to eliminate *all* English satire, which had a well-established history of orthodox engagement with English ideology, but rather as a political mandate to stem a particularly unorthodox (and increasingly popular) mode of formal verse satire, a structurally rebellious, ideologically iconoclastic, and philosophically nihilistic mode executed in imitation of the Roman satirist Juvenal, a mode which appeared poised to overwhelm the more traditional and sanctioned modes of cultural critique, particularly, the Horatianist strain.[8] In short, the ban was less an *ad hoc* response to any singular transgression, and more a symptom of an ideological crisis over how Elizabethan society could be (or, more precisely, could not be) represented satirically, a clear priority for Elizabeth's government as indicated by the passage of such legal statutes as the 1563 proclamation against defaming images of the queen and the 1580–1581 act criminalizing "seditious words and rumours uttered against the Queen's most excellent majesty."[9] Not coincidentally, as Elizabeth's counselors struggled with numerous and varied political and economic dilemmas, her cultural arbiters chose to act against the Juvenalian mode's activistic function to proffer centrifugal representations of Elizabethan society, a situation which Annabel Patterson describes as a struggle "not only for the popular imagination but also, obviously, for control of the media by which that imagination was stimulated" (*Shakespeare* 76).

The Nature of the Bishops' Ban: "To Pacify so Great a Goddess's Ire"[10]

The Juvenalian satires that appear most prominently in the Bishops' recall and burn order certainly represent the most egregious offenders, those that provoked the majority of the government's "ire"; however, intriguingly, the order includes a range of works that appear to span a variety of genres. For example, alongside the Juvenalian imitative verse satires of John Marston, Joseph Hall, Everard Guilpin, and, to a lesser degree, Thomas Middleton, the Bishops single out John Davies' *Epigrams* (published with Christopher Marlowe's Ovidian *Elegies*), Torquato and Hercole Tasso's polemical dialogue *Of Marriage and Wiving*, the anti-feminist tract *The XV Joys of Marriage*, the erotic allegory *Caltha Poetarum*, and, oddly, all existing and planned works by Gabriel Harvey and Thomas Nashe, a duo notable for their acrimonious published disputes. Yet where the modern perspective sees a puzzling generic variety in the list of recalled works, it is not at all clear that the Bishops made the same distinction. Although apparently variegated, all of the recalled works contain the kind of satiric potential that could constitute, in the eyes of the authorities, an ideological threat. In other words, the apparent generic heterogeneity of the list suggests that the categorization of a work as satire in the period (just as today) was determined in no small part by the activistic nature of the mode, by its trans-ideological goal-orientation (either stated or tacit) to support, or to reimagine, authorized images of society.

While denigrating ridicule has been the foundation of English satire for centuries, many of the listed works are uniquely extreme in both their modes of criticism and their choice of targets. For example, Richard Aldington describes the *The XV Joys of Marriage* as an ironic "satire directed against the feminine mind" (37), while F. P. Wilson defines both *The XV Joys* and the Tassi's *Of Marriage and Wiving* as "satires" whose common method of vilifying women is part of their larger project of critiquing Elizabethan customs and structures of authority.[11] The only causal phrase in the entire order, the description of the Tassi's dialogue as "the book against women," implies that this objection on the basis of misogyny may be symptomatic of a larger objection to the work as a covert political satire directed at Elizabeth or at the ideology unique to her as a female monarch.[12] Although the tradition of English satire certainly includes an extensive history of anti-feminist critiques, such satires take on potentially intolerable political dimensions when published during the reign of a female monarch whose ideologies of personal independence and bodily integrity were seen, by some, as a threat to the continuation of the State.

The most pervasive motivational explanation for the ban is that of linguistic indecency, a position derived from the inarguable fact that the order was issued by the leaders of the Church of England. Oscar Campbell, for example, contends that the ban represents "the interposition of the ecclesiastical authorities acting in the interest of offended morality" (15), and Dustin Griffin agrees, stating, "the Bishops' Ban was probably aimed not at satire's social or political criticism but at its indecency" (149).[13] However, while works such as *The XV Joys*, *Caltha Poetarum*, and Davies' *Epigrams* certainly contain erotic images and crude language, there is not the kind of sustained indecency in the majority Juvenalian works that would rouse the Bishops' ire, and even if there were, the indecency position ignores the inextricable union of religion and politics within Elizabeth's government. In 1599, John Whitgift was not just the Archbishop of Canterbury, but also a member of Queen Elizabeth's Privy Council, and Richard Bancroft was not just the Bishop of London, but also the head of the Queen's High Commission, and as such, objections over indecent language connote both moral and political transgression:

> The idea that the bishops acted to some extent independently of the government is contrary to what we know of Tudor policy and law. No ban could be issued for any reason whatsoever without the approval and consent of either the Privy Council or the High Commission, and in this case the clauses concerning 'histories' certainly seem to indicate Council involvement.
>
> (McCabe 189)

68 *Satire Unleashed*

Indeed, the ban's prohibition against prose "English histories" and "plays" unlicensed by the Queen's Privy Council underlines not a moral objection, but the Bishops' alertness to any and all genres capable of seditious sociopolitical representation, with satire as the most overt offender. With regard to representational transgression in prose histories, in February 1599, the Bishops' office censored John Hayward's *The Life and Raigne of Henry IIII*, demanding the removal of Hayward's dedicatory epistle lauding Robert Devereux, the Second Earl of Essex, as "a great man... both in the present judgment and in the expectation of a future time."[14] This initial action apparently calmed the Bishops' fears as Hayward's prose history was then licensed for publication, and a second edition appeared in late May. However, in the months after Essex's departure for Ireland in late March 1599 to quell the rebellion of the Earl of Tyrone, the danger of the reading public creating historical parallels of Essex as a new Henry IV and Elizabeth as the despotic King Richard II apparently became too vivid; the second edition was recalled and burned around the same time as the issuance of the ban on satire.[15] As for drama, Shakespeare's *Henry V* was subjected to the scrutiny of the Master of the Revels in early- to mid-1599 for some potentially politically destabilizing analogical representations of current events: censored scenes and characters include the opening scene with the Bishops of Ely and Canterbury, the excision of the Irish soldier Macmorris, and all speeches by The Chorus, who, in the introduction to Act Five, likens Henry's triumphant return to England to Essex's anticipated return from Ireland. In short, wittingly or not, the works of Hayward and Shakespeare had threatened to degrade the image of sovereign authority cultivated by Elizabeth and her advisors in favor of the Earl of Essex, a clearly intolerable perceptual translation that came at an especially sensitive historical moment.[16]

The argument for libel as the Bishops' central motivation has come to eclipse the indecency explanation, with scholars such as Lindsay Kaplan and John Huntington describing the ban as an attempt to limit "the slanderous effect of contemporary references found in these poems."[17] Cyndia Clegg offers perhaps the most compelling version of the libel argument, positing the ban as an effort to quell any analogical readings of the generalized vice figures in the satires that could be applied retroactively not to the Queen, but to Whitgift's friend Essex and his failing military campaign in Ireland. Among other evidence, Clegg points to the satiric image of "Foelix," an ambitious noble *poseur* and hypocrite, in Satire One of Guilpin's banned *Skialetheia*, as "a passage that has been widely read as satirizing the Earl of Essex" (211):

> For when great *Foelix*, passing through the street,
> Vaileth his cap to each one he doth meet,
> And when no broom-man that will pray for him,

Shall have less truage then his bonnets brim,
Who would not think him perfect courtesy?
Or the honey-suckle of humility?
The devil he is as soon: he is the devil,
Brightly accoustred to bemist his evil.[18]

Clegg's argument that such portraits unintentionally anticipated events such as Essex's triumphant public departure for Ireland, thus motivating Whitgift to silence all subsequent *ad hominem* analogies on behalf of his friend, is possible, but limiting. On the one hand, as argued in Chapter 1, satire's inclusive chronotope draws power from comparisons between the vices of the past and the reader's present; yet on the other hand, after months and even years in public circulation, the satiric portraits had been scrutinized thoroughly enough to resist specific anachronistic applications. By June of 1599, the first three books of Hall's satire had been available for over two years, the second three books, for over a year, and both Marston's *Scourge* and Guilpin's *Skialetheia* for nearly nine months, thus while any analogical parallels might have been noteworthy, they would likely appear more coincidental than intentional.

Furthermore, from a historical standpoint, there would have been little need to protect Essex from potentially libelous applications in the summer of 1599; as late as July 16, Essex received a congratulatory letter from the Privy Council expressing their contentment at the success of his expedition. Essex did not receive private notice of Elizabeth's displeasure with his campaign until late July, and the dishonorable cease-fire Essex negotiated with the Irish rebels did not become public knowledge until September.[19] And if the Bishops were only concerned with potential libels of Essex, why not simply order particular lines struck, or require the offending sections removed, as was done with Hayward's epistle and Shakespeare's drama? Why attempt to erase all popular satire for such a limited offense? However useful the Foelix figure might have been to Essex's enemies, it is equally possible that the power of this and other typological figures found throughout the banned satires lies in their ideological rather than their libelous unorthodoxy. In essence, what seems more likely (and more potentially objectionable) is the power of a figure like Foelix to transmit a revised, degraded, ridiculous, and thus a centrifugal image of the medieval chivalric ethos held so dear by Elizabeth's flagging courtier culture.

The language of the ban itself expresses its keenest anxiety not over matters of libel or obscenity, but over matters of stylistics, accountability, and the proliferation of Juvenalian-inspired satire in London's bookstalls. The sheer volume of satires available to the reading public could not have escaped the notice of Elizabeth's book censors: in just over two years, beginning in March 1597 with the publication of the first three books (entitled "Toothless Satires") of Hall's *Virgidemiarum*, the publication and consumption of formal verse satires increased dramatically, causing satire to become an increasingly visible and influential literary vogue in the culture. One year after the publication of Hall's first three books of satire, the last three books (entitled "Biting Satires") were entered into the Stationers' Register, followed soon after by William Rankins' *Seven Satyres* (1598; not named in the ban), a second edition of Hall's Toothless Satires (1598), Marston's *The Metamorphosis of Pigmalion's Image and Certain Satires* (1598), the first edition of Marston's *The Scourge of Villanie* (1598), and Guilpin's *Skialetheia, or the Shadow of truth in Epigrams and Satyres* (late 1598). Between January 1 and June 1, 1599, a second edition of Hall's "Biting Satires" was published, as were two more editions of Marston's *Scourge of Villanie* (with the "Satyra Nova" attacking Hall directly), as well as Thomas Middleton's *Micro-Cynicon: Six Snarling Satires*. This is not to imply that formal verse satire was startlingly novel in late Tudor culture; Thomas Wyatt's horatian satires, first published in *Songs and Sonnets* (or *Tottel's Miscellany*) in 1557, were still in the public eye at the time of the ban.[20] Furthermore, John Donne's first four satires were in circulation in manuscript between 1593 and 1599,[21] Thomas Lodge's satire *A Fig for Momus* was published in 1595, and Davies' book of *Epigrams* was published in 1596.[22] What is intriguing, however, is that none of the formal verse satires of Wyatt, Donne, or Lodge, appears in the Bishops' ban; the order seems concerned with silencing only the mode of immoderate Juvenalian verse satire that reached its height in the spring and summer of 1599.

As for stylistics and accountability, the Bishops' command to collect and destroy not merely the listed works but "*any* book of the *nature* of these heretofore expressed," as well as "such books as can be found or are already taken of the *Arguments* aforesaid" (my emphases) employs modal language (nature; arguments) to communicate the Bishops' intolerance of all literary works that participate, directly or indirectly, in the Juvenalian style of unorthodox social representation. The desire for stricter accountability ("to know whether it be their hand or no") informs authors, wardens, and printers alike that the tolerance for anonymous, radical literary challenges to social norms was at an end; however, the requirement also reveals the degree to which the Bishops feared the growing influence of the young generation of avant-garde poets fostered largely by the Inns of Court culture.[23]

The suggestion that the Bishops were anxious over the rising influence of Juvenalianism also helps to account for the ban's rather odd prohibition against the works of Harvey and Nashe. As David McPherson argues, early in their public exchanges, both Harvey and Nashe styled themselves as outspoken, liberally minded satirists, but whereas Harvey soon came to "dislike the role," preferring instead a more conservative, centripetal, moralizing voice, Nashe fashioned his satiric persona consistently in the mode of the contemporary Italian erotic-satirist Pietro Aretino, and by extension, a "modern Juvenal, the lashing satirist" (1553). Despite Harvey's eventual recantation of Nashe's "mold of Aretine, or Rabelais, Archilochus, Aristophanes, Lucian" (1554), it seems likely that the Bishops considered the men's literary quarrelling of a kind with Juvenalian indecorum.[24]

The Spectrum of Juvenalianism: From a "Satyr without Horns" to a "Tamburlaine of Vice"

As contentious as the scholarly arguments are concerning the origin and purpose of the Ban, one factor they all share is a disregard for the importance of the reprieve granted solely to Dymoke's *Caltha Poetarum* and Hall's *Virgidemiarum*. It is difficult to deny the possibility that both works were excused due to private connections: as the brother of the Queen's champion, Dymoke likely had many potential protectors at court, and as for Hall, his father, John Hall, had been deputy to the Earl of Huntingdon, and young Joseph was in training for the clergy in 1599, which doubtless brought him into regular contact with church and government officials. The fact that Hall was ordained and began public preaching just eighteen months after the issuance of the ban suggests his undamaged status in the eyes of his fellow clerical authorities.

Nepotism aside, the fact of a narrowly focused reprieve complicates arguments by Kernan, McCabe, and Clegg describing late Elizabethan satire as a formally homogeneous and uniformly radical "new tradition" in imitation of Juvenal. While the Juvenalian influence in all six books of Hall's formal verse satire is indisputable, as demonstrated by editor Arnold Davenport,[25] the fact of the relative absolution granted to Hall's imitative satire alone suggests the capacity of late-sixteenth-century Juvenalianism to vary along a formal and ideological spectrum, with the radical form of Juvenalianism at one end, and the centralizing form of Horatianism at the other. Fredric Bogel is quite correct when he asserts that the purism behind the Horace-Juvenal dichotomy is largely an artificial construct created by scholars, "because it allows the potentially disruptive energies of satiric aggression to be at once acknowledged and contained" (30); however, while it is true that Horace can be as roughly indignant as Juvenal, and Juvenal can be as urbanely ironic as Horace, for English Renaissance poetic imitators, the dichotomy was vital more for its ideological orientation than for its formal implications. To imitate horatian poetics was to align one's work with an ideologically privileged conservative tradition that reached back for centuries (see Chapter 2), while the tradition of Juvenal as model, as Ben Parsons argues, inherently implies an endorsement of unwarranted *libertas* (freedom), a centrifugal, disruptive, even potentially militant mode of abuse unconcerned with established formal traditions and ideological *schemata*.[26]

72   *Satire Unleashed*

Furthermore, to imitate Horace is to link one's culture to the politically and culturally valued inception of the Roman Empire under Augustus, while to imitate Juvenal is to suggest an analogical connection between the reader's present and the morally and politically dissolute reign of the Roman emperor Domitian.[27] As such, the presence of an openly defiant form of English Juvenalianism in the late 1590s must have seemed to the authorities not just inappropriate, but a direct challenge to the ideological stability of a nation undergoing a range of potentially destabilizing political, economic, social, and religious crises, and as such, could scarcely condone the "decentering of the sources of cultural authority," as Louis Montrose asserts.[28]

For imitative satirists and wary censors alike, the cultural authority for English satire was Horace, and thus what is so remarkable about Hall's satire is its ability to capitalize on the public's interest in Juvenalian ferocity, accessible language, and unrepentant individualism, while simultaneously structuring his imitative style to more closely evoke the sanctioned poetics and centripetal ideology of Horace. A closer inspection of Hall's work reveals it as a liminal mode of English satire, one that constructs a formal and ideological middle space between the tradition of horatian moralistic, socially salutary satire and the new vogue for individualistic, socially iconoclastic Juvenalian satire, with which Hall's hybrid mode participates in name only. The Bishops' reprieve, in essence, sets a standard for satiric form; Hall's meditatively stoic "quiet style" of Juvenalianism receives a begrudging seal of approval, while Marston's violently cynical "censuring vein," as John Weever describes the banned style, remains unforgivably antagonistic to the norms of Elizabethan representation.[29] As such, Hall's mixed style represents not a "failure to separate, even in intention, the two main streams of satire, the comic and the Horatian from the tragic and Juvenalian," but a deliberate rhetorical strategy of sociocultural appeasement achieved largely by rendering his version of Juvenal "toothless," or "impotent," as Horace described his own centripetal style, even when Hall's mode is supposedly at its most "biting."[30]

The programmatic statement prefacing Hall's "Toothless" satires announces his intent to utilize a new imitative style that is conversant with the avant-garde mode of unrestrained Juvenalian "*indignatio*" (outrage), yet seeks to shift that ethos towards the conventionally centripetal norms for English satire such as occur in the horatian tradition:

> In speaking of satire, I seem to have said that satire is born of anger, but I correct myself; this is not enough to say about satire. Anger makes the satire, but what I have left out is that satire moderates anger: Paint your satire with your own blood, then it is satire. Behold the new satire: A Satyr without horns! Rejoice, these monsters are of a new monster, and are both of the Satyrs and of the Satires.[31]

Here, in Latin verse available only to an educated readership, the authorial voice begins by modifying his initial conclusions on the most appropriate generic conventions of satire by referencing Juvenal's famous programmatic statement "outrage makes the verse" (*Satires* 1.79), purposefully shifting individualistic rage against social ills towards the socially supportive purpose characteristic of the horatian tradition: satire may be born of anger, but it must function to temper the anger of others, and by implication, to embrace a purpose that is constructive rather than destructive. "Good" satire must not spill the blood of its targets, but instead must be 'painted' with the blood of the author, a self-sacrificial metaphor that implies the kind of Christian imperative that underpins both Hall's biography and much English satire prior to the late sixteenth century. Consciously referring to the perceived similarity in etymology between "Satyr" and "Satire," the statement ends with the pronouncement that Hall's new mode will exist formally and ideologically in a centrist position between the classical tradition of Old Comedy (the Satyrs) and the new vogue for a satiric "Tamburlaine of vice," a kind of self-emasculated amalgam ("A Satyr without horns!") that is emblematic of Hall's approach to his satiric subjects throughout all six books of the *Virgidemiarum*.[32] Therefore, Davenport's statement that Hall was successful in creating the first "true Juvenalian mode of satire" (xxv) bears further consideration. Decades later, John Milton lambasts Hall's choice as both cowardly and antithetical to the nature and purpose of satire itself:

> For a satire as it was born out of a tragedy, so ought to resemble his parentage, to strike high, and adventure dangerously at the most eminent vices among the greatest persons, and not to creep into every blind tap-house, that fears a constable more than a satire. But that such a poem should be toothless, I still affirm it to be a bull, taking away the essence of that which it calls itself. For if it bite neither the persons nor the vices, how is it a satire? And if it bite either, how is it toothless?[33]

Hall subdivides his books of "Toothless Satires" into three categories, "Poetical," "Academical," and "Moral," a construction which underlines the intellectually distanced and uncontroversial intentionality of the social critiques to follow. Unsurprisingly, throughout the Toothless Satires, decorous humanistic philosophical contemplation overpowers the few direct engagements with recognizable social targets. The effect of such a distancing strategy renders the mode closer to a horatian sermon than to a satire, which is precisely how Hall characterizes his own socially safe style: "go to then ye my sacred *Semones*" (4.1.80). And like Horace's desire to restrain the excessive poetry of his predecessor, Lucilius, Hall admits in a number of programmatic statements that he is unable or unwilling to give full expression to the generic conventions of unfettered Juvenalian satire. For example, in his introductory "Defiance to Envy," Hall's authorial speaker opines, "The ruder Satyre should go rag'd and bare: / And show his rougher and his hairy hide: / Though mine be smooth, and decked in careless pride" (76–78). Elsewhere in the introduction, the speaker describes the paradoxical nature of his hybrid satire as,

> Too good (if ill) to be expos'd to blame:
> Too good, if worse, to shadow shameless vice.
> Ill, if too good, not answering their name:
> So good and ill in fickle censure lies.
> Since in our Satyre lies both good and ill,
> And they and it, in varying readers will.
>
> (67–72)

Hall's witty construction blends moral and aesthetic language to justify the employment of satire, and to defend it against charges of seditious intent. A "good," or morally effective, satire is poetically "ill," yet appropriate to the rough conventions of Juvenalian satire. However, while "good," or socially beneficial and aesthetically pleasing satire, may be accused of not "answer[ing]" the "name," or generic heritage, of satire, the "worse," or more appropriately vituperative satire, is less capable of "shadow[ing]," or reproducing, the vices with which it participates. Horatianism and Juvenalian conventions are thus portrayed "in fickle censure" in Hall's toothless style, and Hall claims the "varying" nature of each individual reader will determine which aspect receives the greater focus.

Such self-conscious and self-defensive formulas occur time and again in *Virgidemiarum* as when, for example, the speaker denies the efficacy of excessive personal liberty in satire ("'Tis better to be bad, than to be bold," "Prologue," 3.14), and most tellingly, in his "Post-script to the Reader," when the authorial voice admits that "a true and natural Satire" (as opposed to his own style) is "both hard of conceit, and harsh of style," as most evident in the works of "Juvenal" and "Persius" (97). Hall goes on to admit that although his first "Biting Satire" (4.1) "doth somewhat resemble the sour and crabbed face of Juvenal's," overall, his hybrid mode self-censors the more disruptive aspects of the Juvenalian conventions in order to avoid reprisals, which, as the reprieve indicates, was apparently effective: "I endeavoring in that [his Juvenalian satire 4.1], did determinately omit in the rest, for these forenamed causes, that so I might have somewhat to stop the mouth of every accuser" (99).

Within the Toothless Satires themselves, Hall downplays the activistic element of satire that engages with recognizable particulars by making both his historicity and his poetics unapologetically anachronistic and homiletic; more often than not, the speaker points the reader backward to images of a decorous English past rather than confronting the reader with startlingly specific images of a decadent and irredeemable present. As one example, in the "Academical" satires, the tangible benefits of adhering to traditional social decorums are presented as an appealing alternative for those who would abuse their intellectual gifts for personal advancement. For example, in Satire 2.6 (a decidedly horatian satire), the speaker ironically and comically juxtaposes the virtues and vices of the "Trencher-Chaplain" hired to instruct the sons of a gentleman "Squire," and urges the reader directly to align with the instructor's better behaviors, just as Horace's "best father" instructed him to learn from bad examples and to emulate good ones (1–2; see Horace's *Sermones* 1.4.105–111). The speaker implores the teacher (and the reader) to content himself with his subservient role, not to take the best bed, not to usurp the father's place at the table, not to overeat, and never to beat a student without the mother's approval, all of which are ironically implied as abuses common to the servant class, and yet all of which are equally portrayed as virtuous behaviors that, if followed, will earn the properly obeisant subject "five marks, and winter livery" (16).

Having demonstrated his mastery of the salutary horatian mode, Hall proclaims an intention in the subsequent three books of "Biting Satires" to indulge in the alternative, less decorous, and more libelously obscure mode of Juvenalian imitation:

> Henceforth I write in crabbed oak-tree rind:
> Search they that mean the secret meaning find.
> Hold out ye guilty, and ye galled hides,
> And meet my far-fetch'd stripes with waiting sides.
>
> ("Conclusion" 43)

However, Hall's scourging mode never makes good on its threats. Hall promises "Hot blood's rage," a tone like a "thunder-clap," "open rhymes" available to all, and unfettered assaults in direct opposition to the pedantic obscurity of "*Flaccus*" [Horace], which are reimagined as appropriate only for the "Trivial floor" of the schoolhouse (91, 171–174). In reality, however, while Hall replicates the moral topics and *figurae* present in the Juvenalian originals, his tone is mild, his couplets rarely vary, the language is consistently elevated, and the contemporary references remain eminently safe, as when the speaker offers an uncontroversial joke against the ailing King Philip II of Spain, who had failed to recapture England a decade earlier: "Yet when he hath my crabbed Pamphlet read / As oftentimes as PHILLIP has been dead" (29–30). In short, Hall's "Biting Satires" invoke Juvenal more than imitate him. The "Biting Satires" purposefully eschew the creation of an authentic English version of Juvenal's ferociously iconoclastic perspective, one motivated by a bona fide desire to stand at the crossroads of contemporary society and challenge the reader with familiar, if augmented, representations of the decadent world they both inhabit.[34]

On the whole, the "Biting Satires" nibble at abstractions of such familiar Christian vices as Ambition (Satire 4.2 and 4.6), Pride (Satire 4.3), Luxury (Satire 4.4), and Greed (Satire 4.5). Yet while some of the satires contain extratextual references to contemporary locales, institutions, and colloquial idioms ("For else how should his son maintained be, / At Inns of Court or of the Chancerie," 4.2.53–54; "The sturdy Ploughman doth the soldier see, / All scarfed with pied colors to the knee... Now he doth inly scorn his Kendal-green, / And his patch't Cockers [leggings] now despised been," 4.6.36–41), generally speaking, these *exempla* from the reader's context are deliberately enervated by their proximity to classical references available to an exclusive minority. In Book Four, satire five, for example, the contemporary hot button topic of usury ("*Tocullio* was a wealthy usurer") is undercut by an obscure comparison available mainly to the upper strata of society: "By Bushels was he wont to mete his coin / As did the old wife of *Trimalcion*," a reference to Petronius's character of the grasping wife Fortunata in Petronius' *Satyricon* (39–42). Later, in Book Six, when the bad poet *Labeo* sets his sights on piercing the speaker's satire "ten leaves at once" with his critical quill, the timely subjects of artistic rivalry and official censorship are safely distanced by the comparison of the offended critic to the Fury *Megaera* in Seneca the Younger's classical tragedy, *Thyestes* (6.1.1–7). "The Satire *should* be like the Porcupine" (my emphasis), Hall admits, "that shoots sharp quills out in each angry line," but the current era is too insecure, too circumspect, and too fearful to digest less ambiguous representations of social orthodoxies delivered by a self-anointed judge, jury, and executioner, as Hall himself makes clear: "Ye Antique Satyres, how I bless your days, / That brook'd your bolder style, their own dispraise...For now our ears been of more brittle mold, / Than those dull earthen ears that were of old" (5.3.1–6).

Hall's most supposedly Juvenalian satire (4.1) initially fulfills the reader's expectations with the required outburst of individualistic rage against those who would accuse the speaker of employing Juvenalianism for his own private grudges rather than for generalized moral instruction:

> Who dares upbraid these open rhymes of mine
> With blindfold *Aquines* or dark *Venusine* [Horace]?
> Or rough-hew'n *Teretismes* writ in th'antique vain
> Like an old Satyre, and new *Flaccian*?
>
> (1–4)

Beyond evoking the defiant rhetorical pose of Juvenal's first satire, Hall alludes to the competing imitative models available to him, and his attempt to navigate amongst them, although he ends with the image of himself as the culture's "new *Flaccian*," i.e. a new English Horace. Furthermore, the speaker rejects the alignment with the indiscriminately violent methods of Juvenal ("blindfold Aquines"), Julius Caesar Scaliger ("rough-hew'n Teretismes"), and Aristophanic Old Comedy ("Like an old Satyre"), and appeals instead to educated humanists capable of uncovering the moral message underlying the supposedly libelous *figurae*: "yet well bethought stoops down, and reads a new: / The best lies low, and loathes the shallow view" (19–20).

Where Hall's last three books come closest to the true activistic nature of satire, or in other words, to the creation of an authentic critical perspective and refracted social engagements meant to motivate action, is his condemnation of the contemporary practices of rack-renting and enclosure among English landholders, which seem to promise a purpose-driven indignation and a resulting centrifugal ideological orientation largely absent from conservative Horatianism. Enclosure and high rents were particularly pressing economic and class issues during the final years of the sixteenth century, as the overall economic prospects for rural tenant farmers was particularly bleak. R. B. Outhwaite cites devastating crop failures between 1596 and 1599, which he describes as the "years of dearth," with food riots in the south occurring in 1595. Statistics on the price of wheat in England between 1596 and 1599 indicate that the average price had decreased by half over this four-year period, while the purchasing power of the annual wage rates for agricultural laborers and craftsman had also declined over the course of the decade.[35] Violent objections to the enclosure of grazing lands by grasping landowners were not unique to the 1590s; economic historian Joan Thirsk cites the "large-scale enclosure movement" as an ongoing concern for lawmakers, as evidenced by reports from the multiple Enclosure Commissions set up to address the problem.[36] However, like the Kett Rebellion of 1549, the 1596 Oxfordshire Enclosure Riots, while quickly quelled, was an alarming symbol of the growing discontent among the working classes over restrictions of time-honored freedoms such as access to common grazing lands. The fact that two anti-enclosure bills were passed by Parliament in the wake of the Oxfordshire uprising suggests the government's awareness of the potentially explosive consequences of allowing the wealthy to continue to inflict economic hardships on the poor.[37]

Hall's mitigated Juvenalian speaker exudes a cautiously revolutionary fervor as he addresses Enclosure unequivocally in "Biting Satires" 4.2 and 5.3, and yet, Hall again employs subtle ironic distancing techniques to avoid government censure and to keep his social engagement safely centripetal. In Satire 4.2, for example, instead of presenting an image of an avaricious nobleman, Hall gives the reader *Lolio*, a Yeoman farmer, an emblem of the prideful, foolish commoner who will do anything to raise his undeserving son to the upper class ("to make his eldest son a Gentleman," 2), including impoverishing himself, spoiling his son, and encouraging contact with preening courtiers. When the neighbors come to visit, they praise Lolio for his foresight, and they fantasize of a time when his noble heirs will "rule and reign in their rich Tenancy" (124). As noblemen, Lolio's imagined descendants will be free to indulge their greed, mainly through exacting the exorbitant rents and land enclosures that currently afflict them:

> When perch't aloft to perfect their estate
> They rack their rents unto a treble rate;
> And hedge in all the neighbor common-lands,
> And clog their slavish tenant with commands,
> Whiles they, poor souls, with feeling sighs complain
> And wish old *Lolio* were alive again.
>
> (125–130)

Oscar Campbell claims that such passages "reveal the moral ardor with which the satirists attacked contemporary economic abuses and suggest that they adopted the tone of Juvenal because their own indignation was as hot as his" (42). However, while a more overtly indignant and realistic depiction of the economic suffering caused by such practices might have clearly aligned Hall's satiric ideology with that of the oppressed classes, instead, Hall's evocation of the enclosure crisis is just one of a range of carefully chosen *exempla* of excess which function not as an attack on a particular economic practice, but as an ironic promotion of virtues such as thrift, temperance, and industry among the lower classes. In short, the target here is not the greed of the landowners, but the greed of the aspiring tenant farmers. The descent of Lolio's son from "the very Embleme of good husbandrie" (22) to a morally void "Brasse Gentlemen" (148) delivers an ideologically sustaining message of the benefits of the status quo rather than a destabilizing condemnation of the iniquitous behavior of the upper classes.

Similarly, *Satire* 5.3 ponders the futility of enclosure and the morality of defending ancient grazing rights in a manner which could not help but invoke controversial historical incidents such as the Oxfordshire uprising: "For what mought [might] that avail / That my field might not fill my neighbor's payle [i.e. fencepost]... If they were thriftless, mote [might] not we amend, / And with more care our dangered fields defend?" (44–51) Yet once again, this engagement with a topical issue is rendered inert, as so often occurs in Hall's satires, by a preference for the past over the present; in this instance, the blame falls not on the greed of the nobility, but the greed of the nomadic farmers of old who were not content with open fields and no restrictions "save for the furrows of their husbandry" (39), and chose to demarcate property to which they were not entitled: "some headless cross they digged on their lea, / Or roll'd some marked Meare-stone in the way. Poor simple men" (42–44).

Eventually, as in Satire 4.2, Hall creates a relatively neutral ideological image of the enclosure issue that will ensure both the stability of the status quo and the inoffensiveness of Hall's satire: the speaker promises praise for any enclosures constructed by the "thrifty Yeoman" (62), provided that he strikes a balance between the public needs of the peasant farmer class and his own private advantages:

> So be, thou stake not up the common stile;
> So be thou hedge in nought, but what's thine own,
> So be thou pay what tithes they neighbor's done,
> So be thou let not lie in fallowed plain,
> That which was wont yield Usury of grain.
>
> (65–69)

By producing a monologic, tractable version of Juvenal, Hall neutralizes Juvenal's potentially disruptive influence for the benefit of the governing classes.[38]

This Horatianist brand of Juvenalianism is more akin to the "revolutionary conservative" approach adopted by Sir Thomas Wyatt in "Mine Own John Poyntz" than it is to Marston's mode, an approach that presents itself as a radical challenge to orthodox positions, but in fact, the relationship between the targets and the satiric intentionality is ironized so as to support the ideology of the dominant social fields. The Bishops had little to fear from this form of satiric cultural representation, and thus the 'stay' issued to Hall's mode seems almost inevitable.

Before turning to an analysis of Marston's radical counter-mode, the prefatory statement found in another banned and reprieved work, *Caltha Poetarum*, is worth noting briefly because it is emblematic of the crisis in the late sixteenth century over the 'proper' form of sociopolitical representation, or the struggle, to return to Patterson's language, over the popular imagination and control of the media that influences it. In the work's preface, Dymoke makes a rather modernist argument that questions the efficacy of continuing to imitate revered classical models like Horace in order to appeal solely to fellow learned poets and vigilant censors, and suggests instead the benefits of adopting a more populist approach in order to provide the most moral improvement to the widest audience. In short, Dymoke, like Marston, is wary of poets like Hall who employ monologic poetics with an eye towards a synergy with the dominant forces in the literary and social fields at the expense of both accessibility and the reformatory imperative so important to satire.

Dymoke begins by offering a list of familiar, socially sanctioned models from across a variety of genres, with a strong glance towards satire:

> For *Homer*, who imitated none, and *Archilocus*, who is compared with *Homer*, because they only finished their works in their life.

And *Virgil*, the curious Ape of *Homer. Ovid* the Amorous, *Martial* the licentious, *Horace*, the mixed betwixt the modest and *Satiric* vein. The flower of our age, sweet pleasing *Sidney. Tasso* the grave. Polished *Daniel* the Historic. *Spencer* the Truth's Faith.[39]

The speaker's depiction of Horace as "mixed betwixt the modest and Satiric vein" is wholly in line with the traditional construction of Horace as the centripetal satirist of empire appropriate for poetic imitation in the same manner as Homer, Virgil, and the other classical models Dymoke describes as "admired and deified almost by the wisest, the learnedst, and the deepest sighted into great matters, the ignorant not being able to attain unto them."[40] Juvenal and Persius are conspicuous in this formulation by their absence.

Dymoke then advocates for populism in imitative poetics in a manner wholly embraced by Marston's neoteric Juvenalian mode. Dymoke laments that poets like himself who embrace "low," commonplace subjects and demotic language are delegitimized by cultural authorities: "So we are held among the inferior spirits, and are the little Penates, to country, homely, and low reaching wits, admired by such, and religiously read, though never taken into the others' [the erudite authors'] hands." However, Dymoke then issues a defiant summons to other 'low-minded' poets to embrace styles and subjects that prefer familiar, rustic Englishness over erudite continental models as, presumably, the more ethically effective poetics: "Gentlemen & others, I pray you let us hold together for the preservation of our reputation, and maintain the prescription of our low subjects, least *Apollo's* music do quite drown poor *Pan*, and the country Hornpipe be laid aside."[41]

Marston's banned mode, executed most explicitly in *The Scourge of Villanie*, takes Dymoke's recommendations to heart, its unabsolved and unrepentant radicalism the result of a complete rejection of the rhetorical, philosophical, and ideological norms for imitative satire that Hall embraced through his so-called "quiet" horatianist mode. James Baumlin argues persuasively that Marston used Hall's hybrid mode as a negative model against which he defined his radically centrifugal version of Juvenal as the most appropriate style for English satire: "by imitating and in the same poem rejecting the Horatian attitude toward vice, Marston demonstrates his familiarity with the model, points out its inability to deal effectively with the graver vices, and so justifies his ultimate choice of Juvenal."[42] In an act of clear defiance of the government's desire for affinity between cultural and political representations, Marston chooses to construct a cynical, populist, "barking satirist" *persona* named W. Kinsayder to deliver a new decorum of indecorum for English imitative satire, a mode whose central tenet is Juvenalian "freedom."

Marston asserts the authority of the individual will free of traditional restrictions, free to use demotic language rather than deceptive poetic artifice, free to reverse Horace's preference for *"ridiculum"* over *"acri"* (humor over bitter hatred) in his critiques, free to turn to the individual conscience rather than to the church or state to judge what is good and what is evil (a principle Marston terms "Synderesis"), and free to offer his own perceptual translations of orthodox subjects not as the authorities would have them, but as they truly are: "I am myself," writes Marston, "so is my poesie" ("To Detraction," 24).[43] Such a solipsistic challenge to the tradition of centripetal Horatianism (among other challenges) must have seemed more than just indecorous to Elizabeth's censors, but a potentially seditious, if not an utterly treasonous assault on approved sociocultural *ethoi*. As cited by Cyndia Clegg, in his 1600 speech to the Star Chamber, Thomas Egerton, The Lord Keeper, seems to refer to the seditious quality of the banned satires when he requests punishment for those "libelers who by tongue and by pen did not spare to censure states, etc. And such of late have slandered her Majesty's officers by libel" (215–216). Although many assume that "libel" refers to references to Essex, Egerton's reference to the negative affect on the "states" should not be overlooked: whether "states" refers to a violation of class distinctions or to the diminution of the national image, the central objection remains an ideological one.

Marston's claim to unrestrained freedom by way of Juvenal, and by extension, by way of Juvenal's own model, the Roman republican era satirist Lucilius is no mere rhetorical pose; to align one's satire with Lucilius has ideological as well as rhetorical implications. Lucilius's rhetorical freedom is associated with the relative openness of Roman republican democracy, and as such, Juvenal desires to "blaze and roar" freely, like Lucilius, against his own dissolute society, yet he understands the risks such freedom poses in the oppressive era of Domitian (See Juvenal 1.165–168 and 155–156).[44] Marston, via Kinsayder,[45] espouses a much more cavalier expression of anger in a manner largely unconcerned for both his personal safety ("No gloomy Juvenal, / Though to thy fortunes I disastrous fall," 1.3.195–196) and the scorn of those he attacks ("Who'll cool my rage? Who'll stay my itching fist / But I will plague and torture whom I list?" 1.2.9–10), because the sheer ubiquity of sin and vice throughout the empire of "Albion" (50) requires the freedom to assault anything and anyone with no regard for traditional orthodoxies:

> Yet I should rail upon
> This fusty world, that now dare put in ure
> To make JEHOVA but a coverture,
> To shade rank filth, loose conscience is free,
> From all conscience, what else hath liberty?
> As't please the Thracian Boreas to blow,
> So turns our airy conscience, to and fro.
>
> (1.2.12–18)

Here, Marston overturns the entire horatian tradition: the unorthodox Juvenalian libertine fashions himself as the sole voice of reason capable of passing judgment on the entire culture, the isolated cynic, answerable to no patron in a culture that relies on systems of patronage, and thus under no constraints to mollify his anger. He has no intention to instruct or to support, in the horatian sense, as Hall does. The cynic perspective has no interest in pressing the reader to choose the virtuous example over the vicious one, because in the decadent, irredeemable world he represents, there are no virtuous alternatives, not even the satirist speaker himself; the best he can offer are provocative images to spur awareness of the nation's true social ills lurking behind the veil of hypocritical dogma. For the Bishops to allow this kind of unbridled iconoclasm, this use of art to transmit a 'tragic' image, in Kernan's view, of society would be equivalent to endorsing the kind of 'seditious words uttered against the Queen's most excellent majesty' outlawed nearly two decades before (192).

Perhaps the most alarming (from the Bishop's perspective) aspect of the mode is Marston's stated intention to target his nation specifically, which suggests a satiric ideological orientation hostile to orthodox sociopolitical economies. The unflinching Juvenalian will "bear the scourge of just *Rhamnusia*, / Lashing the lewdness of *Britania*," his self-appointed role likened to that of the Greek goddess Nemesis come to punish rather than to amend the vices of England (Proemium 1.1–2); what clear-eyed poet "can abstain," Marston wonders, from making "his shamefac'd Muse a scold" when the evidence is so plain that "dead's the strength of England's yeomanrie" (1.2.142–143 & 139). Whereas Hall carefully controls the degree of overt historicity evoked by his satiric representations through culturally approved classical allusions, Marston finds more "pleasure" in reversing such "sharp control," as the conventional employment of "good subjects" clothed in "true poesie" is judged as hypocritical at best, corruptive at worst (Proemium 1.8 & 6). In essence, because Marston deems the use of erudite obscurity to be immoral, distanced historical references are translated into more plain, familiar, and thus more ideologically unstable representations that reflect the true scope of the immoral conditions that jeopardize both the reader and the satirist: "Think'st thou that I in melting poesie / Will pamper itching sensualitie? / (That in the body's scum all fatally / Entombs the soul's most sacred faculty.)" (2.6.19–22).

Another key rhetorical convention of this radical ideology is its validation of the everyday language of the *vulgus* (the common people), an authorial choice which reinforces the mode's populist orientation, and which provoked Ben Jonson's scorn in his ideologically conservative horatian drama, *Poetaster*.[46] However, Marston's choice of language is as eminently logical as it is politically daring: unorthodox visions of English society are best delivered with words that are equally unorthodox, such as the command to "Quake guzzell dogs, that live on putrid slime, / Skud from the lashes of my yerking rhyme" (Proemium 1.20). And while poetic traditionalists and cultural arbiters might be shocked by street phrases like "dung-scum," "bitcherie," "Oyster-wenches," "jobbernoul," "gurnet's head," and "[William] Kemp's jig" in classically inspired satire, in context, the effect is more authentic, more efficacious, and ironically, more moral for a cynic dedicated to an activistic engagement with the vices of the living present.[47]

In Bakhtin's terms, Marston chooses to present a linguistic alternative to "concrete verbal and ideological centralization" preferred by authorities invested in protecting the ideological image of enduring imperial authority from cultural products that familiarize and degrade that image through 'crude, familiar' contact with the evolving multi-valent language of the present (*DI* 271–273). The ideological effect of the insertion of the demotic languages of the clown and of the street fair, is centrifugal; power is spun away from official verbal ideologies (Horatianism, for one) into a more heterogeneous sociolinguistic context in close contact with the readers' experience. As discussed in Chapter 1, Bakhtin contends that such satiric dialogism allows the satirist to investigate, without pretense to poetic and ideological norms, the true moral state of the subject in compelling ways (See *DI* 23, 35).

Such a deliberate reorientation of the imitative tradition in satire attracted the attention of more than just the Bishops: the university students who wrote and staged the three parodic *Parnassus* plays at St. John's College, Cambridge, between late 1598 and late 1601 reference Marston's radicalism directly.[48] In *The Second Part of the Return from Parnassus*, the typological characters Ingenioso and Judicio debate the merits of major cultural figures, and when their discussion touches on the relative merits of Marston, both characters assault him for his destabilizing ideological and rhetorical indecorum. Judicio begins with the usual comparison of Marston's cynic style to a barking dog, but a dog whose venom, in this case, befouls the entire world ("What, *Monsieur Kinsayder*, lifting up your leg and pissing against the world? Put up man, put up for shame"; 267–268), while Ingenioso lays the blame on the ignobility of Marston himself ("withouten bands or garters ornament"). The immodest, demotic language (his 'ruffian style' and "plain naked words") is also condemned as failing to fulfill satire's traditional imperative to restrain excess freedom in support of the status quo:

> He quaffs a cup of Frenchman's Helicon,
> Then royster doyster [swaggers; blusters] in his oily terms,
> Cuts, thrusts, and foins [stabs] at whomsoever he meets,
> And strews about Ram-alley[49] meditations.
> Tut, what cares he for modest close-couched terms,
> Cleanly to gird our looser libertines?

84　*Satire Unleashed*

> Give him plain naked words stripped of their shirts
> That might beseem plain dealing Aretine.[50]
>
> (269–278)

Marston himself is unapologetic concerning both his unorthodox language and his belief that good satire preferences social purpose over empty rhetorical flourishes. In his programmatic address to "Judicial Perusers," Marston acknowledges conventional assumptions about the need for decorous distance in satiric imitation, and then flatly rejects them as antithetical to satire's activistic nature: "know I hate to affect too much obscurity and harshness because they profit no sense. To note vices so that no man can understand them is as fond as the French execution in picture" (1–4). He then notes the bias that all satires that employ comprehensible images that "come within their [critics'] reach" are "bastard" (4–6), and admits the cultural penchant for a "seemly decorum" and "peculiar kind of speech" conventional for the "Satyre's lips" (28–30). However, he defiantly refuses to ascribe to such restrictions as they fail to represent the true ugliness of vice and sin in a way that could impel social change: "let me have the substance rough, not the shadow. I cannot, nay I will not delude your sight with mists; yet I dare defend my plainness 'gainst the verjuice [bitter] face of the crabbed'st Satyrist that ever stuttered" (28–35).

What potentially moves such defiance from nonconformism to sedition, in the eyes of the authorities, is the effort to create a consensual community between the critic and the masses. As Patrick Buckridge[51] argues, Marston frequently exposes the counterproductive nature of elitist devices in satire, and defends their opposites:

> Marston contests the historical authority of both these precepts ['darkness' and 'roughness']... his main point being that when they are put into practice (as, for example, in the satires of his older contemporary, Joseph Hall), they are conducive to bad reading for they encourage "decoding" habits.
>
> (60)

In the opening address to Utterly Unfit Readers ("*In Lectores prorsus indignos*"), Marston constructs a generically typical, yet ideologically purposeful, "quasi-dramatic" dialogue intended to advance his populist philosophy.[52] "Phylo," the Interlocutor who, as his typological name suggests, will argue as a 'lover' of the elitist satiric style, argues with "Satyre" (The Satirist), who argues for accessibility as a requirement of satire's purpose-driven nature. *Phylo* opens by imagining depraved readers from across a range of class levels, all of whom misinterpret the raging Juvenalian mode for their own benefit, implying that the satirist should restrict himself and his poetics to the fit reader alone, as the centripetal traditions demands: "Fie Satyre fie, shall each mechanic slave, / Each dunghill peasant, free perusal have / Of thy well labor'd lines?" (1–3). The Satirist responds that his mode is purposefully inclusive, welcoming all to view their likenesses in language available not only those who can read, but those who can hear, too; all levels of society deserve retribution for their moral transgressions, and so the Satirist will spare (and fear) no one:

> Aye *Phylo*, Aye, I'll keep an open hall,
> A common, and a sumptuous festival,
> Welcome all eyes, all ears, all tongues to me,
> Gnaw peasants on my scraps of poesie.
>
> (27–30)

Although the Satirist knows the majority of the society will misjudge his critiques, he will tolerate its mistakes "with my full consent" because his intention to forthrightly expose the true images of vice to all and sundry overrides the potential dangers of misreading and mockery:

> So you will never conceive, and yet dispraise,
> That which you ne'er conceived, and laughter raise:
> Where I but strive in honest seriousness,
> To scourge some soul-polluting beastliness.
>
> (63–68)

Marston's centrifugal ideological orientation also extends itself dangerously into the realm of religious philosophy, part of what R. C. Horne describes as the tendency in Marston's Juvenalian mode for repudiating "every current school of ethical thought, including Neo-Stoicism, Empiricism, Calvinism, and Cynicism itself" (23). Alvin Kernan and Scott Colley have argued independently for Marston's unorthodox satiric mode as radically Calvinist in nature, a position that both Caputi and Horne reject. For Colley, the radicalism of Marston's Calvinism is evident in is intensely paradoxical nature; notions of free will are futile in the face of divine providence, as Calvinists would have it, and yet the dissolute world compels humans to choose, and then condemns them when they do; in Marston's satires, "people cannot merely await the inevitable; they must stand accountable and responsible for all of their actions… In one sense a person is a kind of puppet; and in another sense a person is a free agent" (Colley 87). Marston frequently blends the official and oppositional doctrines of Anglicanism, Calvinism, and Puritanism often at odds in the reader's society by blurring familiar notions of "freedom and inevitability," reprobation and election, works and faith; all come crashing together, sometimes within the same satire. However, instead of resolving such apparent contradictions in a manner either complementary or antagonistic to Anglican doctrine, Marston frequently allows them to devolve into an all-consuming despair that "his best efforts at satire may be useless to amend the behavior of the already damned" (Colley 86). Such despair is reminiscent, Kernan argues, of the persistent pessimism and desire for sweeping reforms espoused by puritanical forces in Elizabethan society (123–124).[53]

As Horne points out, as each philosophy is raised, as each consensual community of like-minded thinkers is proposed, it is quickly rejected as insufficient in the face of man's self-defeating choice of vice over the potential for divine Grace. Examples of Marston's distrust of nearly all philosophical dogmas are numerous: "Preach not the Stoics patience to me," the spokesman rails (1.2.5); "I *can*" live well by having faith in the "thwarting Cynics" views, says an Interlocutor, to which Marston replies, "thou may'st," but lack the strength of will to do so (1.4.146–147); and Marston declares that, "Sure Grace is infus'd / By divine favor, not by actions us'd, which is as permanent as heaven's bliss" (117–119), a rigid Calvinist position complicated by the conditional nature of Grace (it is only for the elect "them that have it," 120) and the fact of God's indifference to the rest, which leaves them with no recourse but to indulge the animal rather than the intellectual parts of the soul.

> Vice, from privation of that sacred Grace,
> Which God withdraws, but puts not vice in place.
> Who says the sun is cause of ugly night?
> Yet when he veils our eyes from his fair sight,
> The gloomy curtain of the night is spread.
>
> (123–127)

As a result, mankind "hath no soul," no remnant of the divine rationality proposed by Aristotle "the Stagerite," only the "sensual action" (2.7.66–68) proposed by the philosopher "Porphyry" (1.4.139), who argued for the soul as often incapable of transcending the sensual, animal realm.[54] The absence of God has left the irrational human animal not only without Synderesis, but without essence; humans are translated from the image of God's central creation to mere *"Apparitions, / Ignes Fatui, Glowworms, Fictions, / Meteors, Rats of Nilus, Fantasies"* (2.7.13–15), and as such, Marston accepts the potential purposelessness of his activistic translations, their inability to motivate change because the vacuous target has lost all potential for good. Ultimately, such existential despair is reminiscent of Nietzsche's brand of philosophical Nihilism, which accords with other centrifugal qualities in Marston's mode, specifically, his "resistance to systems, to traditional wisdom, to accepted views of human experience" (Colley 95).

While Nihilism, like Atheism, could represent a political threat in the judgment of Elizabeth's government, the nihilism of the mode becomes a more evident threat when viewed as an expression of the manifold sociopolitical and philosophical instabilities of the late 1500s. In addition to the intense social crises of the time (including the succession issue, the specter of another Spanish invasion and Spanish support for the Irish rebellion, alterations in class relations brought on by the growth of capitalist systems, the *fin de siècle* consciousness, and the manifold economic deprivations noted earlier), the era was remarkable as a time of a general spiritual crisis characterized by extreme efforts to find new systems of meaning and purpose. As I. A. A. Thompson has argued, the late 1590s saw, on the one hand, "melancholia, skepticism, atheism, withdrawal from the active world of politics and a picaresque rejection of established values," and on the other hand, "a 'moralizing puritanism,' the revival of Augustinian salvationism, and neo-Stoicism," all of which represent efforts to remake established systems of belief into "a new social ethic and a rehabilitation of the military ethos" (276). Such a volatile philosophical environment, according to Anthony Esler, was the perfect environment to foster the rise of Juvenalian satire as the preeminent imitative model for the young generation of Elizabethan poets; it was the culture's "melancholy mood," states Esler, that prompted the shift in literary tastes "from romance to realism, from realism to satire, from satire to nausea."[55] Kernan draws a similar correlation between the philosophical uncertainty of the time, the rise of Juvenalianism, and the correlation between late Elizabethan era and the decay of the Roman Empire (66–67).

Although admittedly a more extreme view than Kernan's, Hiram Haydn[56] argues for the imitation of Juvenal, the "favorite model" for satirists largely from the Inns of Court (107), as part of the larger "ideological revolution" (xiv), or "Counter-Renaissance" of the period that "originated as a protest against the basic principles of the classical renaissance, as well as against those of medieval Scholasticism," principles that the radical Juvenalian presents as romanticized failures (11). "If the 'plain-speaking' tradition of the Elizabethan satirists derives largely from the example of Roman satire," writes Haydn, "it is nevertheless conscious of its ultimate debt to Cynic-Stoic primitivism, with the latter's antagonism to all the artifices of civilization, culture, and society" (107). Similarly, Finkelpearl writes that, "the youthful, self-conscious cynicism nurtured in the catalytic atmosphere of the law schools," with its "disenchanted resolve to be at all costs realistic, to show things as they really are and to describe them (as Jonson put it) in 'language such as men do use'" more than likely appeared openly seditious to the Bishops' office tasked with the maintenance of centripetal representations of national ideologies (73). The established tradition of stabilizing decorum in imitative satire was in danger of falling before a poetically indecorous, philosophically indifferent, and ideologically challenging mode advanced by a secular group of ambitious young men bent on testing, critiquing, and revising the values of the culture at an historical moment when those values were most imperiled and, in the eyes of the Bishops, most in need.

All these centrifugal features are evident in Marston's "A Cynic Satire" (2.7). In true Juvenalian fashion, Marston places himself at the crossroads of imperial Britannia, where the satirist engages in a combination of disputation and diatribe with Linceus, the ideologist for maintaining the centripetal images of the various examples of faultless Englishness that parade past them. As one might expect, the Cynic does not merely reject the centripetal traditionalism of the Interlocutor as fatuous, but completely translates each recognizable ideologist from an ennobling image into the most degenerate images possible, taking down with them the twin ideologies of spiritual and national exceptionalism fostered by apprehensive authorities.

The satire opens with Marston's parodic proclamation, "A Man, a man, a kingdom for a man," which simultaneously mocks Shakespeare's notorious rhetorical flourish from *Richard III*, and ironically introduces the iconoclastic contention that the divinity of mankind is reducible to its animal component. Linceus responds incredulously that the "streets do swarm / With troops of men," to which the "currish mad Athenian" satirist replies with a translated image of these "men" as sensual beasts whose spirits are devoid of the divine "radiant shine," and are instead infused with the "souls of swine" (2–12). As his initial example of the disconnect between appearance and essence, a concern frequently addressed by Elizabethan authorities in everything from sermons to statutes such as the Sumptuary Laws, Marston focuses the satirist's withering gaze on "yon gallant in sumptuous clothes," who he quickly reduces to an "incarnate devil" who embraces all misguiding semblances, rather than admit the "Sodom beastliness" at the center of his being (18–27). But the gallant is then further reduced to less than a beast: he is a vacuum, a mere shadow of humanity's lost divinity: "for naught but shades I see, / Resemblances of men inhabit thee" (141–142).

All of the subsequent iconoclastic and nihilistic perceptual translations are linked by a rejection of core humanistic ideological principles, particularly, the concept of the centrality of the human position within the divinely ordained Great Chain of Being, the essential rectitude of the human spirit, and the presence of the divine spark that would allow for the amelioration of the human condition. For Linceus, human images reflect "a complete soul, of all perfection" (29); men are "the shade of *Nestor* in sad gravity" which no "sour Satirist" can "unman" (47 & 50–51), paragons of martial valor whose inherent radiance will stop the cynic's "barking chops" (101–102). Women, too, are represented with the accustomed Petrarchan iconized images of their gender as "a celestial Angel, fair refined" (163). Alternatively, Marston demands that the traditionalist look beyond the surface, beyond the orthodox, and into the true images of man's irredeemable condition: "Can'st thou not, Linceus, cast thy searching eye / And spy his imminent Catastrophe?" (56–57) The grave advisor *Nestor*, clearly a type for corrupt systems of patronage, is reimagined as a "sponge" living off his benefactor, and just as quickly discarded, his "liquor" squeezed out by "greatness's fist" (58–60 & 74–75); legislators (93), the symbol of divine "faire Justice course" (90) are, in reality, mere slippery "eels," mutable and duplicitous "John-a-style" whose "dilatory pleas" obscure their vicious intentions through meaningless legal babble: "the language that they speak, / Is the pure barbarous blacksaunt of the *Geate*" (78 & 81–87); the emblem of chivalric martial prowess is nothing but French oaths and "misshapen Swizer's clothes" (116–117), his "divine part soaked away in sin" (123); and the woman is no angel, but "the devil as soon" (166), her mystical appearance merely a lie composed of Sulphur and "lemon juice" (167), her spiritual divinity held at bay by her adherence to the social dictates of fashion: "Alas, her soul struts about her neck, / Her seat of sense is her rebato [her ruff] set... Nothing but clothes, and simpering preciseness" (176–179).

The iconoclastic translations end with a sweeping pronouncement that the gulf between the reality of human bestiality and the ideal of human divinity has become too wide to bridge:

> Sure I never think those axioms to be true,
> That souls of men from that great soul ensue,
> And of his essence do participate
> As't were by pipes, when so degenerate,
> So adverse is our nature's motion,
> To his immaculate condition:
> That such foul filth from such fair purity,
> Such sensual acts from such a Deity,
> Can ne'er proceed.
>
> (188–196)

The commonplace metaphor of pipes connecting humanity to the divine along the Great Chain of Being is augmented by the rather vulgar (in the sense of familiar) image of them as currently blocked thanks to the human preference for illicit sensuality over divine grace, or as the unorthodox perspective would have it, "the slime that from our souls do flow, / Have stop't those pipes by which it was conveyed" (197–198). Despite the acknowledgment of God's purity, such a complete rejection of so many religious and ideological doctrines central to the Elizabethan ethos could only have signaled, in the judgment of the clerical authorities, not merely an indecorous mode of social critique, but a potentially heretical poetic challenge to, as Horne puts it, "the validity of all received systems of belief" (23). For a society with as many causes for concern

90 *Satire Unleashed*

as England had near what would turn out to be the end of Elizabeth's reign, Marston's brand of Juvenalianism is too revolutionary in both the formal and ideological senses, and as such, an act of censorship such as the Bishops' ban, while autocratic, is comprehensible.

Countering the Counter-Discourse: John Weever's Poetic Response to Marston's Mode

In support of her position that the Bishops' focus was the regulation of defamatory language, Debora Shuger perceptively cites three "verse responses" to the Bishops' ban known collectively as *The Whipper Pamphlets* (106). Published in quick succession in 1601, and comprised of Weever's assault on Marston, Guilpin, and Ben Jonson in *The Whipping of the Satyre*, Guilpin's reply to Weever in *The Whipper of the Satyre*, and Nicholas Breton's conciliatory *No Whipping, nor Tripping: but a Kind Friendly Snipping*, these pamphlets are significant as the only contemporary refractions of the government's concerns penned by artists with a vested interest in the prohibition. As described in Chapter 1, Weever's *Whipping* wholeheartedly defends the Bishops' censorious actions as wholly justified by the 'unholy' nature of the Juvenalians' challenges to ideological norms; however, Weever's poetic engagement with the Juvenalian threat is even more comprehensive. Weever consistently depicts the centrifugal mode as a cultural threat that shifted the traditionally salutary imperative of satire from "balm" to "blame."[57] As opposed to the ideology of horatian satire, Weever contends there is no restorative impulse in Marston's mode; the culture it represents remains in a constant state of decline and fall, much like Juvenal's Domitian-era Rome, and the banned satirists' claims to improve society are just a disguise for their true intent to undermine the stability of the nation and its leaders.

Weever's conservative defense of the ban is central to *Faunus and Melliflora* (1600), a poem which, over the course of nearly two thousand lines, establishes itself as a mildly erotic pastoral in the style of Sir Philip Sidney's *Arcadia* before awkwardly presenting English translations of the first satires of Horace, Persius, and Juvenal. The poem's use of multiple genres constitute what Arnold Davenport believes was Weever's attempt "to evade the ban by cobbling together his two works in such a way that the erotic poem might pass as a mythological account of the origin of satire and the satires themselves be presented as a deprecation of satire" (vi). After referencing the Bishops' prohibition in the thinnest of allegories, the work ends with a gleeful valediction to the reign of the Juvenalian "sly scoffing critics, jeering Lucianists, / Stern censuring Catos, full gorg'd Lucilians, / Envy swollen Cynics" ("Prophecy" 2–4). In order to demarcate his own imitative ideology as diametrically opposed to the prohibited mode, Weever's speaker intentionally informs the reader of his "hate" for the "censuring vein" of Marston's "Rhamnusian *Scourge of Villanie*," preferring instead the reprieved mode of Joseph Hall: "If this praise-worthy be, then first of all / Place I the Satyre Academical" (1079–1086).

Soon after Weever abandons his translation of Juvenal, citing the will of Venus (i.e. Queen Elizabeth) that Juvenal should be silent, he depicts the ban as appropriate moral "revengement" for the Juvenalians' "detraction" of Elizabeth's "Godhead" (1604–1607). What follows is an elaborate justification for the repression of Marston's unorthodox influence:

> Hearing before the Satyres enmity,
> 'Gainst her [Elizabeth's] proceedings and her deity...
> Polluting with her [Satyre's] damned luxury,
> All ears which vow'd were unto chastity...
> Which 'fore she asked, this boon to her was giving,
> That all Satyres then in England living
> Should sacrificed be in the burning fire,
> To pacify so great a goddess' ire,
> And from their Cinders should a Satyre rise,
> Which their Satyric snarling should despise.
>   (1662–1677)

Again, Weever depicts the ban as necessitated by the conflict between the requirements of cultural stability and the presumptuous excesses of Marston's form of Juvenalian imitation. The analogical Elizabeth is imagined as aware of the satirist's attack on her authority and on her iconic sovereign image ("her proceedings and her deity"), and also aware of the morally corrupting effect that the unrestrained and base style has on her people ("polluting with her damned luxury, / All ears which vow'd were unto chastity"). Weever's use of the term "chastity" is an intentionally loaded choice, as Elizabeth's iconic image as the chaste Virgin Queen was well established by 1599, and thus the invocation of the term returns the reader to the image of Marston's mode as contaminating the image of Elizabeth and her subjects in the imagination of the readership. The final perceptual translation of the Juvenalians immolated like heretics at the public stake is meant to ensure the return of iconic stability to an outraged Elizabethan state, as well as to anticipate the Phoenix-like rebirth of a centripetal form of English satire antithetical to the style and goals of the banned mode.

The Bishops' ban is a stark symbol of the incessant contentious dialogue between artists who choose to raise questions about their society's fundamental beliefs, and those authorities who, depending on historical conditions, feel compelled to react to such questioning with varying degrees of severity. For the Juvenalian satirists, only a cultural revolution

92 Satire Unleashed

could save their degenerate society, while the conservative forces, both arbiter or artist, perceived such representational liberality as equally revolutionary.

Notes

1 The core of this chapter consists of my article, "The 1599 Bishops' Ban and the Ideology of English Satire," published in the online academic journal *Literature Compass*, vol. 7/5, 2010, pp. 332–346. Certain sections have been omitted, and others augmented. The article is used with the permission of the editors of *Literature Compass* (Editor-in-Chief: Stuart Christie). Research from my 2004 dissertation also appears in this chapter.
2 See Chapter 1, pp. 9–11, note 13.
3 For a full transcription of the ban, see Arber, Edward. *A Transcript of the Company of Stationers of London; 1554–1640 A.D.*, vol. 3, Peter Smith, 1950, pp. 316–316b. I have regularized some of the more idiosyncratic spelling, including Satire as "Satyre," an intentional misspelling which demonstrates the early modern misconception of a link between the Latin tradition of *satura* and the Greek tradition of Satyrs. However, I maintain the Renaissance spelling where this link is pertinent.
4 Patterson, Annabel. *Censorship and Interpretation: The Conditions of Writing and Reading in Early Modern England*. University of Wisconsin Press, 1984. See p. 44.
5 Bourdieu, Pierre. *Language and Symbolic Power*. Edited by John B. Thompson, translated by Gino Raymond and Matthew Adamson, Harvard University Press, 1991. See p. 137.
6 For more detailed information on the Stationers' responsibility to oversee printed materials, see Clegg, pp. 46–58.
7 McCabe, Richard. "Elizabethan Satire and the Bishops' Ban of 1599." *The Yearbook of English Studies*, vol. 11, 1981, pp. 188–193. See pp. 189–190.
8 See Alvin Kernan's description of the Juvenalian mode in *The Cankered Muse*, pp. 64–82.
9 Patterson, Annabel. *Shakespeare and the Popular Voice*, Basil Blackwell, 1989. See p. 86.
10 Quotation is from John Weever's *Faunus and Melliflora* (1600). Edited by Arnold Davenport, University Press of Liverpool, 1948, 1675.
11 *The Bachelor's Banquet*. Edited by F. P. Wilson, Clarendon Press, 1929. See pp. xxii and xxxiii.
12 See Chapter 4 for a detailed engagement with the banned anti-feminist satires.
13 For other obscenity arguments, see Finkelpearl, Philip. *John Marston of the Middle Temple: An Elizabethan Dramatist in His Social Setting*, Harvard University Press, 1969 and Boose, Lynda "The 1599 Bishops' Ban, Elizabethan Pornography, and the Sexualization of the Jacobean State." *Enclosure Acts: Sexuality, Property, and Culture in Early Modern England*, edited by Richard Burt and John M. Archer, Cornell University Press, 1994.
14 See Clare, Janet. *"Art Made Tongue-Tied by Authority": Elizabethan and Jacobean Dramatic Censorship*, Manchester University Press, 1990. See p. 83. See also Clegg, Cyndia S. *Press Censorship in Elizabethan England*, Cambridge University Press, 1997. See p. 204.
15 See Clegg, p. 204 for a timeline detailing the censorship of Hayward's history.
16 In his Arden Three edition of *Henry V*, T. W. Craik proposes that the play was acted in March 1599 (3). For comments on the censorship of the play,

see Clare, pp. 71–74. The allusion to the Essex expedition in the choral opening to Act Five occurs at lines 29–35.
17 See Huntington, John. *Ambition, Rank, and Poetry in 1590s England*, University of Illinois Press, 2001 and Kaplan, Lindsay. *The Culture of Slander in Early Modern England*, Cambridge University Press, 1997. Quotation is by Kaplan, p. 30.
18 Quotations from Guilpin's *Skialetheia* are taken from an unlineated facsimile edited by Alexander B. Grosart. Charles E. Simms, 1878.
19 The dates relevant to the Essex expedition have been drawn from Harrison, G. B. *The Life and Death of Robert Devereux, Earl of Essex*, H. Holt and Company, 1937.
20 See Rollins, Hyder E. "Introduction." *Richard Tottel's Tottel's Miscellany (1557–1587)*, vol. 2, Harvard University Press, 1965, pp. 1–37.
21 See Alden, Raymond M. *The Rise of Formal Satire in England under Classical Influence* (1899), University of Pennsylvania Press, 1961, pp. 70–80.
22 The 1596 date for Davies' *Epigrams*, published with Marlowe's Ovidian *Elegies* is taken from a 1973 facsimile edition published by The Scolar Press. Editor A. J. Smith contends that the book was most likely published in London with a false imprint of "Middleburgh" around 1596, and was still readily available in the summer of 1599.
23 Caputi notes that, by 1599, the literary circle of the Inns of Court counted a number of the banned satirists among their ranks, including John Marston, Everard Guilpin, Thomas Middleton, Joseph Hall, and John Davies (7–8). Other satirists of the time not implicated in the ban, such as John Weever and Ben Jonson, had close associations with the Inns. Caputi, Anthony. *John Marston, Satirist*, Cornell University Press, 1961.
24 See McPherson, David C. "Aretino and the Harvey-Nashe Quarrel." *PMLA*, vol. 84, 1969, pp. 1551–1558. Quotations are from pp. 1553 and 1554, respectively.
25 The current chapter makes extensive use of Arnold Davenport's thoroughly annotated editions of Hall's and Marston's poems. See *The Poems of Joseph Hall, Bishop of Exeter and Norwich*, Liverpool University Press, 1969. Also, *The Poems of John Marston*, Liverpool University Press, 1961.
26 See Parsons, Ben. "'A Riotous Spray of Words': Rethinking the Medieval Theory of Satire." *Exemplaria*, vol. 21, 2009, pp. 105–128. See p. 113.
27 As Gilbert Highet illustrates, although Juvenal produced his satires during the relatively quiescent reigns of Trajan, and/or Hadrian, during his youth, Juvenal likely experienced, or at least was well aware of, Domitian's worst deprivations. See Highet. *Juvenal the Satirist: A Study*, Oxford University Press, 1954. pp. 1–41.
28 In *The Purpose of Playing*, The University of Chicago Press, 1996, Louis Montrose summarizes the range of social, economic, political, and religious changes of the late sixteenth century as follows: "the combination of population growth, price inflation…transformation in agrarian modes of production and disruptions of traditional rural communities and values… widespread geographic mobility and rapid social mobility…Furthermore, the technological, socioeconomic, and ideological conjunction of printing, literacy, Protestantism, and entrepreneurial capitalism," not to mention anxiety over the issue of royal succession. pp. 21–22.
29 Hall uses the descriptive term "quiet style" in *Virgidemiarum* 5.3.13; Weever's comments on Marston's style are taken from *Faunus and Melliflora* (1600), line 1085.
30 Patterson, Annabel. *Hermogenes and the Renaissance: Seven Ideas of Style*. Princeton University Press, 1970. See p. 104. For Horace's comment on his poetic "impotence," see Chapter 2, note 21.

31 The translation is mine. For Hall's Latin text, see Davenport, p. 10.
32 See Guilpin's *Skialetheia*, "Preludium." "Tamburlaine" is a reference to Christopher Marlowe's two plays on the subject (late 1580s). Hall mocks *Tamburlaine* and Marlowe in *Virgidemiarum*, 1.3.11–18.
33 See Milton's "An Apology for Smectymnuus" (1642), Section 6, in *The Prose Works of John Milton*, edited by Rufus W. Griswold, 2 vols., John W. Moore, 1847,oll.libertyfund.org/titles/milton-the-prose-works-of-john-milton-vol-1.
34 See Juvenal's Satire 1, lines 63–72.
35 See Outhwaite, R. B. "Dearth, the English Crown and the 'Crisis of the 1590s.'" *The European Crisis of the 1590s: Essays in Comparative History*, edited by Peter Clark, George Allen & Unwin, 1985. See pp. 17–18 and 27–29. See also *The Agrarian History of England and Wales*. Edited by Joan Thirsk, vol. 4, Cambridge University Press, 1967. See pp. 814–865.
36 See Thirsk, note 43, p. 240. Thirsk reports that Enclosure Commissions convened in 1517, 1548, 1566, and 1607.
37 See Mark Overton, *Agricultural Revolution in England: The Transformation of the Agrarian Economy, 1500–1850*, Cambridge University Press, 1996, p. 190. See also Thirsk, p. 4.
38 This contention is at odds with Richard McCabe's interpretation of the same satire in his book-length study of Hall's poetry, *Joseph Hall: A Study in Satire and Meditation*, Oxford University Press, 1982. On pp. 47–48, McCabe writes, "In order to demonstrate its futility, he turns the art of contrived obscurity against itself. Satire, he asserts, should affect the conscience thereby producing a moral reaction, but this is possible only if it can be clearly understood." I am suggesting instead that there is a gulf between the programmatic statements of the satirist-speaker and the actual execution of the poem. Hall's speaker claims to be a 'plain speaker,' but the reality of the poem indicates greater interests in irony and decorum.
39 Quotes from the prefatory epistle to *Caltha Poetarum or The Bumble Bee* are taken from a photocopy prepared by the British Library. I have regularized the spelling and punctuation.
40 See Chapter 2 for details on the medieval and Renaissance valuation of Horace, and for a discussion of Dante's "beautiful school" of virtuous 'pagan' poets.
41 It is perhaps not too far-reaching to associate Cutwode's invocation of the god Apollo with high poetic genres in the Aristotelian sense, and the rural Satyr-god Pan with low genres such as satire.
42 See Baumlin, James. "Generic Contexts of Elizabethan Satire: Rhetoric, Poetic Theory, and Imitation," *Renaissance Genres: Essays on Theory, History, and Interpretation*, edited by Barbara K. Lewalski, Harvard University Press, 1986. See p. 457.
43 The quote is from Steven R. Shelburne, "Principled Satire: Decorum in John Marston's *The Metamorphosis of Pigmalions Image and Certaine Satyres*." *Studies in Philology*, vol. 86, 1989, pp. 198–218. See p. 210. Juvenal discusses his desire for free expression in Satire 1, lines 147–171. Marston uses the term "Synderesis" in *SV* 3.8.211 and 3.11.236; the definition is from "Synderesis." *Internet Encyclopedia of Philosophy*, edited by James Feiser and Bradley Dowden, www.iep.utm.edu. The reference to the "barking satirist" can be found in Marston's *Certain Satires*, "The Author in Praise of his Precedent Poem," line 46.
44 Anderson, William S. *Essays on Roman Satire*, Princeton University Press, 1982, p. 30. Horace criticizes Lucilius' freedoms in Satire 1.4.1–13 and 1.10.1–5. For a perspective on Lucilian freedom and associations with

Empire, see Rosen, Ralph M. "Satire in the Republic: From Lucilius to Horace." *A Companion to Persius and Juvenal*, edited by Susanna Braund and Josiah Osgood, Wiley-Blackwell, 2012. See pp. 19–40.
45 As discussed in Chapter 1, the conflation of author and speaker here is deliberate, as stylistics and choice of targets are tied to authorial intention.
46 For a full engagement with Jonson's *Poetaster*, see Chapter 5.
47 Marston's language (in order) can be found at 3.10.15, 1.4.88, Proemium, Book Two, line 15, 2.6.41 & 42, and 3.11.31. "Kemp's jig," of course, refers to William Kemp, a comic actor and dancer with Shakespeare's Lord Chamberlain's Men. Jobbernowl's and Gurnet's head refer to idiots and men with ugly fish heads.
48 See "Introduction." *The Three Parnassus Plays (1598–1601)*, edited by J. B. Leishman, Nicholson and Watson, 1949. The three plays are *The Pilgrimage to Parnassus* (late 1598), *The First Part of the Return from Parnassus* (1599/1600), and *The Second Part of the Return from Parnassus* (late 1601).
49 A notorious alleyway running between The Temple and Fleet Street.
50 A reference to, again, the Juvenalian Italian satirist Pietro Aretino.
51 Patrick Buckridge, "True Reading and How to Get It: John Marston's Primer for Satire." *Southern Review*, vol. 23, 1990, pp. 58–67.
52 See Mary Claire Randolph, "The Structural Design of Formal Verse Satire." *Philological Quarterly*, vol. 21, no. 4, 1942, pp. 369–384. See pp. 372–374.
53 See Colley, Scott. "Marston, Calvinism, and Satire." *Medieval and Renaissance Drama in England*, vol. 1, 1984, pp. 85–96. See Horne, R. C. "Voices of Alienation: The Moral Significance of Marston's Satiric Strategy." *Modern Language Review*, vol. 81, 1986, pp. 18–33.
54 See Davenport's extensive commentary on such issues, pp. 310–313.
55 Esler, Anthony. *The Aspiring Mind of the Elizabethan Younger Generation*, Duke University Press, 1966, p. 228.
56 Haydn, Hiram. *The Counter-Renaissance*, Charles Scribner's Sons, 1950.
57 Weever, John. "In Satyrum," *The Whipping of the Satyre*, line 490. Weever's references to the Juvenalian's "pride" can be found throughout this work, but particularly at lines 277–300.

4 Anti-Feminist Satire and the Bishops' Ban

In the late summer of 2016, former First Lady, Senator, and Secretary of State, Hillary Rodham Clinton secured the Democratic Party's nomination for the presidency of the United States. As the first female nominee within the historically male-dominated field of American political power, it should come as little surprise that her elevation sparked contentious reactions within nearly every segment of American society, reactions that, more often than not, centered around the issue of Clinton's gender: economic markets scrutinized Clinton's projected policy focus on the so-called 'women's issues' of pay inequality and extending Paid Family Leave; religious and social groups objected to Clinton's candidacy as a violation of traditional "family values"; military leaders debated the potential ramifications of serving under a female Commander in Chief; and pundits engaged in heated philosophical debates over the relationship between gender and power. For example, former Secretary of State Madeleine Albright and feminist activist Gloria Steinem urged solidarity among women voters in order to advance both Secretary Clinton and the cause of women's social empowerment, while author Marc Rudov mocked the idea of women in power on the basis of long-standing biological stereotypes. Revealingly, behind Rudov's misogyny lay the much deeper patriarchal anxiety that the rise of a "Feminist in Chief," to use Rudov's terms, must necessarily result in the marginalization of male interests, and by extension, male power.[1]

The producers of satire, both conservative and liberal, were quick to engage with such an important potential inversion of the sociopolitical field. Both communities used the activistic power of satire to undermine, in some cases, or to reinforce, in other cases, the gender-based ideologies polarized around the issue of a female president. Armed with their own forms of satire, groups for and against Clinton acted less to change the perceptions of the opposing side (although swaying undecided voters was considered a potential benefit) and more to delineate their communities and to consolidate their preferred forms of perceptual discourse. For example, Clinton's supporters donned t-shirts bearing ironic slogans that utilized established feminist language to argue not just for Clinton's candidacy, but more broadly, for women's capacity to assume roles so frequently denied them. Such slogans included "A Woman's Place is in the White House" and "Yes, She Can," an homage to Barack Obama's 2008 slogan, "Yes, We Can."

While such commendatory slogans do not necessarily qualify as satire, a number of feminist satirists were quite successful in using the mode both to realign and to deflate much of the sexist rhetoric targeted at Clinton. Parodic counter-slogans were created to ameliorate misogynistic invectives such as "Bitch" and "Tramp," two ideologically saturated epithets whose social history infuses them with the intent to degrade women for the benefit of paternal authority. Another particularly savvy example of such ideological reorientation was the response to a viral social media photo of a marquee warning against Clinton's "vagenda ['vagina' and 'agenda'] of manocide [man and homicide]," a contextually unironic phrase quickly appropriated by pro-Clinton supporters. Meanwhile, satirists such as Sara Schaefer used satire to weaken the conservative agenda behind such hyperbolic sexism by distributing highly ironized vagenda "to-do lists" across various social media platforms: "2:55 PM: text Jenny for her scrotum-infused kombucha recipe. Commit vehicular manocide in the parking lot; 4:30 PM: Kill a football team," etc.[2] Yet despite such efforts, the opposing side of conservative satirists and media producers at the highest levels of the social, political, and economic fields unleashed a barrage of particularly vehement gender–conscious satire meant to appeal to Clinton's detractors; although difficult to quantify, it is reasonable to assume that such efforts to degrade Clinton's public image through satire contributed, at least in some small way, to her eventual political defeat.[3]

Sensationalist examples aside, the conservative, or to return to Bakhtin's terms, ideologically patriarchal satire sought to translate Clinton's image pejoratively in two ways: some satiric assaults were restricted to matters of politics rather than gender, focusing on Clinton's involvement in such contentious public incidents as the 2012 assault on the U.S. diplomatic compound in Benghazi, Libya, and Clinton's use of private email servers during her time as Secretary of State, both events summed up by t-shirts and buttons bearing relatively straightforward slogans such as "Hillary for Prison," "Hillocchio" (i.e. Clinton as a Pinocchio-style liar), "Wanted" posters accusing Clinton of treason, and Donald Trump's repeated typological invective, "Crooked Hillary." However, the more ubiquitous efforts to use satire as a conservative activistic weapon employed misogynistic language to degrade Clinton's image. For example, campaign materials bearing such slogans as "Trump That Bitch," "Life's a Bitch, Don't Elect One," and representations of Clinton as The Wicked Witch of the West from *The Wizard of Oz* were sold not just at Trump rallies, but through a considerable number of Internet retailers.

More troubling were the satiric slogans that carried such misogyny to exorbitant levels, namely, sexualized attacks that invoked Hillary Clinton's personal relationships, as well as some that invoked long-standing assumptions about her sexual orientation. Most common were historical references to her husband, former U.S. President Bill Clinton, and his extramarital affair with White House intern Monica Lewinsky in 1995, as signaled by lewd mottos like, "Hillary Sucks, But Not as Much as Monica," "Say No to Monica's Ex-Boyfriend's Wife in 2016," and "Even Bill Doesn't Want Me." Clearly, the ideological intention informing this type of misogynistic satire was to promulgate an image of Clinton as an unsuitable leader based on her supposed sexual failures as a wife, and by extension, her imagined failure to fulfill her normative or 'natural' role as a woman, as patriarchal norms require. Similar satiric images flourished in mid-2016 after Huma Abedin, Clinton's political advisor, gave a glowing interview about Clinton to *People* magazine, which conservative pundits and satirists immediately refashioned into 'evidence' not just of Clinton's indifference to her husband's needs, but 'proof' of Clinton's lesbianism, an assumption fed by the patrilineal narrative of a woman's desire for power as only comprehensible when linked to a desire to transgress the 'natural' heteronormative hierarchy.[4]

For a woman like Hillary Clinton, who occupied many important positions in fields of public service for decades, this kind of satirically expressed "unease with a powerful woman and anxiety about changing gender norms," as Charlotte Templin describes it, was nothing new, particularly those satiric assaults intended to reify the image of Clinton as a transgressive figure outside of gender and sexual standards.[5] Templin points out that during her time as First Lady of the United States (1993–2001), Clinton was frequently subjected to conservative satiric assaults via editorial cartoons (among other media) that attempted to revise her image into that of a power-hungry virago who routinely emasculated her hapless husband: "of over 400 cartoons that appeared between November 1992 and July 1996, nearly half fall into a category that could be called 'Hillary is Taking Over,'" including images of Mrs. Clinton as a puppet master with her husband as the puppet, Mrs. Clinton in a man's suit signing important documents while a cross-dressed President Bill Clinton clutches a handbag, etc. (24; 26). "The crux of the matter," writes Templin, "is the belief that Hillary Clinton, a 'failed woman,' is not fulfilling the requirements of heterosexism, which, as [Judith] Butler's analysis illustrates, is compulsory in our culture and, according to [Germaine] Greer, an obligatory requirement of the First Lady" (25).

Butler's influential work, *Gender Trouble*, further suggests that the motivation for such centripetal satiric assaults is not simply the supposed heteronormative failures of transgressive women, but an anxiety over classification provoked by women's imagined rejection of regulatory systems meant to insure the stabilizing performance of those sexual and gender norms that "govern culturally intelligible notions of identity." Butler writes,

> Inasmuch as "identity" is assured through the stabilizing concepts of sex, gender, and sexuality, the very notion of "the person" is called into question by the cultural emergence of those "incoherent" or "discontinuous" gendered beings who appear to be persons but who fail to conform to the gendered norms of cultural intelligibility by which persons are defined.[6]

Butler's view implies that Clinton's anxious detractors rendered her as unfit not simply because she was either too feminine or too unfeminine, but because she was incomprehensible, and thus uncontrollable, which represents a threat to those patriarchal economies that rely on such categorizations. The anti-feminist satiric agenda often relies on images of female incoherence and its consequences, particularly the masculine impotence that must inevitably result from the blurring of traditionally defined gender identities and roles, as evident in the cartoon depictions of a crossed-dressed Hillary Clinton and an emasculated Bill Clinton.

In the summer of 2016, as the prospect of a female American president became seemingly inexorable, conservative satirists amplified the ideologically charged image of Clinton's 'discontinuous' identity into a distorted typology of Clinton as a grotesque consequence of the failure of patriarchal regulation, a failure which not only blurred comfortable and comforting sureties of Clinton's identity, but also threatened the patriarchal identity of the nation she might soon represent.[7] Earlier translations of Clinton's identity as incoherent devolved into an hybrid image of Clinton as not just a lesbian, but a monstrous one as well, fully committed to castrating the male electorate. Men who would dare to transgress their own gender boundaries by supporting a female presidential nominee were subjected to shaming invectives labeling them as unpatriotic traitors, impotent "*castratos*," their masculinity forever imprisoned in a "testicle lockbox."[8] Such masculinized discourse implies that Clinton was bent not only on satisfying her inhuman sexual desires, but on annihilating the phallocratic order, to employ Luce Irigaray's conceptions, to the point that the standard paternal ideology itself was threatened with irrelevance: "the masculine would no longer be 'everything.' That it could no longer, all by itself, define, circumvent, circumscribe the properties of any thing and everything."[9]

This anxiety of impotence is intrinsic to Butler's explication of the ideological implications of the category of "Lesbian," which represents in the mind of the paternal order an inscrutable and threatening "third gender... that radically problematizes both sex and gender as stable political categories of description":

> A lesbian, [Wittig] claims, in refusing heterosexuality is no longer defined in terms of that oppositional relation. Indeed, a lesbian, she maintains, transcends the binary opposition between woman and man; a lesbian is neither a woman nor a man. But further, a lesbian has no sex; she is beyond the categories of sex. Through the lesbian refusal of those categories, the lesbian exposes (pronouns are a problem here) the contingent cultural constitution of those categories and the tacit yet abiding presumption of the heterosexual matrix.
>
> (113)

Thus, for the anti-feminist satirist, whose ultimate purpose is to reinforce the traditional gender hierarchy and empower masculine identity, as Felicity Nussbaum posits, the Lesbian typology is an especially useful activistic tool, one with the explicit or implied intent to motivate masculine readers to protect their personal and social relevance from gender nonconformists:

> Satire... helps men to survive their fears, to remain potent when threatened with impotence, both real and imagined. The formalized ritual of the anti-feminist satire within the tradition reassures the threatened male minority. The myth of satires against women includes the myth that women create chaos, and the imposition of form (satire) on formlessness provides meaning and rationality when the fear of meaninglessness and insanity arises.[10]

From a Presentist standpoint, the ideological threat of masculine irrelevance inherent in the Lesbian typology is reminiscent of the way the figure of the Amazon was utilized by patriarchal authors in early modern culture. Although the fictive Amazon race was occasionally represented positively as "picturesque ornaments to a pageant or a romance" due to their unique combination of feminine beauty and masculine military prowess, far more often, their matriarchal social system was employed satirically to symbolize a "violation of that traditional order under which 'women are born to thralldom and penance / And to been under man's governance.'"[11] Mary Villeponteaux notes the simultaneously compelling and repelling "monstrous side" of the Amazon image as a kind of lesbian "no sex" existing beyond conventional gender identities; Amazons are desired by men for their combination of male fortitude and female reproductive capabilities, but are also feared due to the disruptive nature of their inverted society, which includes castrating or murdering male captives, not to mention the Amazon's rejection of their 'natural' social role as mothers evinced by their practice of cutting off one breast: "the Amazons are good examples of *virtu* [masculine merit]... but that manliness destroys their feminine virtue; the two cannot easily coexist...a mother who is also a public figure exercising manly virtues poses the possibility of monstrosity."[12] In essence, the category of Amazon, like the category of Lesbian, represents the apogee of monstrous imperfection in womankind, neither woman nor man, an ungovernable cipher whose autonomy threatens to destroy male sovereignty on both the domestic and national levels.

Anti-feminist satire, replete with these kinds of misogynistic typologies, has a long and unpleasant literary provenance. From the vitriolic iambics of Semonides (seventh century B.C.E.), who types women by their various animal natures, to aspects of Aristophanes' scathing comedies such as *Lysistrata*, to Juvenal's "Sixth Satire," to the Christian ascetic diatribes of Tertullian and Jerome, to aspects of Jonathan Swift's and Alexander Pope's poetry, the list of satires enumerating the supposed deficiencies of women's natures is nearly endless.[13] Yet despite the fact that each of these and many more examples of anti-feminist satire has its own unique historicity and intentionality, the fact of satire's inclusive dialogic chronotope allows readers to harmonize the criticisms of the past with criticisms of the present and vice versa with surprisingly little need to adjust for topological changes. As such, both ancient misogynistic critiques and contemporary gender-based criticisms reveal correlations which suggest that the anti-feminist satires of the past were more than just humorous rhetorical exercises, just as they were more than mere "jokes" in the summer of 2016; anti-feminist satire was and is an activistic part of a patriarchal regulatory system that extends through multiple cultural, social, and political fields. Marxist critic Fredric Jameson describes such systems as 'mediatory cultural codes' used to construct "ideologies of Otherness" in order to safeguard the political and financial economies of the governing (in this case, masculine) class.[14] However, in response to Jameson's silence on feminist responses to such regulatory systems, Kathleen Martindale posits the need for more critical attention to "a feminist materialist ethics" capable of identifying acts of ideological resistance to such mediatory codes, what Martindale terms, "feminist performances of negative ideological critique."[15] One such performance, I would argue, was the censorious response of the Elizabethan government to the anti-feminist satires ordered recalled and burned by the Bishops' ban of 1599.

Anti-Feminism and Social Regulation

To reiterate, for the cultural products that make up the anti-feminist satiric tradition, the ideological purpose behind corrective mockery of the vices imagined as specifically female is to reinvigorate male identity and authority as much as to regulate female 'excess.'[16] As Mark Breitenberg argues, "the identities of men are upheld by the construction of woman as Other, thus producing a gendered subject/object relationship in which female desire and sexuality is simultaneously (in a mutually validating way) construed as either non-existent or excessive."[17] The intransigent Katherine in Shakespeare's *Taming of the Shrew*, Spenser's emasculating Amazon Radigund, the terrifying Lesbian democratic nominee for president, all serve as satiric types whose supposed deviations justify the submission of female desire to the desires of the husband and of the patriarchy. However, the man who cannot or will not act to prevent women from indulging their natural excesses is often presented as the true source of female transgression, as Diane Purkiss has argued: in the early modern period in particular, "the social problem of female unruliness is figured as a defect in man," as evidenced by satiric illustrations from the time depicting shameful inversions of the 'natural order,' such as a husband riding backwards on his horse, or a wife beating her husband (or in our own era, a cartoon of a First Lady signing a bill into law as a powerless president looks on).[18] When the husband and/or the arbiters of society fail to regulate the woman's gender performance, like traitorous "*castratos*," they enable women to blur gender categories and roles to the detriment of traditionally masculine economies, as implied in the anti-feminist satiric pamphlet "*Hic Mulier: or the Man-Woman*" (pub. 1620):

> For since the days of *Adam*, women were never so Masculine; masculine in their genders and whole generations, from the mother to the youngest daughter; Masculine in Number, from one to multitudes; Masculine in Case [clothing], even from the head to the foot; Masculine in Mood, from bold speech to impudent action; and Masculine in Tense: for (without redress) they were, and are, and will be still most Masculine, most mankind, and most monstrous.[19]

The anonymous pamphleteer ends by imploring "Father, Husbands, or Sustainers" to deny the "necessary maintenance" (i.e. the money and the permissiveness) that supports the usurping behavior of these "new *Hermaphrodites*," a pejorative category of gender incoherence in the early modern period which, as Carla Freccero has shown, is distinct from the more socially constructive category of the "Androgyne": "the former [androgyne] being a spiritualized union of male and female aspects, the latter [hermaphrodite] connoting a monstrous hybrid, characterized not only by a merging of the two sexes, but by the deformation of each required to effect the union."[20]

Whichever ideologist figure anti-feminist satirists choose to adopt for their attack, the Shrew, Witch, Whore, Lesbian, Amazon, Hermaphrodite, etc., men are imagined as responsible for making such types of "female disorderliness," as Natalie Davis describes them, coherent again through socially sanctioned mediatory systems meant to safeguard the established power fields. These social systems, reinforced by cultural products like satire, include "selective education" (delivered primarily through religious sermons) on women's moral duties and natural roles, "honest work," and often violent and humiliating "laws and constraints that made her subject to her husband."[21] Phallocentric fields accept the need for women as an inescapable requirement of the primogeniture system, but women are imagined as a necessary evil best kept under foot, socially and culturally, if the man is to maintain his authority unquestioned.

It should come as little surprise that the regulatory satiric images of women, ranging as they do on a spectrum from troublesome to monstrous, were produced and consumed for centuries with relatively few public challenges due to the fact that, for centuries, women were fashioned ideologically as unfit for participation in a variety of influential social fields, even as the historical evidence demonstrates that women were active participants in many, if not all of those same fields, an oxymoronic social role which Dympna Callaghan terms the "excluded participant."[22] Consequently, the possibility for women to perform their own negative ideological critiques in a public forum was problematic, if not impossible, prior to the advancement of more progressive social systems. While it is certainly true that a number of early feminist works such as Christine de Pisan's *City of Ladies* (circa 1405) worked valiantly to reinscribe the traditional image of women as monsters, negative poetic critiques of phallocentric standards such as Amelia Lanyer's *Salve Deus Rex Judeorum* (1611), Aphra Behn's dramas and her mock-pastoral poem "The Disappointment" (1680), and Lady Mary Wortley Montagu's scathing assault on the English legal system ("Epistle from Mrs. Yonge to her Husband," w. 1724), appeared with more regularity as the relative social openness of the Restoration period worked in dialogue with the acceptance of women as a legitimate social force. Such satirists went beyond simply responding to the long tradition of anti-feminist satire, argues Rosalind Ballaster; instead, they and others like them "self-consciously, I would suggest, set out to develop and 'authorize' a position for the female satirist other than that of meta-satirist."[23]

However, in the English Tudor era, anti-feminist satire seemed generally accepted as a kind of cultural commonplace, and was permitted to advance its regulatory agenda with relative impunity, despite the presence of England's first female monarch (arguably): Mary I, Elizabeth's elder half-sister, who took the throne in 1553. Despite the wealth of misogynistic satire within the culture she oversaw, Mary and her officials seemed more troubled by political and religious references in satire (i.e. her Catholicism) than by any potentially anti-feminist elements. To cite the most infamous example, Marian censors changed the lines "where Christ is given in prey / For money, poison, and treason—at Rome" in Sir Thomas Wyatt's epistolary satire "Mine Own John Poyntz" (pub. 1557 in Tottel's *Miscellany*) to "where *truth* is given in prey / For money, poison, and treason—*of some*" (my italics; see Chapter 2) in an attempt to bolster the ideology of Catholic sovereignty for Queen Mary and the English nation, while ignoring the dour depictions of women in Wyatt's other satires and lyric poems. Well after Elizabeth came to power, the misogynistic elements in Shakespeare's *The Taming of the Shrew* (1593) and *A Midsummer Night's Dream* (1595) failed to arouse the ire of Edmund Tilney, the queen's censorious Master of the Revels, despite the fact that both plays feature a man humiliating a woman in order to render her a more compliant wife. Yet in that same year, Tilney likely ordered the fourth act of Shakespeare's *Richard II* struck for its politically sensitive representation of the deposition of a consecrated monarch.[24]

That is not to say that there was no official effort to challenge the phallocentric regulatory impulse of anti-feminist satire in the Elizabethan age. As stated, the most striking example is the inclusion of two anti-feminist satires in the 1599 Bishops' ban against the further publication of satires and unexamined histories and plays. The first of the banned anti-feminist works is a translation of Hercole and Torquato Tasso's polemical dialogue (or "philosophical controversie," as announced on the title page) entitled *Of Marriage and Wiving* (*Dello Ammogliarsi* in the original Italian text). The second satire is an anonymous English translation of the early-fifteenth-century French satire *Le Quinze Joyes de Mariage*, entitled *The XV Joys of Marriage*, a satire whose English versions enjoyed uncontroversial popularity in the first decade of the sixteenth century and again after Elizabeth's death in 1603.[25]

The rationale for the inclusion of the two anti-feminist satires in the Bishops' prohibition is a matter for debate. Andrew Keener is rightly puzzled by the inclusion of *Of Marriage and Wiving* in the ban, arguing that despite the work's 'possible' misogyny, it is "potentially less transgressive than the other books burned in Stationers' Hall."[26] However, if the banned anti-feminist satires were, in fact, less transgressive than the Juvenalian satires, it seems unlikely that the Bishops would bother to include them in this particular act of censorship. However, Keener does identify one particular transgression: in an era when anti-feminist satire was common, the Bishops' censorious eyes were drawn, at least with regard to *Of Marriage and Wiving*, not by misogyny, but by the "Italian provenance" of the work, which is a reasonable assumption (509). The conservative Elizabethan satirist John Weever, for example, frequently demonstrates concern with the Italianate character of the banned satires and its negative influence on the culture: "If travelers this year of Jubilee, / Bring her nor o'er again from Italy: / Which if they do, no sooner see her float, / But Satyres pinch her spangled Petticoat" (*F&M* 1680–1683). Furthermore, as argued in Chapter 2, Wyatt's "Mine Own John Poyntz" reacts, at least in part, to the influence of continental-style

Machiavellianism on the image of sovereign Englishness in the court of Henry VIII.

However, in the case of *Of Marriage* and *The XV Joys*, it is less their national origins and more the dissonance between their activistic ideology of gender regulation and the sociopolitical conditions they inhabit that best accounts for their appearance in the Bishops' ban. While the Bishops' attempt to silence the Juvenalian perspective was likely a conservative response intended to fortify national precepts against defamatory social images produced at a delicate historical moment, when directed at the anti-feminist satires, this same censorious edict has both conservative and progressive qualities. As an official expression of Elizabeth's displeasure, the prohibition of the anti-feminist satires functions as a form of nuanced feminist negative ideological critique, a repression of an established cultural system of gender regulation which now threatened to weaken, rather than strengthen, the stable conveyance of the monarch's ideological image.

Elizabeth, like Secretary Clinton and countless other female authorities across the centuries, was no stranger to such efforts to degrade her public image through misogynistic satire and other publicly minded forms of critical discourse, from sermons, to pamphlets, poems, political tracts, and (again) to caricatures.[27] Such works often praised the virtues of marriage for women in the hope of influencing Elizabeth either to marry or to name a successor, but Elizabeth remained committed to her personal independence. Between 1558 and 1576, Parliament formerly petitioned Elizabeth to marry no fewer than four times; however, Elizabeth resisted a secular allegiance by "rendering her relationship with her English subjects as a mystical marriage," effectively ensuring her personal and political autonomy from outside incursion (Callaghan 10). Although Elizabeth remained no doubt sensitive to the topic of marriage, by 1599, the edicts, poems, and pamphlets pressing the issue, positively and negatively, were likely less significant to the queen; she had long before constructed her identity as inviolably linked to her country, rejecting the traditional marital strictures that woman, as an 'unreasonable creature,' is only made whole by submitting her will, her identity, and her property to male authority.[28]

Typically, as Barbara Feichtinger argues, pro-marriage political tracts were composed of three central elements: "a strict concentration on the male perspective, emphasis on procreation as the sole purpose of marriage, and a close link with normative misogyny."[29] With this in mind, it is unsurprising that those tracts that injudiciously linked the virtues of marriage to misogynistic images of women's 'natural' imperfections provoked a stern response from Elizabeth's government. For example, 1598 saw the posthumous publication of a tract by Sir Peter Wentworth, a particularly zealous Member of Parliament, entitled *A Pithy Exhortation to her Majesty for Establishing her Successor to the Crown*, which not only encouraged Elizabeth to marry in decidedly indecorous terms, but more seriously, derided her intransigence as equivalent to an unnatural mother abusing her offspring: "And seeing that God hath ordained you our nursing mother, we your children cry upon you and most earnestly beseech you that by neglecting this motion, you unnaturally leave us not unto the evident spoil of the merciless bloody sword."[30] This image of Elizabeth as both wife and mother to her nation (rather than to a male) was one cultivated by Elizabeth herself as part of her nonconformist gender ideology; as recorded by William Camden in his *Annales* (1625), Elizabeth responded to critics of her personal independence in Parliament with, "I am already bound unto an Husband, which is the Kingdom of England... And reproach me no more, (quoth she) that I have no children: for every one of you, and as many as are English, are my children and kinsfolk," an ideology which lends the appearance of correspondence to gender norms, while also authorizing the unorthodoxy of a female monarch with no aspirations to marriage. Wentworth's metaphor of Elizabeth as unnatural mother thus becomes a direct challenge to that aspect of her ideology.[31]

Decades earlier, Stubbs' argument in *A Gaping Gulf* against Elizabeth's possible marriage to the French Duke of Anjou similarly invoked Elizabeth's maternal responsibilities to her people and to the Anglican Church; however, the core of Stubbs "alarmist rhetoric" was, as Ilona Bell argues, regulatory anxiety over the social chaos that accompanies unrestrained female bodily desire, or as Bell puts it, "the gender unconscious—inciting fears that the queen's female body is threatening the social order."[32] Drawing on the familiar biblical image of women as the "weaker vessel" (1 Peter 3:7), Stubbs expresses deep concern that women's inherently corrupt nature and natural subservience as dictated by God will not just make Elizabeth's body easy prey for a foreign nobleman, but that her injudicious choice of husband would leave her body and her nation open to an invasive French Catholic force determined to overthrow the sovereignty of England:

> And if woman, that weaker vessel, be strong enough to draw man through the advantage which the devil hath within our bosom... how much more forcibly shall the stronger vessel pull weak woman, considering that with the inequality of strength there is joined as great or more readiness to Idolatry and superstition. And if the husband which is the head be drawn aside by his wife over whom nevertheless he hath authority and rule: how much more easily shall the wife be perverted by her husband to whom she is subject by the law of God.

Elizabeth was less than forgiving of Stubbs' and Wentworth's presumptuous and misogynistic depictions of her body, mind, and country as both corrupt and corruptible: Stubbs and his distributor, William Page, had their right hands cut off, while Wentworth languished in the Tower of London for nearly four years between the time when Elizabeth learned of his pamphlet in early 1593 and his death in late 1596.

The anti-feminist satires in the Bishops' ban suffered a similar fate due to a similar conflict between the regulatory ideology of misogynistic satiric poetics (i.e. women as socially unfit due to inherent defects, deficiencies, and excesses) and the dictates of Elizabeth's state ideology. By 1599, Elizabeth had been in power for over forty years, long enough to consolidate a gender-fluid ideological system (supported by a range of cultural products) that clearly clashed with the misogyny and regulatory goals of the anti-feminist satiric tradition.[33] To be fair, the 'true' intentions of the translators of *The XV Joys* and *Of Marriage and Wiving* was less likely to create a libelous satiric assault on Elizabeth's ideology, and more to fulfill a nationalistic desire to "English" part of a long-standing literary tradition from the continent, just as Wyatt had done decades earlier with Horatian poetry. However, the decision to promulgate these two particular anti-feminist satires at this particular time was ill-advised because the political and ideological conditions that satire is always compelled to engage had changed so as to lend rather heretical and treasonous intentionalities to the anti-feminist satires.

The Bishops' designation of *Of Marriage and Wiving* as a "book against women" suggests its inclusion was the result of a female monarch provoked by sexist literature, which is certainly a possibility; the government had several legal edicts in place to protect Elizabeth from "seditious words" and "deforming images." However, the larger issue was that Elizabeth, in a manner unique from her half-sister Mary before her, chose to create an unorthodox gender ideology for herself and for her nation that the anti-feminist satires, deliberately or not, translated pejoratively, potentially disrupting the stable conveyance of meaning monitored closely by Elizabeth's counselors. Louis Montrose notes Elizabeth's propensity for using public edicts like the Bishops' ban to secure images of "hierarchical and homological order" as part of her desire "to concentrate authority and power, both temporal and spiritual, in the person of the monarch" in response to "unprecedented changes affecting English society" in the late 1590s (21).[34] In such an environment, the conventional satiric types of female imperfection populating the banned anti-feminist satires were no longer just comic expressions of patriarchal anxieties, but activistic challenges to ideological sureties that the monarchy and the nation had relied on for decades.

The XV Joys of Marriage

As the licit status of the English *XV Joys* both before and after Elizabeth's reign suggests, the sudden impermissibility of the satire in 1599 most likely derives from an incompatibility between the satire's activistic agenda and aspects of Elizabethan self-representation in a manner conversant with the banned Juvenalian satires. On the formal level, *The XV Joys* is stylistically incongruous with the declamatory, outraged, and sweepingly nihilistic rhetoric characteristic of the Juvenalian mode; however, both *The XV Joys* and the majority of the banned satirists employ the familiar Chaucerian-inspired Heroic Couplet style. The decision to use Heroic Couplets not only helps nativize the foreign source material, but for *The XV Joys*, the form also serves to 'elevate' and 'regularize' the "raucous bourgeois and sub-bourgeois voice" of the French original, rendering the 'Englished' version (at least before Elizabeth came to power) ideologically 'safer' than the continental version's indecorous, demotic heteroglossia and thematic emphasis on individual liberty: "the uniformity of the English verse masks and never finally conveys the narratological hybridity and disruptiveness of the French work" (Coldiron 117). In fact, several times, the English translator breaks the fiction by informing the reader that his version consciously deviates from the original due to material he deems too controversial or too inflammatory to include in his version: "For I will not those words put in rhyme / But hold my tongue and speak when it is time" (2398–2399).

Structurally, *The XV Joys* (as the title suggests) consists of fifteen discrete domestically focused vignettes delivered by a narrator in the style of the medieval French fabliaux, occasionally reporting dialogue through free indirect discourse in a manner (for English readers) once again reminiscent of Chaucer. Despite the comic trappings, the text reports relentlessly on the supposedly inherent defects in women's nature, with particular attention paid to the gap between what women say and what they do. Furthermore, wives are not the sole target for accusations of hypocrisy, but mothers, daughters, midwives, and gossips, too, which creates an ironic intentionality targeting less the institution of marriage and more the threat women pose to "the common good," as Coldiron suggests (135). In support of this centripetal phallocentric agenda, the satiric typology of both the women and the men in the poem is unambiguous: the women are uncharacteristically powerful, "cautelous [crafty], willful, and eke malicious / forward, wanton, nice, and disdainous… fail will she not to have the sovereignty" (1986–1997), while the men are presented in dialogic opposition to the women, namely, "right well tamed" (758), an impotent fish caught inextricably in "the leap" (i.e. a basket) of marriage, unable to prevent women's monstrous excesses.

Stylistically, *The XV Joys* clearly does not fit within either the Horatian or Juvenalian verse traditions; however, aspects of the work's narrative episodic structure reflect the style and function of "serio-comical" genres such as menippean satire. Kernan defines the menippean form as any satire written in the third person or "managed under cover of a fable" (13), while M. M. Bakhtin posits *menippea* as an organizing

Anti-Feminist Satire and the Bishops' Ban 109

principle in which the seriousness of myth is undermined by carnivalized contact with the "living present." Stylistic unity gives way to inserted genres, hetero-voiced narration replaces high rhetoric, and fanciful, scandalous, even unnatural states of being are put on display, all in the service of "testing" and/or "echoing the ideological issues of the day" (*PD* 107–118).

The original French *XV Joys* is clearly more conversant with the menippean tropes and their centrifugal philosophical effects than the English version, due, as Coldiron demonstrates, to the French version's unrestricted generic play, its rich rhetorical heteroglossia, its gleeful parodies of religious hagiography,[35] its unabashed erotics, and its ideological syncrisis (the dialogic juxtaposition of alternative perspectives), which comes in the form of anticipated objections to the misogynistic elements tendered by female readers. The overall effect is not a condemnation of marriage or women, but a genuinely carnivalesque exploration of the "connection between political and domestic liberty" as symbolized by marriage (Coldiron 136). While aspects of the English version take advantage of certain menippean strategies, conscious authorial changes, particularly, the omission of all "apologetic deflections" and the resulting dominance of the monologic, patriarchal perspective, render the English *XV Joys* not a strict translation but a "nakedly misogynistic" adaptation less interested in exploring notions of personal liberty and more invested in promoting the standard phallocentric ideology in a manner hostile to late Elizabethan ideological conditions.[36]

The few menippean characteristics retained in the English *XV Joys* seem chosen for their comic qualities, yet they also retain their hortatory focus on the male readership. For example, the contemporary settings increase the relevance of the scandalous behaviors, the inserted genres (complaint, sermons, domestic drama, Romance and Epic parodies) allow for direct and indirect examples of female transgression, and the carnivalesque spirit, inherent in each tale's 'comic' display of inverted gender norms, magnifies the dangers posed by the tales' ideologists, the 'mannish' wives and 'womanish' husbands. Finally, at the heart of each episode is the exploration of the social implications of an ideological issue of great importance to Tudor society and to Elizabeth's personal ideology: chastity.

It should come as little surprise that anti-feminist satire should take such an interest in violations of chastity because the concept was one of central importance to so many fields throughout the medieval and early modern periods. The maintenance of political, economic, and social hegemonies hinged on the legal system of Primogeniture (goods and titles passing to the first-born son), which in turn required the regulation of women's reproductive power in order to ensure the legitimate transmission of both property and authority. Thus, the philosophy of chastity, itself a regulatory ideology of natural female submission and unending fealty to the authority of the husband and the patriarchy, was thoroughly codified and celebrated through a series of intermediary forces (mainly religion and the law) and supported through cultural products. Breitenberg concurs, arguing that the ubiquity of chastity in the literature of the period is explicable because the vice of inconstancy (chastity's opposite), like later conceptions of the incoherent female, represents a foundational threat to masculine economies that rely on stable images of male supremacy. Consequently, the patriarchal economy fetishized the concept of chastity "as extremely important to women" in order to control women's power to affect those social codes central to patriarchal economies: "Honor and reputation are important to both genders, yet clearly it is women who confirm male honor and not the reverse" (382). Conduct and Marriage Manuals of the period, such as *The Mirror of Modestie* (1580) and *A Discourse of Marriage and Wiving* (1615), were produced, Breitenberg contends, at least in part to provide men with an "outward set of interpretable signs" that will allow them to verify women's claims to fidelity, and the same holds true for *The XV Joys*.

At the center of nearly every episode are direct and indirect demonstrations of how women mask their transgressive "appetite," as the narrator terms it, for the benefit of a male readership keen to avoid the dishonor that accompanies unchaste behavior (2797). For example, in the first episode, the narrator reports that the credulous husband is "all eased" by his wife's tearful claim of unerring fidelity, yet fails to act when "in mind is he displeased supposing / that of nature she is cold of body chaste / and deal with no man would"; unfortunately for him, his wariness is overcome by his "piteous heart and mind" (261–269). The first direct *exemplum* of female infidelity comes soon after by way of the wife's desire to transcend her social station, or more specifically, her refusal to obediently submit to her husband's rank as required by the marital strictures:

And thus she sayeth…
"In twenty places or more I had be married
If I so would, but like a fool I tarried
For where I might great honour and avail
Have had, and riches, thereof now I fail"…
Thus she complaineth her withouten care
Of her husband or how the good man fare,
For wholly she hath set her mind upon
Her own estate, and shortly she is gone
Unto this marriage.

(394–419)

All of the wife's subsequent actions reinforce her unchaste nature and the need to strengthen the traditional gender power hierarchy: for example, her demands for a gown richer than she merits (a violation of sumptuary laws), her withholding of sex as a bargaining tool (a violation of St. Paul's dictates in 1 Corinthians 7:4), her refusal to share the profits of her land with her husband (a violation of the English common law concept of Coverture), etc. (79–81, 244, and 182–194) Yet, as rebellious as she is, the husband's powerlessness before her illicit desires is depicted as equally shameful, if not more so.

The other Joys offer similar direct and indirect images of the personal and social instability that accompanies unchecked female inconstancy. For example, in "Joy Seven," the narrator warns the implied male readership that

> know ye may, though she [a wife] be good / as ye have heard me say / And of her body chaste or otherwise… For every wife believeth verily / and holdeth this opinion steadfastly/ That her husband the weakest creature/ And most wretched is
>
> (2352–2361)

The derision of women's fidelity in "Joy Ten" is more direct: "And women both yet will they not live chaste/ But ease themselves by other means in haste" (2994–2995). Unsurprisingly, every Joy abounds with 'comic' tales of women's unregulated appetites: a wife foolishly granted permission to go on a pilgrimage receives the undue attentions of other men ("Joy Two"); a woman of high estate conspires with her maidservant to cheat on her husband both literally and figuratively ("Joy Five"); a wife brings shame to her husband through her selfishness and inhospitality ("Joys Three and Six"); a lustful unmarried young woman entraps a man by convincing him that the child she carries is his ("Joy Eleven"); a parodic Penelope cuckolds and then remarries quickly on the mistaken assumption that her husband has been killed in war ("Joys Twelve and Thirteen"); and an entire community vouches for a cheating wife, even after the hapless husband witnesses the transgression with his own eyes ("Joy Fifteen"). As a result, the paternal narrator ceaselessly exhorts the male readership to search for those signs that will ensure he and his community avoid "his proper shame / None other wight thereof is for to blame" (599–600).

As opposed to the 1599 English version, the fact that the 1509 adaptation of *The XV Joys* was not subjected to censorship supports the possibility that the satire's misogynistic ideology was more amenable to the social conditions at that time, particularly the social instability surrounding Henry VIII's quest for an heir; as Coldiron points out, "the poem's elaborate extended metaphors of marriage as a trap or prison—a scathing indictment of men foolish enough to marry—might have harmonized oddly with the moment's national imperative and chronic concern for the succession" (132). However, the fact that, in 1509,

England had yet to experience the domination of a female political force could have made the hortative warnings in *The XV Joys* more theoretical than actual. Yet by 1599, England had experienced not one but two (or three, if one includes Lady Jane Grey) instances of the inversion of the supposedly divinely ordained gender hierarchy in the form of consecrated female monarchs, each with their own approach to the proprieties of gender performance. Whereas Queen Mary had chastely submitted her authority to King Phillip II of Spain in 1554, Elizabeth chose to turn the dogma of female chastity on its head, and thus cultural products like anti-feminist satire that asserted the morality and utility of female submission to masculine dominance suddenly 'harmonized oddly with the moment's national imperative.'

Because chastity was a central component of Elizabeth's ideological persona, authors, politicians, and church officials were well advised to engage the subject delicately or risk the consequences, as the cases of Stubbs and Wentworth clearly demonstrate. Early in Elizabeth's reign, the question of whether or not the young queen would conform to gender standards, especially the convention of chaste submission, as her half-sister had done before her, was considered of central importance. For Elizabeth's male counselors seeking to strengthen the Protestant sociopolitical fields, the right kind of marriage "promised a solution to the problem posed by female rule. It offered a means by which Protestant rectitude and Tudor royal blood conjoined... and a king constituted, ambiguously through the marriage itself or through issue."[37] Thus, the young queen Elizabeth's "strongest card" was her presumed ability to produce a male heir once married to a Protestant nobleman from England, or some other country equally adverse to Catholic influence (McLaren 268). "'Be a sort of Christ unto us,' pleaded one of Elizabeth's councilors in 1562 as he begged her to marry, 'Mortify your own affections'"; in other words, the councilor asks Elizabeth to subsume her desires to a male for the good of the *patria* (McLaren 268).

Elizabeth, however, had other plans. In an ingenious political move, she revised the mediatory systems of chastity to preserve her own and her country's autonomy. Her iconographic self-construction as the Marian "Virgin Queen," her body and will unquestionably spotless, allowed her to circumscribe the convention that alliance with a male was necessary to control women's naturally inconstant desires, while her related claim to be chastely beholden only unto "the Kingdom of England" promoted her as a figure of national chastity, sovereign, complete, with no need for submission to outside authorities. As noted by Carole Levin, this image rendered Elizabeth "both woman and man in one," a being "beyond the categories of sex," as Butler writes, a divine androgyne to some, and a kind of Amazonian hermaphrodite, or in a modern sense, an incoherent lesbian "no sex" to others (120; 1).

As suggested, both conservative politicians and anti-feminist satirists were quick to respond to such an unorthodox ideology, with the government attempting to oversee and approve all images of the royal person, as indicated by the numerous legal acts issued in defense of Elizabeth's sanctioned ideology. For example, the draft proclamation of 1563 prohibited 'deforming images' of the queen in portraiture, the 1596 Privy Council order prohibited "Unauthorized Portraits of the Queen," the 1581 statute attempted to regulate "Seditious Words and Rumors Uttered Against the Queen," and various edicts derived from the 1559 Act of Supremacy all gave Elizabeth's councilors the authority to "reform, redress, order, correct, and amend all such errors, heresies, schisms, abuses, offences, contempts, and enormities whatsoever" caused by printed materials or other media that could threaten "the increase of virtue, and the conservation of the peace and unity of this realm" (Clegg 36).

Yet despite the government's sensitivity to the activistic power of unsanctioned versions of the royal image, satirists had limited success in producing both verbally and pictorially subversive perceptual translations of Elizabeth's preferred iconography, or as Rob Content describes them, "monstrous composite-imagery" of the queen. Content's examples include verses condemning the excessive amorous idolization of Elizabeth's image in Sir Philip Sidney's *Old Arcadia* (circa 1581), and a parodic drawing found in William Wodwall's *The Actes of Queen Elizabeth Allegorized* (1595), in which Elizabeth is reimagined as a kind of ostentatious "hideous composite bird... 'contrary to all other of [its] kind.'"[38] In short, while conceptions of gender incoherence and hybridity proved useful to Elizabeth, they were useful to her satiric detractors as well.

However disquieting Elizabeth's unorthodox gender image was to some, her unique iconography allowed her to assert not only her own political legitimacy, but also the legitimacy of her nation as an imperial power. Tracing Elizabeth's preferred ideological symbol, Astrea, the virgin goddess of purity, from its classical origins through its early modern manifestations, Frances Yates shows how the symbol amalgamates figures of matriarchal authority with notions of masculine imperial authority.[39] Astrea blends "the Carthaginian Queen of Heaven, Virgo Caelestis, with the Mother of the Gods, with Ceres, Atargatis, the Syrian goddess, yet she is still the just virgin of the golden age... Her worship has taken on a state aspect; she represents *Virtus* and *Pax*, those much emphasized features of Roman imperial rule" (32). Thus the adoption of the blended Astrea iconography early in Elizabeth's reign meant much more than a means to resist enforced marriage; Astrea reflects "a universal claim—the tradition of sacred empire," an image bolstered after the shocking defeat of the Spanish Armada in 1588. As both religion and history had proved England to be sovereign, so too, Elizabeth's body, and the nation to which she was chastely beholden, was presented as holy, inviolable, and independent: "the monarch who is One and sovereign within his own domains has imperial religious rights, and he [or she] can achieve the imperial reform independently of the Pope" (56).

Still, despite such efforts, courtiers hoping for a return to masculine authority and national identity continued to assert the morality of traditional gender norms by staging elaborate allegorical dramas, pageants, and masques, including *Gorboduc* (1561), *The Masque of Pallas* (1562), and *The Misfortunes of Arthur* (1588), which like the anti-feminist satires, often dramatized the devastating consequences of Elizabeth's decision to remain an autonomous "no sex" (Axton 40). However, by 1599, such conservative pressures gave way to a grudging acceptance of Elizabeth's unflagging ideologies of national chastity and corporate integrity. Thus, the figure of the Astrea Virgin was augmented (if not replaced) by the ideological figures of Diana, goddess of chastity and the hunt, and Cynthia, another name for Artemis, Diana's Greek counterpart and goddess of the moon: "as Elizabeth grew older and hope of offspring faded, Diana or Cynthia as a public image found reluctant acceptance" as a means to "transmit [the] perpetuity" of Elizabeth's sacred body politic (Axton 60). Thus the aging Elizabeth is allegorized as the chaste goddess Diana in such works as the reprieved *Caltha Poetarum*, and more importantly, Edmund Spenser's *The Faerie Queene* (1590), in which Spenser praises Elizabeth's "own excellent conceit of Cynthia (Phoebe and Cynthia being both names of Diana)" ("A Letter of the Authors" 737). In short, because "chastity, not the morality of marriage, becomes a national virtue" by 1599, to project female inconstancy as a vice common to all women requiring more strenuous regulation of their independence, as occurs consistently throughout *The XV Joys*, was more than just libel, but a potentially treasonous rejection of a concept central to the heavily monitored national image (Axton 60; 70).

Of Marriage and Wiving

The second anti-feminist satire, *Of Marriage and Wiving*, is a prose translation of a 'debate' between "the two famous Tassi now living," as the title page announces, "the one Hercules the Philosopher, the other, Torquato the Poet," with Torquato Tasso acting as the defender of women and the institution of marriage, and his cousin, Hercole Tasso, acting as the detractor. As mentioned, *Of Marriage* is the only work in the ban to receive any explanatory language from the Bishops justifying its inclusion in the prohibition. The tract's offense is defined not in terms of its derision of marriage, but as "the book against women viz, *of marriage and wyving*"; clearly, the Bishops' central objection is the work's misogyny and not its misogamy. Furthermore, while the work's unique "form, its content, and its status as a translated work of literature" suggest that it "differs significantly from the other banned books," in fact, those very same factors, coupled with the satire's ideologically antagonistic dialogism, render it as much of a satiric threat to the maintenance of the Elizabethan image as the banned verse satires and *The XV Joys of Marriage* (Keener 508).

The formal qualities of *Of Marriage and Wiving* adhere to the classical sophistic pro-contra argument tradition: Hercole's section denigrates the topic of marriage ("*pars destruens*," literally pulling down), while Torquato's section endorses it ("*pars construens*," building up; Keener 510). As conventional as the form appears, surprisingly, in his opening dedication, Hercole suggests that his polemic "against women" (an appraisal echoed by the Bishops) should not be taken at face value. Hercole implies an ironic intention behind the hyperbolically scathing treatment of the subject, an intention available only to the reader who can "well mark and have but an eye unto the beginning and the end of the matter from whence the manner of writers is to draw and borrow their purpose and inventions." However, the Bishops' special notation of the work's offense makes it clear that Hercole's effort to represent his side as a paradoxical censure or "mock disputation" was either rhetorically or politically insufficient to warrant a "stay"; the Bishops likely could not (and obviously did not) excuse the subversive gender politics at the heart of the satire (Keener 514). The work's translator, Robert Tofte, even goes so far as to insert a direct praise of Elizabeth late in the defamatory section in a rather obvious attempt to defuse the subversive potential of the satire's misogyny. Obviously, Tofte's clumsy characterization of the "Virgin and Maiden Queen" as "different and exempt from all such defects before rehearsed" failed, as Cyndia Clegg notes, "to contain the text's uncomplimentary (at least to her [Elizabeth]) coupling of misogyny with praises of marriage" (199; see *Wiving* 34).

Despite its claims to the contrary, Hercole's argument (and Tofte's translation) is simply too ferociously declamatory and too rooted in the history of misogynistic theology, literature, and biology to be excusable as comic irony.[40] Instead, such factors render Hercole's contribution correlative with the most extreme examples of anti-feminist satire, particularly Juvenal's deeply misogynistic "Sixth Satire". This is not to suggest that Hercole's contribution should be read as an imitative prose version of the Juvenalian original, however, the similarities in tone, *exempla*, and regulatory focus place Tofte's translation on a par with the radical Juvenalian mode disallowed by Elizabeth's censors.

As brazen as the misogyny is in both *Of Marriage* and Juvenal Six, Hercole augments what are, by the late sixteenth century, the standard vices attributed to women and their negative effect on the patriarchy (or as Hercole puts it, the "Political, Moral, and Economical" havoc wrought by their monstrous natures, 3) by adding a particularly damning ontological focus that strikes at the heart of Elizabeth's person and her ideology.[41] To frame this attack, Hercole, like Juvenal before him, uses marriage as a framework to declaim against women's characters in an unequivocally vituperative tone. Although Hercole's nominal goal is to dissuade auditors from marrying, the effect is one of gender regulation and the defense of masculine identity, much like how Juvenal weakly structures his diatribe against women's excesses as an ostensible attempt to convince Postumus to remain single. Furthermore, as in *The XV Joys*, Hercole focuses on numerous *exempla* of women's natural lack of chastity rather than focusing on a more general condemnation of the marital institution; thus for Hercole, marriage is only imperfect because women are inconstant "old she-Satans" who corrupt the "honor and the infamy of Man" with their duplicitous "black swan-like chastity" (7; 29).[42]

For Juvenal, marriage is to be avoided because all women lack a stabilizing sense of shame; homosexual relations, the speaker argues, are far preferable to the fruitless search for a chaste female. Hercole concurs (although he substitutes celibacy for homosexuality as a viable alternative), yet his argument goes a step farther, rejecting marriage on the basis of "the base indignity and corrupt wickedness of women's nature," which cannot help but lead men to ruin (10): "If we will not be defiled," argues Hercole, revising Ecclesiasticus 13:1 as applicable to women rather than to powerful men, "let us touch no pitch: if not polluted, let us not handle filth: if we mean to live pleasantly, let us never marry" (4).

Juvenal, too, decries the threat women's immodesty poses to patriarchal systems, but his *exempla* are ultimately explained away as a political rather than an ontological failure: the cause of female wantonness is presented as due less to women's inherent imperfection and more to the success of the empire, or more precisely, its effeminizing wealth ("*divitiae molles*," 300), which has given women the latitude (and men the indolence) to subvert their 'natural' social roles (cf. lines 85–87 and 110–112). The wives and daughters of the Roman upper classes, no longer restrained by the patriarchal proprieties of rank, have been permitted to become not just men's tormentors, but monstrous inversions of the social order, or '*dominae*,' i.e. female rulers, as Juvenal puts it (30).

Hercole's contribution shares a number of regulatory *exempla* with Juvenal Six that dramatize women's natural inconstancy and male complacency, including women subverting male authority in the household, depriving men of their male companions, women's mothers acting as panderers, invocations of Messalina and Clytemnestra, the duplicitous use of cosmetics, the disruption of masculine lineage through infidelity, etc. However, Hercole and his translator add to these conventional misogynistic types a vituperative strain of biblical and biological 'proofs' drawn from selective readings of Solomon, the Disciples, Aristotle, Galen, and others to suggest that the threat to the continuance of male identity and authority comes not because of how women are allowed to indulge their natural excesses, but because of their nugatory quiddity, meaning their valueless, meaningless essence. The accompanying perceptual translations of women are particularly odious and politically provocative: women are reduced to "slavish inferiors," "imperfect and

Anti-Feminist Satire and the Bishops' Ban 117

vile," "demi-men," "monsters," and most disruptive of all to Elizabeth's ideological image, "things that have no being" (16, 11, 17, 12).

Buoyed by classical authorities, Hercole's opening dismissal of marriage is quickly and completely overtaken by a comprehensive inversion of the image of women as ontologically legitimate. Beginning with the issue of women's bodies, Hercole adulterates the familiar biblical depiction invoked decades before by Stubbs of women as the weaker, yet still important, vessel (1 Peter 3:7) with the perception of women as "worse than a weak vessel of brittle glass" unfit to be "men's companions" (a direct contradiction of Genesis 2:20), before degrading the image further into the female vessel as only useful as a "receptacle of some of our Excremental humours, standing us in the same stead as the Bladder, the Gall, and such other uncleanly members of our body" (29; 15; 11).[43]

The popular theory of the four bodily humours next leads the speaker to extend his attacks on the worthlessness of women's bodies into a rather standard derogation of women's physicality as contrary both to men's bodies and men's affairs. As one would expect, the female bodily humours are presented as predominately "cold and moist" rather than hot and dry, as in males, but what shocks is the fulsome list of physical infirmities resulting from women's inferior humours, including "dropping distillations," "rheumatic Catars," "gouty swellings," "scurvy scabs," hysteria, and (strangely) the total inversion of bowel function, which Hercole terms the "Iliack passion." Psychologically, the humorous defects in women are to blame for such stereotypical female character traits as "sleepy and heavy," "unmindful and forgetful," "simple and sottish," "carping and biting," traits which precipitate the kinds of behaviors antithetical to the maintenance of masculine authority: female humours, readers are told, lead women to be more "malicious and envious," "jealous and suspicious," "miserable and covetous," "bold and impudent" than the masculine alternative (12–13).

Subsequently, Hercole erases all possibility of autonomy, for good or ill, from women's flawed physicality by representing that physicality as an unfinished and imperfect rendition of the male; in fact, the very category of woman is presented as a misnomer, as there are only men and "demi-men." This biological bias in the satire is derived from such sources as medieval and early modern theology, and also from a selective reorientation of concepts found in the influential medical texts of the day, particularly, *The Problems of Aristotle*, "a popular Elizabethan medical guide... incorporating Galenic elements into its fundamentally Aristotelian perspective" (Montrose 140–141). According to Ian Maclean,[44] the Aristotelian and Galenic understanding of women was of a being characterized by "deprived, passive, and material traits," an unfinished entity "not carried through to its final [i.e. male] conclusion," and as such, one who seeks "completion by intercourse with the male" (131). However, in response to the question of whether or not such images of women's bodies as incomplete and thus inferior were fully accepted in early modern society, Maclean cites a number of contemporary accounts that laud, rather than condemn, women's physical differences as a logical aid to procreation. "By 1600," Maclean writes, "in nearly all medical circles, the peripatetic claim that the female is an imperfect persun [sic] of the male is banished from the textbooks," and "none but satirical or facetious texts support the proposition of [female] monstrosity" (134; 131). Of course, an anti-feminist satire like Hercole's bent on creating a phallocentric image of women as insufficient need not trouble itself with contradictory viewpoints; the purpose of the satire is all, and despite objections to the contrary, early modern culture still produced a wealth of philosophical, medical, and theological material from which to cherry-pick the best *exempla* of female deficiency as a means to safeguard the established gender power hierarchy.

Moving to the inextricable link between the female body and the female spirit, Hercole reiterates many conventional theological perspectives on the challenges to female salvation, however, he delivers them in a tone of Tertullian-like conservative ferocity and rhetorical monologism that closes off the discourse to all but the most negative spiritual outcomes for both women and the men who associate with them. Hercole magnifies arguments from Christian church fathers (Solomon, the apostles Mark, Matthew, Luke, and Peter, Saints John, Augustine, Jerome, etc.) to 'prove' both the inadequacy of the female spirit and, more importantly, its threat to male salvation: women are the usual "subtle sex of Eve... the Overthrowers of Mankind" (7), but also inhuman beasts unblessed by "his [God's] own image and likeness" (13), as well as "stumbling blocks to hinder us [males] from returning once more back again unto heaven, our allotted country" (32). Such scathing satiric images recall Nussbaum's supposition that the project of anti-feminist satire is one in which images of women as the creators of chaos serve 'to reassure the threatened male minority,' to impose a sense of meaning when the fear of meaninglessness arises. As is characteristic of anti-feminist satire, Hercole projects the masculine fears of social and ontological irrelevance onto the bodies, souls, and the essentialism of women.

The charges of bodily and spiritual imperfection lead naturally to charges of essential monstrosity and absence. Hercole modifies the Aristotelian theory of woman as an unfinished male into the image of woman as a "defiled" being, their subhuman nature the result of "the defect of the *Vertue Operative*, or the working of the power of Nature, as Monsters are brought forth through defect, or through superabundance of matter" (11–12). Thus women are, once again, marked by both excess and deficiency, striving to achieve a meaningful perfection unavailable to them, i.e. to become "a Man, [just] as every deformed wretch [would be a] goodly and fair creature" (12). Because she will never be perfect, never be male, the woman uses marriage not just to supplant the male, but to become him, as far as she is able: "because then the wife becomes as a mixed substance with him whom she weddeth (every one of them as a new *Salmare* with her Hermites, renewing daily *Hermophradites*)" (16). Although not likely intentional, here, the Elizabethan ideology of a holy and sovereign androgyne English monarchy is dialogized with the traditional phallocentric image of monstrous female incoherence: the hermaphrodite, the usurping, imperfect, destabilizing force that both exists beyond and destroys those clear binary relations key to masculine governing economies (see Butler 125–126).

As potentially parodic and provocative as such images are to Elizabeth's personal history and official self-representation (women as objects for males, women as diseased, women as usurpers of male authority, women as unholy), perhaps the most politically subversive element is Hercole's claim that women's complete oppositional relationship to masculine perfection is so profound that it constitutes an ontological state of nonexistence, or "not being." Women do not simply lack the Galenic elements of masculine heat or penile development, they *are* lack, "false and impossible," "dark and obscure," the antithesis of the substance and light that link masculine economies to the divine good:

> The Woman that hath no being, but only what is given unto her (as it were of Alms) from the rib of Man, shall without doubt fall under this infamous consideration of such a *Non Ens* [not being]: being Nothing, or a thing without substance.
>
> (11)[45]

As ontological ciphers, women lack the kind of teleological purpose that grants meaning; in fact, Hercole presents women as "Accidental things, [which] are by the Philosopher [i.e. Aristotle] compared a little before unto the aforesaid things that have no being" (12). In other words, if all that which has substance inherently tends towards perfection, as Aristotle posits, which in gender terms is equivalent to the masculine ("the same not consenting unto ought but to that which is best, and more perfect in their kind, which is Man"), then the non-male must certainly *ipso facto* constitute not merely "a hateful monster," but a being so incoherent, so totally opposed to perfection that it must ultimately denote the very absence of being.

Such effacing rhetoric anticipates much of Butler's examination of the ways in which masculine discourse like *Of Marriage and Wiving* negates female ontology for the benefit of patriarchal identities and social economies. Butler cites the views of Simone de Beauvoir and Monique Wittig that the idea of woman is as a figure marked linguistically as the Other, an oppositional relation by which male identity is constituted. However, Butler then complicates this view with Luce Irigary's "post-Lacanian reformulation of Freud" (27) that the category of women does not even constitute oppositional demarcation as she exists outside the "closed circle of signifier and signified," as the only universal sign is the male (11; 20). Thus the concept of "Woman" is more than just deficiency, it is "a point of linguistic absence" (10), "unrepresentable," the thing that is "not 'one,'" in other words, a semiotic *Non ens* (9).

For Hercole, the need to exclude such nonentities from the traditionally phallogocentric political and social economies is best exemplified by the examples of classical female rulers whose complete moral vacuity set empires at peril: Pasiphae, Messalina, Faustina, Cleopatra, all queens who supposedly "followed so much the brutish appetite of their inordinate and insatiable lust, as some of them, not being content with mankind, would needs put in practice to enjoy the detested company of most loathsome, deformed, and four-footed beasts" (21). Despite the claim that Elizabeth is the exception to this rule, the images of women in power as beyond all categories of sexual definition, and thus beyond all moral propriety, could not go unaddressed by a government vigilant to challenges to Elizabeth's image as expressions of her personal and political authority.

One final centrifugal element of Hercole's nullifying gender ideology is its hostility to Elizabeth's unique employment of the theory of the monarch's inseparable material and immaterial bodies, the ideological linchpin of Tudor sovereignty. As Marie Axton demonstrates, the controversial political concept of the monarch's two bodies was developed in the middle ages as a legal response to the paradox of a monarch's unavoidable mortality and the fact of a country that required rule *in perpetuum*. Upon succession, the eternal body politic melds with the mortal body natural, ensuring the succession of the family bloodline as a matter of divine will rather than secular inheritance:

> the king's death is simply the death of the body natural, the body politic endures, and as such, the matter of inheritance is null and void; the royal blood of the son causes him to *succeed* the father and incorporate the body politic in himself.
>
> (Axton 37)

Before the accession of Queens Mary and Elizabeth, there had been no gender dissonance in the mortal body natural and the eternal body politic as contiguous expressions of masculine authority, of political power as solely gendered male, as Carole Levin notes. However, after the accession of Mary I, lawmakers were forced to make allowances for a female body natural within the male body politic: in the "1554 Act Concerning the Regal Power,"

> Parliament during Mary I's reign made clear to all 'malicious and ignorant persons' that despite the fact that 'the most ancient statutes

of this realm being made by kings then reigning, do not only attribute and refer all prerogative... unto the name of King, a woman could rule in her own right.

(Levin 121)

However, a problem for phallogocentric systems remained: how to reconcile the 'fact' of an imperfect female body natural with the ideology of divine authority as exclusively male? In other words, how can a 'slavish inferior, imperfect and vile' wield "the name of King," and what obligation did the male subject have to this substandard being? As suggested, the solution for Mary I was a conventional marriage, but for Elizabeth, the answer came through androgyne self-representation, "both woman and man in one, both king and queen together, a male body politic in concept while a female body natural in practice" (Levin 121), or in Elizabeth's own words, the acknowledgment of the unorthodoxy of a ruler whose body natural is "but of a weak and feeble woman," but whose authority is legitimized and glorified by the presence of a male body politic, "the heart and stomach of a king, and of a king of England, too."[46]

However, for what Hannah Betts describes as "the countercult in late Elizabethan England," Elizabeth's gender fluidity represented a victory for the illegitimate female body natural over the legitimate masculine body politic, and questions of allegiance naturally followed.[47] Accusations of ontological and political illegitimacy were no doubt particularly galling to Elizabeth, who had endured humiliating legal challenges to her legitimacy as a ruler and as a human being as the supposed bastard offspring of Henry's second marriage to Anne Boleyn, including the Second Act of Succession (1536), which had "formally bastardized" Elizabeth and (temporarily) barred her from succession, and the Papal Bull of 1570, which declared her a politically illegitimate usurper of Catholic authority, and licensed loyal Catholics to defy her "orders, mandates, and laws."[48] Furthermore, although the illegitimate nature of Elizabeth's female body natural is supposedly legitimized through its union with the divine masculine body politic, if the queen's body natural is represented as nonexistent to the point of meaninglessness, then the concomitant image of the national body politic is equally illegitimate. In addition, for an Elizabethan cultural product to deny women's body natural any connection to the divine could be seen as an intentional abuse of the doctrine of Divine Right, a political theory endorsed by all the Tudors, but one essential to Elizabeth as a woman in power seeking to secure her authority.[49] Without both a coherent national identity and an uncontestable divine mandate, the loyalty of male subjects is difficult for a female ruler to maintain.

Finally, Brian Sheerin explores the republican implications of "ontological absence" within conceptions of Tudor sovereignty.[50] Using

John Fortescue's *Governance of England* (1471) as an exemplary text, Sheerin argues for the primacy of the rhetoric of "presence and absence" in contemporary theories of monarchial authority (793). Motivated by a kind of republican frustration with royal absolutism, Fortescue links good governance with the ideology of the eternal royal presence, and bad governance "to a particular kind of kingly self-cancellation" that "threatens to nullify sovereignty" (793–794). The more the tyrannical monarch strays from the good of the country, the more he is characterized by the kind of ontological absence that negates the subject's obligation to the divine sovereign presence (795–796). However, such sovereignty is more complex for a female ruler, especially if one accepts ontological absence as her natural bodily condition, as forcefully asserted in *Of Marriage and Wiving*. If the ruler's body natural is irreversibly absent, meaningless, what obligation does the male subject have to her sovereignty? Why should he risk his own identity and his nation's, become an impotent '*castrato*,' his masculinity forever imprisoned in a "testicle lockbox," by fealty to a monstrous nothing, an incomprehensible cipher, a blank beyond all normative categories? Whatever their true motivations, Hercole's and Tofte's invalidation of women takes on an almost revolutionary activistic satiric intentionality when viewed in dialogue with the sociocultural conditions they failed to account for:

> Then if in this case we rather covet liberty than bondage, if we would live quietly and not contentiously, if we will be counted virtuous and not wantons, if we love to be free men and not slaves, and if we will seek what is good and shun what is bad, let us (then) let such alone, with whom being (once) yoked, we can never be quiet.
>
> (4)

Notes

1 See Rappeport, Alan. "Gloria Steinem and Madeleine Albright Rebuke Young Women Backing Bernie Sanders." *The New York Times*, uploaded by The New York Times, 7 Feb. 2016, www.nytimes.com/2016/02/08/us/politics/gloria-steinem-madeleine-albright-hillary-clinton-bernie-sanders.html. Vanderbilt University political scientist Cecilia Hyunjung Mo conducted a study that suggested a measurable socially determined bias against accepting a woman in a leadership role. See "Sexism Rules in the Ballot Booth Unless Voters Have More Information." *BioSpace*, uploaded by DHI Service, 11 Nov. 2015, www.biospace.com/News/sexism-rules-in-the-ballot-booth-unless-voters/399084. For comments by Marc Rudov, see Ironside, Andrew. "Marc Rudov on the 'Downside' of a Woman President: 'You Mean Besides the PMS and the Mood Swings, Right?'" *Media Matters for America*, uploaded by Media Matters for America, 11 March 2008, www.mediamatters.org/research/2008/03/11/marc-rudov-on-the-downside-of-a-woman-president/142850.
2 Siese, April. "'Vagenda of Manocide' Marquee is but One of This Gunsmith's Hilariously Offensive Election Signs." *The Dot*, uploaded by The Daily Dot.

24 Aug. 2016, www.dailydot.com/unclick/vagenda-manocide-election-sign/. See also Schaefer, Sara. "Today's Vagenda." saraschaefer.com, uploaded by Medium.com. 26 Aug. 2016, medium.com/@saraschaefer1/todays-vagenda-2747885a4497.
3 See Chapter 1, note 40 for citation of a study demonstrating the impact of satire on public opinion.
4 See Scott, Carl Eric. "Why Did Huma Slip?" *National Review*, uploaded by National Review, 6 April 2016, www.nationalreview.com/postmodern-conservative/433754/huma-abedin-hillary-clinton-rumors.
5 Templin, Charlotte. "Hillary Clinton as Threat to Gender Norms: Cartoon Images of the First Lady." *Journal of Communication Inquiry*, vol. 23, no. 1, 1999, pp. 20–36.
6 Butler, Judith. *Gender Trouble: Feminism and the Subversion of Identity*. Routledge, 1990. See pp. 16–17.
7 See Beinart, Peter. "Fear of a Female President." *The Atlantic*, uploaded by The Atlantic Monthly Group, 8 Sept. 2016, www.theatlantic.com/magazine/archive/2016/10/fear-of-a-female-president/497564/.
8 See Groch-Begley, Hannah. "A Comprehensive Guide to Sexist Attacks on Hillary Clinton from the 2008 Campaign." *Media Matters for America*, uploaded by Media Matters for America, 5 Feb. 2016, www.mediamatters.org/research/2016/02/05/a-comprehensive-guide-to-sexist-attacks-on-hill/199700. Conservative commentator Rush Limbaugh used the term "Testicle Lockbox" on his radio program on 2/14/08, and MSNBC's Chris Matthews called Clinton's supporters "*Castratos* in the Eunuch Chorus" on the program *Hardball* on 12/17/07.
9 See Paglia, Camille. *Sexual Personae: Art and Decadence from Nefertiri to Emily Dickinson*. Yale University Press, 1990. See also Irigaray, Luce. *This Sex Which Is Not One*. Translated by Catherine Porter and Carolyn Burke, Cornell University Press, 1985. See pp. 68 and 80.
10 Nussbaum, Felicity. *The Brink of All We Hate: English Satires on Women: 1660–1750*. The University of Kentucky Press, 1984. See p. 20.
11 Wright, Celeste Turner. "The Amazons in Elizabethan Literature." *Studies in Philology*, vol. 37, no. 3, 1940, pp. 433–456. See p. 456. The interior quotation is from Chaucer's *Man of Law's Tale*, lines 286–287.
12 Villeponteaux, Mary. "'Not as Women Wonted Be: Spenser's Amazon Queen." *Dissing Elizabeth: Negative Representations of Gloriana*, edited by Julia M. Walker, Duke University Press, 1998, pp. 209–225. See pp. 214 and 217.
13 See Rogers, Katherine M. *The Troublesome Helpmate: A History of Misogyny in Literature*. University of Washington Press, 1966; *Woman Defamed and Woman Defended: An Anthology of Medieval Texts*. Edited by Alcuin Blamires et al., Oxford University Press, 1992; *Satiric Advice on Women and Marriage from Plautus to Chaucer*. Edited by Warren S. Smith. University of Michigan Press, 2005.
14 Jameson, Fredric. *The Political Unconscious: Narrative as a Socially Symbolic Act*. Cornell University Press, 1981. See pp. 39–43 and 225–227.
15 Martindale, Kathleen. "Jameson's Critique of Ethical Criticism: A Deconstructed Marxist Feminist Response." *Feminist Critical Negotiations*, edited by Alice A. Parker and Elizabeth A. Meese, John Benjamins Publishing, 1992, pp. 33–43. See pp. 41 and 38.
16 See Chapter 1 for M. M. Bakhtin's theories of satiric laughter as a social "corrective."
17 Breitenberg, Mark. "Anxious Masculinity: Sexual Jealousy in Early Modern England." *Feminist Studies*, vol. 19, no. 2, 1993, pp. 377–398. See p. 382.

18. Purkiss, Diane. "Material Girls: The Seventeenth-Century Woman Debate." *Women, texts, and Histories: 1575–1760*, edited by Clare Brant and Diane Purkiss, Routledge, 1992, pp. 69–101. See p. 80.
19. Anon. *Hic Mulier: or, the Man-Woman* and *Haec-Vir: or, the Womanish-Man*. The Scolar Press Limited, 1973.
20. Freccero, Carla. "The Other and the Same: The Image of the Hermaphrodite in Rabelais." *Rewriting the Renaissance: The Discourses of Sexual Difference in Early Modern Europe*, edited by Margaret W. Ferguson et al., The University of Chicago Press, 1986, pp. 145–158. See p. 149.
21. Davis, Natalie Zemon. "Women on Top." *Feminism and Renaissance Studies*, edited by Lorna Hutson, Oxford University Press, 1999, pp. 156–185. See p. 157.
22. Callaghan, Dympna. "Introduction." *The Impact of Feminism in English Renaissance Studies*, Palgrave Macmillan, 2007. See p. 7.
23. Ballaster, Rosalind. "Manl(e)y Forms: Sex and the Female Satirist." In *Women, Texts, and Histories: 1575–1760* (see note 18 above), pp. 215–238. Quote is from p. 218.
24. See Hammer, Paul E. J. "Shakespeare's *Richard II*, the Play of 7 February 1601, and the Essex Rising." *Shakespeare Quarterly*, vol. 59, no. 1, 2008, pp. 1–35. See also Clare, Janet. *"Art Made Tongue-Tied by Authority": Elizabethan and Jacobean Dramatic Censorship*. Manchester University Press, 1990.
25. Coldiron, Anne E. B. *English Printing, Verse Translation, and the Battle of the Sexes, 1476–1557*. Ashgate Publishing, 2009. See pp. 113–114. See also *The XV Joys of Marriage*. Translated by Brent A. Pitts, Peter Lang, 1985. Coldiron reports that only three editions of the early Sixteenth-Century English version of *The XV Joys of Marriage* are still in existence: "one complete copy of 329 pages/Pierpont Morgan Library), one incomplete copy (Folger Library/UMI microfilm, STC 15258), and one fragment (Bodleian Library, Douce C.10)," none of which has been edited (114). Because no version of the 1599 *Fifteen Joys* is extant, the current study employs examples from Coldiron's essay, an online version of Wynkyn de Worde's 1509 translation (www.otago.ac.nz/english-linguistics/tudor/fyftene_ioyes15258.html), and also extrapolates from the French text translated by Pitts. For the Tassi's *Of Marriage and Wiving*, the current study employs the online version supplied by Early English Books Online (EEBO; http://quod.lib.umich.edu/e/eebo/A13383.0001?rgn=main;view=fulltext), which I have compared to the original document held at the Huntington Library in Pasadena, CA (Rare Books, call number 14110).
26. Keener, Andrew S. "Robert Tofte's *Of Marriage and Wiving* and the Bishops' Ban of 1599." *Studies in Philology*, vol. 110, no. 3, 2013, pp. 506–532. See pp. 508 and 509.
27. See Julia Walker's anthology of essays, *Dissing Elizabeth: Negative Representations of Gloriana*, note 12 above.
28. See T. E. (Thomas Edgar?). "The Lawes Resolutions of Women's Rights (1632; likely prepared in 1603." *LSE Digital Library*, uploaded by LSE, no date, digital.library.lse.ac.uk/objects/lse:sor474mew. p. 148; 26.
29. Feichtinger, Barbara. "Change and Continuity in Pagan and Christian (Invective) Thought on Women and Marriage from Antiquity to the Middle Ages." *Satiric Advice on Women and Marriage From Plautus to Chaucer*, edited by Warren S. Smith, University of Michigan Press, 2005, pp. 182–209. Quotation is from p. 184.
30. In Lyons, Tara L. "Male Birth Fantasies and Maternal Monarchs: The Queen's Men and *The Troublesome Raigne of King John*." *Locating the*

Queen's Men, 1583–1603: Material Practices and Conditions of Playing, edited by Helen Ostovich et al., Routledge, 2016, pp. 183–200. Quote is from p. 196. See "Sir Peter Wentworth, Knight." *Tudor Place*, www.tudorplace.com.ar/Bios/PeterWentworth.htm.

31 Quoted in Axton, Marie. *The Queen's Two Bodies: Drama and the Elizabethan Succession*. Royal Historical Society, 1977. See pp. 38–39.

32 Bell, Ilona. "'Sovereaigne Lord of Lordly Lady of this Land': Elizabeth, Stubbs, and the *Gaping Gulf*." *Dissing Elizabeth*, pp. 99–117. See p. 100. Quotes from Stubbs' pamphlet are taken from the copy held at The Huntington Library, Pasadena, CA (Rare Books number 69569).

33 See, for example, Strong, Roy. *The Cult of Elizabeth*, Random House, 1999, as well as Yates, Francis A. "Elizabeth as Astraea," note 39. The cultural products referred to include pageants, ceremonies, poetry, songs, public spectacles, chivalric contests, paintings, and dramas.

34 Montrose, Louis. *The Purpose of Playing: Shakespeare and the Cultural Politics of the Elizabethan Theatre*. The University of Chicago Press, 1996. See pp. 21–23.

35 William Kibler describes the title as "an irreverent pun on the widespread *Les XV Joyes de Notre Dame* (a popular enumeration of the fifteen joys of [The Virgin] Mary's life." The various excesses of women in the French text thus carry a parodic connection to religious hagiography. See Kibler, William. "Review." Review of Joan Crow's *Les Quinze Joyes de marriage*, Basil Blackwell, 1969. *French Review*, vol. 44, no. 2, 1970, pp. 465–466. Quote is on p. 465.

36 Coldiron (note 25) points out that although the epilogue to the French original is "framed with apologetic deflections of anticipated blame from female readers...the English [versions] make no closing gesture to women readers" (138). Because of this and other conscious changes in the English translation, Coldiron concludes, the English text is far more misogynistic than the French original (139).

37 McLaren, Anne. "The Quest for a King: Gender, Marriage, and Succession in Elizabethan England." *Journal of British Studies*, vol. 41, no. 3, 2002, pp. 259–290. See pp. 267–268.

38 Content, Rob. "Faire is Fowl: Interpreting Anti-Elizabethan Composite Portraiture." *Dissing Elizabeth*, pp. 229–251. Quotations are from pp. 237 and 239.

39 Yates, Frances A. "Queen Elizabeth as Astrea." *Journal of the Warburg and Courtauld Institutes*, vol. 10, 1947, pp. 27–82.

40 Selene Scarsi notes that Tofte translated Ariosto's vitriolic *Satyres* in 1608. See "Tofte's Boiardo: *Orlando Inamorato*" in *Translating Women in Early Modern England: Gender in the Elizabethan Versions of Boiardo, Ariosto, and Tasso*. Ashgate, 2010. See p. 127.

41 I refer to the derogatory speaker as "Hercole" because, as I argue in Chapter 1, the intentional selection of a target for public attack must, at some level, imply an endorsement of that perspective.

42 Juvenal also uses the paradoxical image of the black swan at line 165 to symbolize the rarity of finding a chaste woman. For the counter-argument on Juvenal Six as misogamistic, see Highet, Gilbert. *Juvenal The Satirist*. Oxford University Press, 1954, pp. 91–103. See also Anderson, William. *Essays on Roman Satire*. Princeton University Press, 1982, pp. 255–276.

43 This grotesque image is sometimes attributed to Saint Augustine.

44 Maclean, Ian. "The Notion of Woman in Medicine, Anatomy, and Physiology." *Feminism and Renaissance Studies*, edited by Lorna Hutson, Oxford University Press, 1999, pp. 127–155.

126 Anti-Feminist Satire and the Bishops' Ban

45 I am indebted to UCSC Professor Mary-Kay Gamel for her assistance with the definition of "*Non Ens*": The Lewis and Short dictionary entry reads as follows: "*ens, entis*, neuter. [sum] a thing; formed, like *essentia*, after the Greek *ousia* ("being"). So *ens* is singular, not plural, "not being."
46 See "Elizabeth's Tillbury Speech, 1588." *British Library*, uploaded by The British Library Board, n.d., www.bl.uk/learning/timeline/item102878.html.
47 See Betts' "'The Image of this Queene so quaynt'" and Villeponteaux's "'Not as Women wonted be'" in *Dissing Elizabeth*, pp. 153–184 and 209–228, respectively. See pp. 176 and 212, specifically.
48 See Perry, Maria. *The Word of a Prince: The Life of Elizabeth I from Contemporary Documents*. Boydell Press, 1996. See also "Pope Pius' Bull against Elizabeth (1570)." Uploaded by *Tudor History.Org Blog*, tudorhistory.org/primary/papalbull.html.
49 Burgess, Glenn. "The Divine Right of Kings Reconsidered." *The English Historical Review*, vol. 107, no. 425, 1992, pp. 837–861. JSTOR, www.jstor.org/stable/574219.
50 Sheerin, Brian. "Making Use of Nothing: The Sovereignties of *King Lear*." *Studies in Philology*, vol. 110, no. 4, 2013, pp. 789–811. See p. 795. Hadfield notes how the latter half of Elizabeth's reign was remarkable for its "sea change" in republican challenges to the absolutist ideology of holy sovereignty. See Hadfield, Andrew. *Shakespeare and Republicanism*. Cambridge University Press, 2005, p. 25.

5 Shakespearean Satire
Redux

> Dost thou think I care for a satire or an epigram? No, if a man will be beaten with brains, 'a shall wear nothing handsome about him.
> —Benedick, *Much Ado about Nothing*, 5.4.102–104[1]

If it is reasonable to discuss the stylistic and ideological vacillation of Tudor satiric modes from Wyatt's imperialistic Horatian satires, to Hall's centripetal hybrid satires, to Marston's centrifugal Juvenalian satires, to anti-feminist satires, to Ben Jonson's retrogressive Horatian dramatic satires, then one must ask, is it equally reasonable (or even possible) to discuss, with any degree of precision, the form and function of Shakespearean satire in the period? Judging by nineteenth-century biographical scholarship, the answer, generally speaking, is no; Benedick's assertion that the 'un-handsome' nature of satire is aesthetically inferior to the celebratory nature of comedy was an opinion often accorded to Shakespeare himself. For example, in *Shakespeare: A Critical Study of His Mind and Art* (1875), Edward Dowden argues that the "contemptuous depreciation of life" prevalent in cynical works such as *Troilus and Cressida* (1601) was only possible after events late in Shakespeare's life had driven out his ability to "smile genially, and when he must be either ironical, or else take a deep, passionate, and tragical view of life."[2] Similarly, Kenneth Deighton and W. W. Lawrence contend that satire was simply incompatible with Shakespeare's personality; the derogatory impulse of the mode was, according to Deighton, "alien from his nature, alien from his conception of the dramatic scope, alien from his practice."[3] Any satire that can be found lurking around the edges of Shakespeare's plays, such critics suggest, is incidental rather than intentional.

Yet even as critics advanced a romantic image of Shakespeare as above the kind of negative perceptual translations typical of satire in the late 1590s, Frederick Fleay (1886) challenged this conventional view by arguing that Shakespeare not only employed satire, but used it to participate in the so-called "*Poetomachia*" or "Poets' War" (also known as "The War of the Theatres"), an exchange of targeted lampoons provoked by Ben Jonson's *Every Man Out of His Humour*, which was staged by Shakespeare's own company in the months following the June 1599 ban. According to James Bednarz, Shakespeare's dramatic contributions to the Poets' War contain carefully coded satiric replies to insults present in contemporary dramas such as Jonson's *Poetaster* (1601), John Marston's *Histriomastix* (1599) and *What You Will* (1601), and Thomas Dekker's *Satiromastix* (1601), from which the term *Poetomachia* derives: "I care not much if I make description (before thy universality) of that terrible *Poetomachia*, lately commenc'd between Horace the second [i.e. Jonson], and a band of lean-witted Poetasters."[4] For Fleay, the comment by "Kempe" in *The Second Part of the Return from Parnassus* (late 1601/early 1602) that, as retribution for Jonson's censures of his fellow playwrights, Shakespeare "hath given him [Jonson] a purge that made him beray his credit" (1772–1773), proves conclusively that Shakespeare embraced invective satire in order to "take part in this controversy, and it is in the plays dating 1599–1602 that we must look for his contributions to it," while simultaneously suggesting that Shakespeare's lampoons somehow avoided the personal and ideological bias that usually accompanies activistic satire: "one thing, however, is certain, that he did not act as a violent partisan."[5] However, the highly speculative nature of Fleay's subsequent *Roman-à-clef* interpretations of Shakespeare's Poets' War characters, and the more credible assertion of Shakespeare's ideological impartiality, make it difficult to speak with confidence about both the nature and degree of Shakespeare's participation in the War and the nature of Shakespearean satire in general. One is left to wonder, as David Bevington does, if the highly ambiguous nature of Shakespeare's supposed antipathy to his fellow satirists and their styles does not suggest that perhaps Shakespeare used satire for a "consciously different kind of social critique from that of Jonsonian humours comedy."[6]

In the early twentieth century, Oscar Campbell's influential study, *Comicall Satyre and Shakespeare's Troilus and Cressida* (1938) posited much clearer parameters for Shakespearean satire than Fleay's study by comparing the form and intent of Jonson's neoclassical mode to similar elements in Shakespeare's Trojan War drama. Campbell was among the first to argue that, in the immediate aftermath of the Bishops' ban, the prohibited mode of Juvenalian verse satire made an obligatory transition from one rather hostile cultural field to a more receptive one, that is, from the medium of print to the public stages, which "simply—but very carefully—took over as the principal medium of satiric expression."[7] Under the censorious eye of The Master of the Revels, Jonson adapted many of the conventions of the English Humour play, a genre popularized by George Chapman's *An Humorous Daye's Mirth* (1597) and refined by Jonson himself in *Every Man in His Humour* (1598), in an attempt to revivify as many of the conventions of pre-ban English verse satire as he could, thus circumventing the Bishops' prohibition (Campbell 1–10).[8] David Riggs concurs, arguing that Jonson's deliberate erudition (especially his stated commitment to imitations of the traditional centripetal satiric mode of Horace) functioned "to disarm potential accusers by showing that he [Jonson] had not exceeded the license granted to classical authors."[9]

Thus, in the wake of the ban, Jonson took great pains to reassure the public that his dramatic mode was more a return to the salutary satire of Horace's "middle way" than a reassertion of the banned mode. As such, the ideological agenda behind Jonson's satiric design is less a covert endorsement of Juvenalian iconoclasm than a combination of Juvenalian indignation and Horatian decorum governed by a socially centripetal didactic purpose. Campbell characterizes this dialogic dramatic structure and its centripetal effect as the result of Jonson's deliberate juxtaposition of dialectical satiric types, the most disruptive of which are either reformed and integrated into the restorative aspects of the play, or banished completely: "without the presence of a character to establish ethical and social standards and to mark deviations from them, the intent of the author's ridicule and correction would remain obscure" (54). Shakespeare, Campbell contends, was quick to adopt Jonson's new literary mode, readily "employing and enriching the conventions which Jonson and Marston had established in their efforts to make their satiric plays effective dramatic equivalents of the forbidden satires" (185). In Campbell's view, Shakespearean satire is a socially stabilizing form that emulates rather than innovates.

While Campbell largely restricts his analysis to *Troilus and Cressida* as the most pertinent example of Shakespeare's ascription to Jonsonian satiric principles, five years after *Comicall Satyre*, Campbell penned another study whose unambiguous title, *Shakespeare's Satire*,[10] demonstrates his expanded belief in the degree to which Shakespeare's entire corpus displays not only the Jonsonian mode of the post-ban period, but "all forms of derision which satirists, ancient, medieval, or Elizabethan, had made conventional by Shakespeare's day" (x). Despite the stated intention "not to stretch the conventional conception of satire unjustifiably" (ix), Campbell includes under the heading of Shakespearean Satire a staggering range of plays and characters that exhibit even the faintest hint of a critical nature. For example, Campbell identifies the "disillusioned temper" of the Juvenalian mode as the defining feature of plays as stylistically diverse as *Measure for Measure, Hamlet, Coriolanus,* and *Timon of Athens* (viii); he likens the social commentaries of Philip (the Bastard) Faulconbridge in *King John*, Mercutio in *Romeo and Juliet*, and Sir John Falstaff in the *Henry IV* plays to the satiric function of the medieval vice figure; and he proposes a number of potential topical allusions to the Elizabethan court present in *Love's Labour's Lost*. However, while so much of Shakespeare's work is supposedly inhabited by the cryptically named "satiric spirit" (viii), Campbell is compelled to admit that much of Shakespeare's style lacks the condemnatory "fierce indignation of Juvenal," the "whip of steel" with which Jonson chastises most of his humorous types, as well as the "scorn" and "reformatory zeal" that are the hallmarks of most satiric activism, often preferring instead a disinterested perspective, allowing his characters more self-determination than the typological nature of satire typically allows: "he seldom pronounces direct judgment on his men and women, but prefers to let them all act and speak as they must, without restraint or disapproval from their creator" (vii). The result is a much more confusing picture of "Shakespeare's Satire" than Campbell's earlier study; here, the mode is a catchall, vacillating unpredictably between purposeful and adventitious.

In 2001, Bednarz revised, and in some ways reversed, Campbell's perspectives on the qualities and intentions that constitute Shakespearean satire. In re-historicizing the plays of the period, Bednarz, like Fleay and Campbell, posits Shakespeare as an active participant in the Poets' War, and yet, as opposed to being an advocate for or an emulator of Jonsonian satire, Bednarz argues that Shakespeare employs the mode ironically in order to satirize the vanity, hypocrisy, and banality of Jonson, his satiric mode, and the Poets' War in general. Bednarz claims four of Shakespeare's plays from the period as engaged in this satiric project, *As You Like It* (1600), *Hamlet* (1600), *Twelfth Night* (1601), and *Troilus and Cressida*, and posits a number of potential lampoons of Jonson, Marston, and other dramatists within the characters of Jaques, Thersites, Malvolio, and Ajax. With regard to *Troilus and Cressida*, Bednarz contends that

> the antagonistic symbiosis of Ajax [i.e. Jonson] and Thersites [i.e. Marston] locks them in a combat of invective from which neither can emerge victorious. This, Shakespeare implies, is the outcome of the Poets' War, a skirmish of wits in which Jonson and Marston only managed to expose each other's flaws.
>
> (49)

The overall effect of this study on our understanding of Shakespearean satire is of a reactionary, parodic tool intended, primarily, for personal vindication and aggrandizement, and secondarily, for targeted literary critique.

The evolution of the concept of Shakespearean satire discussed so far, Shakespeare as invective satirist, Shakespeare as Jonsonian votary, Shakespeare as ironic anti-humourist, all tend to rely rather heavily on the degree to which one can 'prove' Shakespeare's satiric intentionality, which is usually accomplished through speculative *ad hominem* readings of Shakespeare's cynical characters. Such an interpretive process is not without contemporary precedents: in the late 1590s, the assumption that the public will subject satiric poems and dramas to the interpretive process of "application," meaning the effort to identify the topical referent intended by a satiric or humorous type, is clearly manifest in the works of Jonson and Marston, both of whom seemed to understand that a great deal of what drew audiences in was the expectation of unmasking the newest set of thinly veiled libelous figures. "Application is now grown a trade with many," writes Jonson in the dedicatory epistle to *Volpone*, "and there are that profess to have a key for the deciphering of everything," while in *The Scourge of Villanie*, Marston claims that while his true intention is to target vices rather than individuals, he knows that the majority of his readers seek only the 'real' private identities behind his latinate types, and subsequently "abuse me with unjust application" ("To Him That Hath Perused Me," 5). Shakespeare, on the other hand, feels little need to offer such *apologia* either to his audience, to his fellow playwrights, or to the censors, suggesting little to no concern that his satiric figures will be assumed to be part of an overarching program of libelous retribution.

Without a doubt, the "curious searchers" (*SV*, "To Him," 20) derided by Marston and Jonson were often guilty of misreading the intentionality behind satire's ideological reproofs as specific lampoons that could be utilized for their own benefit. Yet it is equally clear that the explicit lampoons unleashed by Jonson, Marston, and Dekker themselves fueled the public's perception that, despite claims to the contrary, this new form of dramatic satire was never intended to accomplish either a salutary or a reformatory activistic agenda. Although Jonson claimed a moralizing social imperative ("to spare the persons, and to speak the vices") modeled on the poets of the Augustan Roman era "when wit and arts were at their height," Jonson was unable to shake the perception that his retrogressive mode was nothing more than "mere raillery" bent on revenging private grudges, or as he calls them, "particular imputations."[11] Still, for audiences and critics alike, the application of Jonson's Crispinus to Marston and Dekker's Horace to Jonson is reasonable, indeed necessary, considering the ample parodies provided to the informed playgoer, particularly in *Poetaster*, where the lauded figure of Horace (Jonson himself) forces Crispinus (Marston) to vomit up some of the most recognizable examples of Marston's fustian and demotic satiric language: "Spurious, snotteries, chilblain'd, clumsie, barmy froth, turgidous, ventositous, prorumped, snarling gusts, quaking custard," and so on (5.3.488–525). Furthermore, as mentioned, in response to Jonson's lampoons, Dekker states directly in the opening epistle to *Satiromastix* that his parodic figure of "Horace the Second" should be read in no other way but as an "untrussing of the humourous poet," that is, a brazen assault on Jonson, the self-proclaimed "Horace" of *Poetaster*: "my naked lines... are free from conspiring the least disgrace to any man, but only to our new Horace" (43–45).

132 *Shakespearean Satire*

Thus it is completely understandable that scholars use application as the linchpin for their analyses of the Poets' War dramas; what is surprising, however, is the assumption that the same kind of purposeful application is present in Shakespeare's dramas from the same period. In their own ways, Fleay, Campbell, Bednarz, E. A. J. Honigmann, and Matthew Steggle all propose plausible interpretations of historical persons (possibly) lampooned through some of Jonson's, Marston's, and Dekker's characters: for example, Jonson's Macilente and Clove are lampoons of Marston; Dekker's Asinius Bubo and Jonson's Shift are the poet John Weever; Marston's Lampatho Doria, Brabant Senior, and Chrisoganus are Jonson; Jonson's Demetrius is Dekker, etc. However, similar *ad hominem* efforts to equate, for example, Shakespeare's Malvolio and Ajax with Jonson, an equation based not on direct linguistic parodies but on their mutually bombastic personalities, or Jaques and Thersites with Marston, a link proposed by their common devotion to cynical iconoclasm, remain essentially conjectural, and furthermore, do little to extend the range of Shakespeare's cultural engagement beyond a limited set of untenable particulars.[12] The evidence for the equation of Ajax with Jonson, for example, is especially tenuous, as it is based largely on a punning pronunciation of Ajax as "A-jakes" (a toilet), which constitutes Shakespeare's supposed "purge" of Jonson.[13] Although such an application in Shakespeare's work is not impossible, and certainly could have been fostered through performance, this type of limited referentiality does little to clarify the complex satiric agenda behind a "Problem Play" as multidimensional and ambiguous as *Troilus and Cressida*, nor does it help to clarify the equivocal nature of Shakespearean satire.[14]

History provides another mitigating factor to the supposed clarity of the *ad hominem* intentionality of Shakespeare's Satire. If one were to accept Shakespearean satiric figures as, at their core, lampoons of real historical persons intended as a means for self-promotion, then the resulting image of Shakespeare after the ban is that of an embattled playwright turning to the heavily monitored genre of satire in order to legitimate himself and his work by either aligning himself with or by quashing the younger generation of satiric dramatists. Such an image is not consistent with the evidence of the historical Shakespeare as an "unassailably prominent" notable in the late Elizabethan social and cultural fields, as Katherine Duncan-Jones describes him (*Ungentle*, 107 & 149). At the time, he was the dominant playwright and a successful shareholder in the Lord Chamberlain's Men, an established gentlemen with "a regular annual income of several hundred pounds" or more (when one considers his property holdings in Stratford and gifts for frequent performances at Court), a renowned poet whose high status in the cultural field is made clear by such diverse evidence as the encomiastic poetry of Richard Barnfield, the laudatory prose of Francis Meres, and the gentle ribbing of the *Parnassus* plays. It is difficult to see, as the saying goes, what dog Shakespeare had in the Poets' War fight.

Perhaps there is more merit in conceiving Shakespeare's intermittent and enigmatic engagement with satire to be neither one of replication nor repudiation, but one, as Bevington speculated, of a wholly different type. The evidence suggests that Shakespeare does not so much as engage *in* satire's activistic conventions as engage *with* them. The distinction between this and Bednarz's perspective is a subtle one: whereas Bednarz views Shakespeare as purposefully employing Jonson's own mode to deride it, with the ancillary intent to advance his 'natural' style of cultural criticism over Jonson' "revolutionary" neoclassical standards (106), the debatable nature of Shakespearean application and the correspondent disinterested perspective on his own heterogeneous (rather than typological) characters suggest that the concerns of Shakespearean satire are more comprehensive than particular. Thus, if one shifts the focus of Shakespearean satire away from application and towards ideology, one of the most salient features of satire's activistic nature, then some of the more speculative aspects of Shakespeare's employment of satire during the Poets' War period become less troubling, and the stakes become far greater. Shakespeare's satiric intent appears more publicly than privately minded, more concerned with ideological effects than with personal self-justification, which accords with Bevington's reading of the Poets' War period in general as predominantly an ideological debate over "the proper role of satire in a commonwealth shaken by religious and dynastic uncertainties," a debate likely to attract Shakespeare's attention (Bevington, *Tudor Drama*, 279). At the risk of once again romanticizing the historical image of Shakespeare, it seems reasonable to assert that Shakespeare would have been more intrigued by the implications of satire for the ideological security of the commonwealth (in which he had vested social and economic interests) than by any private desire to use either the Marstonian or the Jonsonian modes to belittle other dramatists.

The supposition that Shakespeare's Poets' War-era drama, *Troilus and Cressida*, engages with the "satiric spirit" of its cultural moment is not in question; what is in question is the form of dialogic exchange characteristic of post-ban Shakespearean satire, as well as the ideological orientation of that exchange as manifest in *Troilus* and in his other equivocal satiric dramas of the period, particularly *As You Like It* and *Timon of Athens*. The satiric agenda that drives *Troilus and Cressida* is obscure to say the least, and its mingled style does little to clarify such obscurity. In their respective editions of the play, Bevington and Anthony Dawson are cautious about labeling the play as a clear example of any one mode of discourse, including the satiric, as is Mark Sacharoff; all note the play's strong tendency towards the satiric, but also note the tragic, romantic, and comic strains that exist in dialogue with the satiric impulse. Furthermore, in their edition of *Timon of Athens*, Dawson and

Gretchen Minton, like Bevington before them, note the play's concern over the "limitations" of the kind of reductive "absolutist viewpoint" typical of Juvenalian and Jonsonian satire, limitations uncommon in Shakespeare's dramatic *oeuvre*; the result for Shakespearean satire, as suggested by Dawson, is not the employment or the rejection of a particular mode, but a dialectical "investigation of satire itself."[15]

I suggest that the activistic intent of Shakespearean satire is neither a typical Juvenalian revision of ideological "stable moral reference points" such as heroics, honor, chivalry, and/or imperial exceptionalism, nor is it, strictly speaking, an attempt to reinforce traditional English ideologies.[16] Instead, there is a recurring pattern of meta-satire within a number of Shakespeare's explicitly socially dialogic dramas from the post-ban period.[17] Plays such as *As You Like It*, *Troilus and Cressida*, and *Timon of Athens* use satire objectively to explore related topics such as the source and function of satiric activism, the pros and cons of unrestricted personal expression, the potentially apocalyptic consequences to society of the translation or reorientation of ideological reference points, and the relationship between satire and misanthropy. Shakespeare's meta-satiric dramas reflect concern over forms and effects of cultural representation, somewhat like the Bishops' ban, and yet, unlike the bishops, Shakespeare does not attempt to stifle the Juvenalian perspective; instead, he allows the audience to witness (with critical distance) aspects of the Juvenalian ideology in dialogue with a number of other competing discourses. Ultimately, in the case of *Troilus* especially, the audience is compelled to observe, without authorial judgment, the pyrrhic victory of the iconoclastic impulse over those centripetal ideologies that can, on the one hand, hamper individual liberty, but that can also, on the other hand, help to maintain a stable sociopolitical image during an uncertain historical period.

Thus, the agenda driving Shakespearean meta-satire is neither to support nor to "defuse" other modes of satire, as critics have suggested (see Bednarz 106), but to convey the consequences of discourses like the Juvenalian mode that fail to offer an ideological balance between the liberty of the individual will and the requirements of an imperiled society. Ulysses' extensive harangue over the disruptive sociopolitical influence of two iconoclasts from his own nation, namely, Thersites, a Juvenalian railer, and Patroclus, a reckless lampoonist, is indicative of the play's interest in the power of the satiric impulse to devalue ideological touchstones to the detriment of such stabilizing images as "the unity and married calm of states" (1.3.100). For Ulysses, the Greek's permissive stance on such an injudicious use of personal liberty can only result in power spun away from the center in a manner dangerous to all:

Take but degree away, untune that string...
Then every thing include itself in power,
Power into will, will into appetite,

And appetite, an universal wolf
(So doubly seconded with will and power),
Must make perforce an universal prey,
And last eat up himself.

(1.3.109–124)

Shakespearean Meta-Satire and the Ideology of the Inns of Court Revels

The hermeneutic designation "meta" in literary studies is so pervasive that to employ the prefix runs the risk of obscuring rather than clarifying the subject to which it is applied. Therefore, a brief overview of the relationship between "meta-satire" and the related theories of metatheatrics and metapoetics will serve to explicate exactly how the term is meant to illustrate Shakespeare's unique dialogue with post-ban satiric modes. Broadly speaking, the appellation "metatheatre" has been used to denote "the theatricalization of theatrics," or in other words, to signal the presence of a dramaturgical strategy intended to draw the viewers' attention to the artifice of theatre itself. The more self-evident examples of metatheatre, such as the play-within-a-play motif of Pyramus and Thisby in *A Midsummer Night's Dream*, "The Mousetrap" in *Hamlet*, and the Wedding Masque in *The Tempest*, force the audience into a self-reflexive relationship with the mimetic art in question, or in the case of the incipient postmodern dramas of Brecht and Pirandello, with art as a whole, by "thematiz[ing] the illusionism of traditional mimetic art."[18] In 1963, the designation "acquired some currency" thanks to Lionel Abel's book, *Metatheatre: A New View of Dramatic Form*, in which metatheatre is distinguished from other referential modes by the appearance of characters who are, to greater and lesser degrees, aware of their place in the dramatic structure, which consequently dissolves "the boundaries between the play as a work of self-contained art and life."[19] James Calderwood argues for Shakespeare's self-reflexive strategies as more metadramatic than metatheatric as the plays' commentaries often consciously dialogize with their social contexts: "Shakespeare's plays are not only about the various moral, social, political, and other thematic issues... but dramatic art itself—its materials, its media of language and theater, its generic forms and conventions, its relationship to truth and the social order" (5). In short, metadramatic forms, which can include meta-satire as a similarly dialogized form, often function as objective sociocultural critiques.

The term meta-satire as applied here to a few of Shakespeare's post-ban plays also contains an element of metapoetics, a concept closely aligned to the aesthetically and socially reflexive metadrama described by Calderwood. Metapoetics, as Peter Steiner defines it, consists of the analysis of poetic forms "analyzed in terms of poetics itself, or more precisely, in terms of the poetic tropes."[20] While the related term "metapoetry" is used to describe "versified criticism" of poetry, as occurs, for example, in Horace's *Ars Poetica*, metapoetics does not necessarily treat poetry in formalist isolation from its social context (Calderwood 8). From a Bakhtinian standpoint, both the poetry and the meta-form engaged with it should be approached as living utterances that have "taken meaning and shape at a particular historical moment in a socially specific environment," and as such, "cannot fail to become an active participant in social dialogue" (*DN* 276). In essence, metapoetics, like metadrama, uses poetry not simply to comment on poetic forms, but to examine the multi-voiced dialogue between the formal tropes and the conditions in which they evolved, between a mode of art and its relationship with the "truths" at the heart of the social order it represents. Thus, Shakespearean meta-satire uses satiric tropes and discourses prevalent in the contemporaneous cultural field in an objectifying rather than participatory manner, compelling the informed reader or playgoer into an extrinsic relationship with texts and social conditions outside the limits of the immediate dramatic structure, which in the case of the post-ban dramas must include the Juvenalian mode banned by Elizabeth's censors.

Deliberate extratextual references to iconoclastic poetics need not be necessarily condemnatory; such an objective relationship can function in both speculative and self-protective manners attractive to artists anxious to maintain their social and cultural capitals. Pierre Bourdieu argues that as the estimation of an author rises in the literary field, bolstered by the approval of the dominant social and economic fields, the author is able to attain the desirable status of bourgeois, and it is reasonable to view Shakespeare's nonpareil status at the turn of the seventeenth century in such economic and class terms. In order to maintain that status, valued producers of culture are often compelled to adopt self-protective forms of "practical metalanguage" which "function as marks of neutralizing distance, which is one of the characteristics of the bourgeois relation to language and to the social world."[21] "Such a mode of expression," argues Bourdieu, is "produced by and for markets requiring axiological neutrality" (85), meaning an author's economically motivated choice to adopt the kind of dispassionate perspective identified over a century ago by Fleay as Shakespeare's 'non-partisan' satiric intentionality.

The idea that Shakespeare was drawn to satire not for its direct activistic potential but as a neutral metalanguage useful for sociocultural interrogation seems characteristically pragmatic. For Shakespeare, either decision to employ or to ignore satire could potentially endanger his bourgeois status; by ignoring satire, Shakespeare risks losing an audience hungry for the mode, and by employing satire, Shakespeare risks retribution from wary noble patrons and/or hypervigilant censors. Instead, his use of meta-satire provides a means to explore, in a disinterested and safe way, the tension between centrifugal and centripetal sociolinguistic forces and their respective values to the culture. This is not to suggest that the satiric elements in *Troilus and Cressida* were intended solely for their intellectual appeal, but if the play was either conceived or reconceived at some point in its development as primarily intended for a bourgeois reading rather than a popular viewing audience, then Bourdieu's perspective becomes all the more applicable: meta-satire both appeals to an erudite readership and offers the author critical distance from the dangerously unorthodox language and centrifugal ideology of the Juvenalian poetics under scrutiny.

So does the designation "meta-satire" mean one must completely discount the targeting of historical individuals in a socially engaged drama like *Troilus and Cressida*? In the absence of more concrete performance evidence, the ambiguity of the metatheatric applications in the play render those markers secondary to the global exploration of the sociocultural impact of the iconoclastic ideology, which must then render the Juvenalian "university men" potentially alluded to in the play not as the targets of the satire, but as ideologists, symbols of the satiric ideologies under observation.[22] From a materialist viewpoint, the problematic publication and performance histories of *Troilus and Cressida* support satire in the play as a readerly metalanguage whose interests extend beyond the libelous concerns of the Poets' War.

As outlined in Bevington's edition of *Troilus and Cressida*, the two 1609 Quarto editions exist in two distinct states: the frontispiece of the first Quarto announces the play as "acted by the Kings Majesties servants at the Globe," while the revised second Quarto makes no mention of the play's performance history, focusing instead on the relationship between the eponymous lovers and the "conceited wooing" of Pandarus, Cressida's meddling uncle. In addition, the second Quarto contains "an enigmatic publicity blurb," penned (presumably) by the publisher, addressed to "a never writer, to an ever reader." In the advertisement, the author informs the "eternall reader" that they hold in their hands a "new play, never stal'd with the Stage, never clapper-claw'd with the palms of the vulgar," but so "full of the palm comical" that it cannot fail to please, especially those who are "most displeased with Plays." Bevington considers this apparent contradiction in performance history easily reconcilable reflections of Shakespeare's desire to appeal both to playgoers and the literate "cognoscenti" who will enshrine his works in the annals of history (1; 401). Jarold Ramsey offers a similar, and equally speculative hypothesis that *Troilus* was a flop with audiences in the early 1600s, but still "attracted a sophisticated following," hence the appearance of the "hucksterish second [Quarto] version" which attempted to re-market the image of the play from a failed entry in the Poets' War to an urbane work of literature worthy of a discriminating upper-class "eternal reader" well-versed enough to make meta-satire possible.[23]

One compelling piece of evidence for Shakespeare as a meta-satirist is his engagement with the ideological implications of Carnival liberty of the type often seen during the Inns of Court Revels ceremonies. As demonstrated, scholars have long suspected a connection between *Troilus* and the Inns' Christmastime festivities, with some arguing for the work as intended for performance during the Revels, and others arguing for the work as written with the Inns' educated readership of law students and would-be courtiers in mind. However, while strong historical evidence exists to prove that Shakespeare's *Comedy of Errors* and *Twelfth Night* were performed as part of the Revels' ceremony at Gray's Inn (1594) and the Middle Temple (1602) respectively, the case for an Inns performance as the prime motivation behind *Troilus and Cressida* is far from settled (Ramsey 225). For example, Campbell argues that the Juvenalian predilections of the young generation of Inns of Court student authors, some of whom were singled out in the Bishops' ban, make the Inns the most receptive venue for Shakespeare's Jonsonian dramatic satire, while Ramsey considers *Troilus* as conceived primarily for a popular audience. Gary Taylor, like Campbell, endorses the Inns occasional work theory, an endorsement which Phebe Jensen flatly rejects. In addition, in *Shakespeare's Troilus and Cressida and the Inns of Court Revels*, W. R. Elton attempts to return the play to an Inns provenance, offering an elaborate explication of the numerous satiric and legalistic components of the play that would be both attractive to and easily understood by the barristers and students.[24]

Among the host of cogent objections to the private Inns performance theory, the influence of the economic field is one of the most persuasive. In response to Elton's study, Ramsey asks, quite reasonably, why Shakespeare would take the time and effort to compose such a complex play for a one-off performance unless offered a sizeable commission, and if that was the case, then "a commission of that size... would pretty certainly have been entered into the minutes of whichever Society had to defray it" (227). Anthony Dawson also sees the economic flaws in Elton's argument:

> I find it hard to accept the implicit assumption that a hard-working dramatist... a sharer in a highly successful theatrical company that depended for its income on performances in the public theatre, would have spent the time and energy required to put together a play such as *Troilus and Cressida* primarily as a one-shot burlesque.[25]

However, even as he argues that Elton's Inns theory "strain[s] credibility," Dawson, like other proponents of the public performance argument, is forced to acknowledge the affinity between elements of *Troilus and Cressida* and the rhetorical and ideological composition of the Inns' Revels, including common interests in "carnivalesque inversion, legal vocabulary, and mordant satire of academic discourse, modes of argumentation, and philosophical reflection" (390). Therefore, if one concedes that *Troilus and Cressida* was not conceived *for* an Inns audience, yet at the same time, displays a keen interest *in* the centrifugal rhetorical and ideological implications of the Inns' saturnalian celebrations, then it is conceivable to approach the issue of Carnival as a topic of interest in Shakespeare's meta-satiric program.

Another key aspect of the Inns provenance theory is that any carnivalized treatment of the Troy legend would have been particularly appealing to the cynical, culturally savvy students at the Inns. However, as Ramsey argues, there was a general resurgence of interest in "the matter of Troy" in the literary culture of the late 1500s (234). Whether intended for a specific or a general audience, Shakespeare's decision to invoke the Troy legend suits the dialogic agenda of meta-satire well. As a setting, Troy represents an opportunity for Shakespeare to step beyond the boundaries of the Poets' War, and to accord a national or imperial dimension to the meta-satiric exploration of satire's ability to translate foundational ideological myths of English culture into nothing more than a "collection of fictions" at a time that could ill-afford to tolerate such translations.[26] As Heather James posits in *Shakespeare's Troy*, Tudor poets and dramatists often deployed the Troy legend in order to examine English national poetics and identity analogically (2–3). For James, the invocation of Troy represents an opportunity for Shakespeare to experiment with "undoing and regluing the idea of England in terms of authoritative books on England's cultural market," which could certainly include the banned satires, whose iconoclastic impulse is bent on undoing English ideology without the subsequent "regluing" process common in Carnival. In short, Shakespeare's unblinking representation of the fall of Troy could have been interpreted by informed readers and auditors as a meditation on the uncertain future of the English state, with satire and as one of the most potent potential catalysts.[27]

As described by Philip Finkelpearl, the Inns of Court Revels (when not canceled due to economic dearth or Plague outbreaks) was a series of entertainments during which, for a proscribed period, the rigid hierarchy of the Inns, with its focus on both legal education and the refinement of aspiring young gentlemen, was replaced by bawdy, parodic versions of the students' daily legal exercises, including mock-disputations, mock-arraignments and pardons, mock-encomia, a whole range of fustian rhetorical flourishes, and other so-called "Law Sports" (42). The tone of these sports, according to Finkelpearl, was by no means solely parodic, but was instead a complex combination of traditional chivalric and mock-heroic rituals, "a mixture, not a compound, of youthful idealism and cynical sophistication," yet a mixture remarkable for its ideologically inverted "disorderly conduct, mock solemnity, and a serious miming of dignified roles" (44; 38).

140 *Shakespearean Satire*

Doubtless, such ceremonies served many practical functions for aspiring young gentlemen, including rhetorical training, social advancement, and public notoriety for the organizers, participants, and artists involved. However, what is most intriguing about the Revels is the overarching ideological function, one similar to the Roman Saturnalia and medieval Feast of Fools celebrations. Marie Axton identifies this function as a sanctioned satiric critique of ruling class conventions and ideologies: "the lawyers created a miniature kingdom and chose a monarch in direct imitation of the government at Whitehall," the pivotal event of which was the election of a parodic "Lord of Misrule" (6). Each of the Inns elected their own temporary ruler, the "Prince of Purpoole"[28] for the 1594–95 Gray's Inn Revels, for example, or the "Prince D'Amour" for the 1597–1598 Middle Temple Revels, who mimicked established royal conventions: they "dubbed knights, staged councils where the prince was advised how to rule, received news of rebellion, sat in judgment, waged war" (Axton 9). The mock-ruler even 'died' or abdicated at the end of his reign as a way to signal the end of the mirror state and the return to the ideological status quo. In essence, like a kind of ideological pressure release valve, the next generation of social leaders was permitted to create translated versions of those institutions central to a national ideology, but only for so long, and only with permission (9).

Similarly, for Bakhtin, the ideological effect of such Carnival rituals is ambivalent as the ephemeral nature of the Carnival world tends to employ centrifugal images of society for a centripetal purpose. The surprising amount of license granted to unorthodox parodies at the Inns, the "temporary suspension of the entire official system with all its prohibitions and hierarchical barriers," as Bakhtin writes, "increased its fantastic nature and utopian radicalism."[29] Yet the satiric liberty inherent in the act of creating a parodic world is tinged with the knowledge of the evanescence of that world and its license to mock. In other words, the carnival nation's power to pull back the veil from social orthodoxies was only as enduring as those same orthodoxies allowed it to be (*Problems*, 122). Bakhtin contends that the idea of a parodic crowning of a parodic Prince simultaneously projects the idea of immanent decrowning and the reintegration of the parodic world as a means to reinforce the status quo: "All the symbolic aspects of this ceremonial of decrowning acquire a second and positive level of meaning—it is not naked, absolute negation and destruction (absolute negation, like absolute affirmation, is unknown to carnival)" (*Problems*, 125). To leave the inverted, centrifugal world intact, as one sees in both the banned Juvenalian mode and in *Troilus and Cressida*, is to allow chaos to supersede the forces of order, to replace ideological surety with libertine nihilism.

As opposed to the largely disinterested meta-satiric structure of *Troilus*, the structures of Ben Jonson's *Every Man Out of His Humour* and *Poetaster* mirror the centripetal project of carnivalized liberation and conservative containment common to the Revels ceremonies. Like several of Shakespeare's plays, Jonson's comical satires have strong connections to the Inns of Court: Jonson dedicates *Every Man Out of His Humour* to the Inns as "the noblest nurseries of humanity and liberty," and Henk Gras confirms that the play was likely seen by the Middle Temple, or was at least very popular with its members, while Randall Martin argues that the play's enthusiastic reception in print (as opposed to its nearly disastrous initial performance at the Globe) taught Jonson that "the educated, exclusively male, and self-consciously intellectual Inns of Court would be more sympathetic to his socially conservative values and high minded artistic ambitions."[30]

In *Every Man Out*, the satiric force of Asper-Macilente, whose names denote the kind of vitriolic, derogating Juvenalian satire practiced by Marston, grants himself the license to reimagine the world he inhabits and welcomes others to do the same, the very activistic process the Bishops' ban had attempted to quell months earlier. In the opening Induction, Mitis and Cordatus, ideologists for the conservative view, beg Asper to restrain the raging *libertas* propelling his unorthodox speech and destabilizing perceptions of society. In response, Asper makes a parodic Marstonian claim for the necessity of individual judgments in the face of overwhelming vice ("Who is so patient of this impious world, / That he can check his spirit, or rein his tongue," 2–3). In reply, Mitis and Cordatus make the stabilizing counterclaim that Asper's liberty lacks the regenerative, and paradoxical, Carnival power to promote chaos in order to bring about order, or in their words, "to melt the world and mold it new again" (46–47). The subsequent dialogic structure of the play itself, according to Jackie Watson, has a surveilling meta-quality about it, as the scenes of satiric abuse are overseen and restrained by the ideologically restorative commentaries of Mitis and Cordatus, the play's Grex or Chorus: "Asper observes everyone metatheatrically, in his adopted role as Macilente; the Grex observe him, and the audience, guided by the Grex, observe them." Yet the effect is equally metatheatric and metapoetic, as the play's overt literary emphasis causes the self-reflexive viewing experience to seem more "akin to reading" than to playgoing, and the texts held most prominently under the readers' wary eyes are "the texts banned by Whitgift and Bancroft," which the play invokes and then disavows.[31]

Unlike Shakespeare's meta-satiric ambivalence, at the end of *Every Man Out*, Jonson reorients his metapoetic dialogism by adopting the kind of didactic centripetal bias preferred by both the Inns' Benchers and the Queen's censors. With his spleen vented and his Fool's reign expired, Macilente makes it clear (in the version revised for publication) that in purging the world of vice, he has purged the vices within himself, and can now return to the world he once sought to devolve: "Now is my soul at peace; / I am as empty of all envy now, / As they of merit to be envied at... I am so far from malicing their states, / That I begin to pity them" (5.6.82–90). In the play's ill-considered original ending, the appearance of Queen Elizabeth, personated by an actor, projects such a transformative image of uncontestable sovereign authority that Macilente's destabilizing impulse is overwhelmed and replaced by an unquestioning (and rather servile) nationalism: "O heaven, that she, whose figure hath effected / This change in me may never suffer change / In her admired and happy government" (5.6.99–101). Such a clumsy epiphany demonstrates a prudent and self-interested "commitment to a moral and corrective theory of satire" conversant with the ongoing intolerance for Juvenalian activism among the culture's arbiters, as the foreboding comments of Mitis and Cordatus make clear: "The days are dangerous, full of exception, / And men are grown impatient of reproof" (Induction, 122–123).[32]

Similarly, in *Poetaster*, the Juvenalian and carnivalesque force of Crispinus is allowed temporary license to degrade all forms of orthodoxy before the status quo is renewed by Horace (Jonson himself) via the purgation of Crispinus' destabilizing language. Furthermore, Horace and Virgil, two of the most celebrated models of centripetal poetics in the English Renaissance, demand Crispinus abandon his imitations of indecorous comic satirists and resist transcending the limits of his scourging art: "neither shall you at any time (ambitiously, affecting the title of the untrussers or whippers of the age) suffer the itch of writing to overrun your performance in libel" (5.3.604–7). Like Crispinus, Inns Revelers who ignored the limits of licensed satire received similar admonitions, and rightly so, Jonson's meta-satire implies: for example, in 1591 and 1592, Inns members Richard Martin and John Davies were censured both for "levying money" and, more significantly, for penning excessively libelous verses (Finkelpearl 47–48). Jonson's centripetal meta-satiric intentionality is clear: carnivalesque mockery of social orthodoxies is allowable only in the service of supporting, rather than undermining, those orthodoxies, and neither Jonson's comical satires nor the Revels break this obligatory pattern.

The meta-satiric elements in Shakespeare's *As You Like It* reflect this centripetal pattern of iconoclastic license and containment, albeit somewhat generally; however, unlike Jonson's centripetal agenda, this early foray into meditations on the motivations and effects of the iconoclastic satiric impulse also displays distinct discomfort with the restrictive pattern of unleashing and then censoring unorthodox expressions. The melancholy Jaques, a character who evokes (if not embodies) Marston's mode of nihilistic Juvenalianism, is granted carnivalized measures of free speech to "blow on whom I please" (2.7.49), to create his own cynical, inverted versions of the sylvan world occupied by Duke Senior's court in exile. However, Shakespeare is quick to

Shakespearean Satire 143

dialogize Jaques' satiric freedom, which his compatriots relish in small doses, with Duke Senior's concerns over the hypocrisy and potentially disruptive social impact inherent in the employment of the unrestricted satiric mode:

> Most mischievous foul sin, in chiding sin:
> For thou thyself hast been a libertine,
> As sensual as the brutish sting itself,
> And all the embossed sores, and headed evils,
> That thou with license of free foot has caught,
> Wouldst thou disgorge into the general world.
>
> (2.7.64–69)

The tension between Jaques' belief in the benefits of carnivalized satiric perspectives to "cleanse the foul body of th' infected world, / If they will patiently receive my medicine" (60–61) and the Duke's concern for the stability of the "general world" embody in microcosm the same cultural tension displayed in both the Revels and in Jonsonian satires, a tension which Deborah Shuger describes as the debate over the capricious boundaries of permissible expression versus impermissible violations of legal and cultural norms, resulting in censorious acts such as the Bishops' ban and the termination of the Revels ceremonies.[33]

At the end of *As You Like*, Shakespeare appears to pick a side in this debate, but seems quite ill at ease with the choice. Despite Shakespeare's usual preference for the dominance of the individual will, Jaques, the Juvenalian cynic, cannot be allowed an indefinite period of unorthodox expression. The convivial "dancing measures" of society both on and off the stage are given precedence, and as such, the centrifugal force is permitted, rather than forced, to retreat to the isolation of the cynic's cave and the aestheticism of the stoic's life. Although Jaques recognizes and accepts his incompatibility with the play's restored sense of order, his self-banishment by no means ensures that the comedic orthodoxies of marriage will bring the kind of social stability the Duke desires. The overall effect seems to be a conventional, socially salutary restoration of order, as Jonsonian comedies and the end of the Revels' ceremonies tended to be, but it is a restoration that Shakespeare seems to find neither wholly sure nor wholly satisfactory:

DUKE SENIOR: Stay Jaques, stay.
JAQUES: To see no pastime I. What you would have I'll stay to know
    at your abandon'd cave. *Exit*
DUKE SENIOR: Proceed, Proceed. We'll begin these rites,
    As we do trust they'll end, in true delights. [*A dance.*] *Exeunt.*

(5.4.194–198)

Meta-Satire in *Troilus and Cressida*: "To Fear the Worst Oft Cures the Worse"

Soon after the uneasy silencing of the iconoclastic perspective in *As You Like It*, Shakespeare turned to the analogous legend of Troy as a means to expand his meta-satiric interest in considering the practical dilemmas of either tolerating or censoring those who posit unorthodox revisions of social ideologies, presumably with an eye towards an audience capable of seeing into the broader project of metapoetic critique. As suggested, the difference between the meta-satiric perspectives of *As You Like It* and *Troilus and Cressida* lies in Shakespeare's revision of the formula of carnival and containment: in *Troilus*, the destabilizing, inverted images espoused by Thersites, Pandarus, and Patroclus are never returned to a stabilizing form, never silenced either by official censorship or by dramatic fiat, but are permitted to remain irredeemably committed to the "redefinition of modern morality" and the rejection of "every current school of ethical thought."[34] As in Jonson's comical satires, Shakespeare places stabilizing counter-discourses in a purposeful dialogic relationship with the iconoclastic impulse, as when Ulysses condemns Patroclus' carnivalesque lampoons for translating military "achievements" into preposterous "paradoxes," or when Nestor laments how the derogatory Thersites takes pleasure in his power "to match us in comparisons with dirt, / To weaken [or] discredit our exposure, / How rank soever rounded in with danger" (1.3.181; 184; 194–196). However, as opposed to taming the centrifugal influence, Shakespeare permits that influence to eclipse centripetal discourses, a meta-satiric strategy used to contemplate the potential consequences to Old and New Troy of unmitigated iconoclasm and unrepentant carnival.

As opposed to the agendas of both Marston and Jonson, Shakespeare endorses neither the centrifugal nor the centripetal ideologies; the meta-satiric structure of the play is like a laboratory experiment in which the variables are permitted to run their course. Ultimately, both systems are found lacking, as the fleeting moments of redemptive possibilities prove incapable of fending off the challenges to their authority, while the Juvenalian impulse fails to offer any ideologically salutary alternatives, or indeed any principles of moral order to mitigate its willfully bleak perceptual translations. All the potential benefits of the *translatio imperii* descending from the rack of Troy are reduced *ad absurdum* to images of moral and social failure, as Thersites' all-encompassing perspective makes clear, "Nothing but lechery! All incontinent varlets!"; "Lechery, lechery, still wars and lechery, nothing else holds fashion" (5.1.97–98; 5.2.194–195).

The meta-satire begins begins with an extratextual gesture through the appearance of the "prologue arm'd" (23), a potentially parodic reference to Jonson's "armed *Prologue*" in *Poetaster* seen months earlier

Shakespearean Satire   145

at the Blackfriars Theatre; in the minds of the informed viewer, this play, it would seem, would deliver an extensive parodic reply to Jonson's insults. However, Shakespeare's Armed Prologue quickly alludes to Jonson's self-important defensive posture, and then expands his own range of meaning and the play's: "A Prologue armed, but not in confidence / Of author's pen or actor's voice, but suited / In like conditions as our argument" (23–25). The argument is, of course, warfare, but not simply the Trojan War or the War of the Theaters: the abandoned parody of Jonson's Prologue effectively alters the expectations of the audience from libelous application to a philosophical meditation on the conflict between systems of social representation and the potential victory of those destabilizing forces that threaten to undermine secure images of national exceptionalism. The Prologue's final shrugging submission to the capricious will of the audience ("do as your pleasures are, / Now good or bad, 'tis but the chance of war," 30–1) not only reorients the grandiloquent language of Epic that opens the speech, but revises the entire tone of the play from the moral absolutism associated with Epic to the moral relativism associated with the libertine Juvenalian ethos, "the errant and self-destructive tendencies of the human will" that can put "all on hazard" (22; see Kaula 271).

The next significant meta-satiric engagement with the iconoclastic impulse comes within the Greek council debate in Act One, scene three. Here, classical figures are redeployed as ideologists in order to speculate on the potentially disastrous consequences of negative valuations of social orthodoxies. Ulysses' traditionalist speech warning of the Greek's tolerance of challenges to "the specialty of rule" (78), challenges spat from the "mastic jaws" of Thersites and the slanderous, lampooning "imitation[s]" of Patroclus (73 & 150), foregrounds the danger to the whole of the individual's ability to undermine ideological certainties, an ability prohibited (albeit ineffectually) by the Bishops' ban years before. "O, when degree is shaked," Ulysses opines, "which is the ladder of all high designs," then the entire Greek-English social "enterprise is sick" (101–103):

> How could communities,
> Degrees in schools, and brotherhoods in cities,
> Peaceful commerce from dividable shores,
> The primogeneity and due of birth,
> Prerogative of age, crowns, scepters, laurels,
> But by degree stand in authentic place?
>
> (103–108)

Even the iconic Achilles, Ulysses informs his colleagues, so overvalues himself that he feels empowered to devalue his nation's endeavors through politically insensitive ridicule ("Having his ear full of his airy fame, / Grows dainty of his worth, and in his tent / Lies mocking our designs," 144–146) and to revel in Patroclus' satirically imitative "pageants" of his superiors (151). Such license to weaken sanctioned images, argues Ulysses, is the very source of the illness weakening the body of the state in a time of war. When, as Nestor states, the self-crowned "imperial voice" (187), can act without regard to "degree, priority, and place," the effect is political and social impotence (86), while for Ulysses, the consequences are far worse: "frights, changes, horrors / Divert and crack, rend and deracinate / The unity and married calm of states / Quite from their fixture!" (99–101).

Following Ulysses' conjectural warnings, Shakespeare provides a tangible example of the iconoclastic impulse in action through the initial appearance of its ideologist, Thersites. Described variously in the play as a deformed "toadstool," a "porpentine" (i.e. a porcupine, an image that harkens back to Hall's depiction of the typical satirist in *Virgidemiarum*),[35] a "slave whose gall coins slanders like a mint" (1.3.193), and (intriguingly) "a privileg'd man" (2.3.57), Thersites embodies all that Ulysses fears. In Act Two, scene one, Thersites' translations of his superiors lays waste to the ideological value associated with classical figures key to the *translatio imperii*: Agamemnon is translated to an image of purulent sores lacking all substance ("matter," 2–9); Ajax is subjected to vulgar epithets even more extreme than those found in Marston's mode, as Thersites variously translates him into a "mongrel beef-witted lord," a "stool [toilet] for a witch," an "asinico" [little ass], and a servile "barbarian slave," among other images (13; 42; 44; 47); and Patroclus, too, has his epic valuation diminished as Theristes re-characterizes him as an effeminizing influence on the omnipotent Achilles: "I will hold my piece when Achilles' brach [bitch; "masculine whore," c.f. 5.1.17] / bids me, shall I?" (114–115) No matter how many beatings Thersites receives from Ajax in return for his abuses, Thersites continues to exert his derogatory 'privilege'; by the end of the scene, Thersites' infectious judgments are born out rather than contradicted, as Hector's challenge goes undelivered, and matters of personal and national honor are left unresolved.

Through meta-satire, the detached reader comes to understand both the importance and the evanescence of the ideological principle under scrutiny, with the satiric perspective offering no beneficial alternative. Nearly every gesture the play makes towards stabilizing discourses (notions of heroism, order, romantic love, etc.) is dialogized with the iconoclastic perspective, much like Marston's preference for polemic dialogues in *The Scourge of Villanie*, where the optimistic social image succumbs to the overwhelming negativity of the nihilistic perception.[36] This radical juxtaposition of perceptions is the very heart of the meta-satiric structure. For example, in Act Three, scene three, Ulysses' plan to convert the kind of solipsistic "stiff-neck't pride" that John Weever identifies in the Marstonian satirists into a socially salutary force rests on a discursive appeal to that very pride, and thus he argues to Achilles that true worth is only meaningful if it shows its influence through the behavior of others:[37]

> A strange fellow here
> Writes me that man, how dearly ever parted,
> How much in having, or without or in,
> Cannot make boast to have that which he hath,
> Nor feels not what he owes, but by reflection;
> As when his virtues, aiming upon others,
> Heat them, and they retort that heat again
> To the first giver.
>
> (95–102)

Yet even as Achilles (and the play) moves tentatively towards this stabilizing ideology, Thersites intrudes into the scene once more, his satiric counter-perspective effectively undermining the truth of the concept in question. Ulysses' canny depiction of reflected virtue is parodically debased by Thersites' report of Ajax's ridiculously prideful behavior on the battlefield: "Why, 'a stalks up and down like a peacock— / a stride and a stand; ruminates like a hostess… The man's undone for ever, for if Hector break not his / neck i' th' combat, he'll break it himself in vainglory" (251–259). As Achilles struggles with the idea of fulfilling his social duty versus indulging his desires ("My mind is troubled, like a fountain stirr'd," 308), the final perspective on the struggle belongs, as it frequently does in the play, to the satiric perspective, which is allowed to overwrite all potential value from the previous exchanges: "Would the fountain of your mind were clear / again, that I might water an ass at it! I had rather be a / tick in a sheep than such a valiant ignorance" (310–312).

Perhaps the most striking example of meta-satiric meditation is Cressida's struggle to resist the advances of Diomedes, her Greek captor, in Act Five, scene two. Similar to the surveilling metatheatric style of Jonson's *Every Man Out*, the scene is structured as a complex, multilayered form of choral commentating: Troilus and Ulysses watch and discuss the exchange between Cressida and her captor, both groups are in turn watched and discussed by Thersites, and all three subjects are watched in turn by the audience. However, whereas the conservative and cautionary judgments of Mitis and Cordatus are endorsed by the play's reformative and stabilizing end, Shakespeare resists the urge to indulge in ideological bias or moral didacticism. Instead, the dramatic irony helps the audience understand that the fault lies less with Cressida and more with her critics, who allow their willful misperceptions to overwhelm any possibility of intrinsic value, either in Cressida, or in the society collapsing around them.

> DIOMEDES: How now, my charge?
> CRESSIDA: Now, my sweet guardian, hark, a word with you.
> TROILUS: Yea, so familiar?
> ULYSSES: She will sing any man at first sight.
> THERSITES: And any man may sing her, if he can
> take her cliff; she's noted.
>
> (6–11)

The audience is presented with a choice of discourses to represent the conflict at hand, and all are found wanting. As the audience knows, Cressida is not, in fact, the tragically ennobling figure of Troilus' self-indulgent, wounded masculine pride ("Cressid is mine, tied with the bonds of heaven; / Instance, O instance, strong as heaven itself, / The bonds of heaven are slipp'd, dissolv'd, and loos'd," 154–156), nor is she "false Cressid! False, false, false!" (178), the quintessence of female infidelity codified in early modern culture, as Thersites' misogynistic images would have her, only worse: "A proof of strength she could not publish more, / Unless she said, 'My mind is now turn'd whore'" (113–114). In short, the meta-satire leaves the tension unresolved, but as usual, the final image comes from the iconoclastic perspective, whose self-interested derogations fail to deliver either solace or certitude: "Patroclus will give me any thing for the intelligence of / this whore. The parrot will do more for an almond / than he for a commodious drab" (192–194).

There can be no expectation of a happy outcome of the final battle for Troy in Act Five; both the literary history and the foundational ideological myth demand that Troy must suffer and fall if Rome and London are to rise. Yet in service of the meta-satiric agenda, Shakespeare alters his sources in ways that serve to emphasize the decidedly hopeless trajectories of Old and New Troy as dictated by the iconoclastic impulse.[38] The "notorious identity," to borrow Linda Charnes' term,[39] of 'False Cressida' is seemingly confirmed, and she and her supposed crime remain alive and unredeemed; an unarmed Troilus does not fall tragically to Achilles and his Myrmidons as Troy falls around him, as described by Caxton and Lydgate, but instead attempts to gratify his pointless "hope of revenge" (5.10.31); and Hector, however, is given Troilus' end before being dragged through the fields of Troy, but not before his belief in intrinsic value is exposed as a "most putrefied core, so fair without" as he allows his personal desire for the Greek warrior's "goodly armor" to supersede his nation's interests (5.8.1–2). Thersites, as one might expect, remains intact, despite his flight from Margarelon, a fellow "bastard" (5.7.16), and finally, the play's concluding speech is delivered by Cressida's salacious uncle, Pandarus, who invokes that most orderly of Renaissance metaphors, the bumblebee, to lament the failure of both orthodox and unorthodox ideological perspectives to fulfill the *translatio imperii*:[40]

> Full merrily the humble-bee doth sing,
> Till he hath lost his honey and his sting;
> And being once subdu'd in armed tail,
> Sweet honey and sweet notes together fail.
>
> (5.10.41–44)

Yet, perhaps Shakespeare has some hope for Troynovant: as Cressida states, to witness social values at their most degraded could lend some perspective to other, less cataclysmic threats to the maintenance of ideological order: "Blind fear that seeing reason leads finds / safer footing than blind reason stumbling without fear. / To fear the worst oft cures the worse" (3.2.71–73).

Timon of Athens: "A Cynic and a Hater of Humanity"[41]

An intriguing moment occurs late in another of Shakespeare's supposed "Problem Plays," *Timon of Athens* (1606–1607), a satiric drama composed years after the turmoil of The Poets' War had died away. In this scene, Timon emerges from his cave in the wilderness to find two unnamed sociocultural types, the "Poet" and the "Painter," who are planning to solicit Timon for gold in the hope that he will return to his former prodigality. The Poet informs the Painter of the type of genre he thinks will most appeal to his misanthropic would-be benefactor:

> I am thinking
> What I shall say I have provided for him.
> It must be a personating of himself;
> A satire against the softness of prosperity,
> With a discovery of the infinite flatteries
> That follow youth and opulency.
>
> (ll.32–37)

The moment is clearly metatheatrical, and yet this particular disruption in the mimetic world of the play also suggests the possibility of metasatire, as the Poet signals that Timon will be 'personated' within a satire written by an outside cultural arbiter. In other words, the Poet plans to turn satirist and write a satire on the topics that the audience or reader has already witnessed throughout this satiric play. The Poet also clearly defines his intended targets as the timidity, even effeminacy, that often comes from a life of opulence, as well as the machinations of disingenuous parasites who prey on the wealthy,[42] and while neither the Poet nor Timon recognize themselves as complicit in the vices the Poet plans to represent, the audience is (once again) fully aware of the irony. Timon's oblivious asides to the audience concerning the would-be satirist's lack of self-awareness ("Must thou needs / Stand for a villain in thine own work?" 37–38) reinforce the possibility of a meta-satiric quality operating both here and throughout the entire work, a quality that, in this case, is devoted to the impartial, even philosophic exploration of the nature of satire and the satirists' relationship to their social context, as dramatized most vividly in the debates between the misanthropic Timon (the villain of his own work) and the Juvenalian Apemantus.

The less pervasive and apocalyptic engagement with satire in *Timon*, as opposed to *Troilus*, is consistent with the development of certain stabilizing elements in the contemporaneous sociocultural fields, including the termination of the satiric wrangling of the Poets' War, the successful resolution of the royal succession issue (if not the social anxieties that accompanied the accession of a 'foreign' monarch), the skirting of a national disaster with the failure of the Gunpowder Plot, and most importantly, Shakespeare's highly increased cultural capital resulting from the royal patronage of King James in 1603. In essence, measures of stability and distance from the turbulent events at the end of Elizabeth's reign, when producers of satire were monitored closely for their ability to affect sanctioned images, grant Shakespeare the luxury to take a more reflective, theoretical approach to the subject of satire. The tone of the meta-satire in *Timon* is less wary than in *As You Like It*, less bleak and frenetic than in *Troilus and Cressida*, and the overall structure less interested in examining the potential impact of the iconoclastic ethos because satire as a sociocultural issue had become far less controversial.

While it is true that, like *Troilus*, *Timon* engages with Juvenalianism through the deliberately Marstonian characterization of Apemantus, Shakespeare, working in collaboration with the more 'satirically skilled' Thomas Middleton,[43] places the Juvenalian ideology in dialogue with the ideology of misanthropy as conceived in the play's sources. The effect of such a dialogue is both "a self-reflexive attempt to highlight the ethics of satire," as Dawson and Minton argue, and an attempt to distinguish what Shakespeare sees as the true source and function of the satiric impulse from the misanthropic impulse (36). As the hater of humanity debates the practiced cynic, Shakespeare reveals key differences between Timon's raillery and the more purposeful, or activistic, aspects of Apemantus's Juvenalianism, a mode that ostensibly despises humanity, but also uses its negative translations to motivate social awareness, perhaps even social change.

In the twenty-eighth novel in *The Palace of Pleasure* (1566), one of Shakespeare's primary sources for the character of Apemantus, William Painter describes Apemantus as an "enemy of mankind... of the very same nature" as the misanthropic Timon.[44] Alternatively, while both Oscar Campbell and Alvin Kernan acknowledge Shakespeare's deliberate depiction of Apemantus as a "bitter cynic" familiar to contemporary readers of satire, both scholars advance Timon as the "true" satirist of the play: "Apemantus," Kernan writes, is presented as "only a freak of nature, the malcontent who rails and curses for the same reason that a dog barks or a snake bites," while Timon's rage is described as more satiric as it "has a moral force behind it" born from an agonizing recognition of his "loss in transformation" (201; 203). However, to accept both characters as either identical misanthropists or identical satirists, one must ignore both the influence of Shakespeare's multiple sources, as well as the pains Shakespeare takes to highlight the differences between Apemantus's satiric cynicism and Timon's erratic misanthropy. The overall meta-satiric effect is, for the most part, an endorsement of the reformative aspects of satire's critical perspectives on society over the misanthropist's self-indulgent and haphazard flagellations.

As stated, readers at the time would no doubt recognize the Marstonian quality of Apemantus' character, as Shakespeare provides a number of metapoetic signals: like Thersites and Marston before him, Apemantus is derided as an "ever angry" "unpeaceable dog" (1.2.29; 1.1.270), a willful, proud philosopher (1.1.188 & 215) who sullenly "rail[s] on society" as part of his self-appointed role as an "opposite to humanity" (1.2.244; 1.1.273). Moreover, these traits are consistently present in the figure of Apemantus, whereas Timon participates in the conventions of cynicism and invective in the second half of the play only. For his construction of the Timon figure, in addition to the *Palace of Pleasure*, Shakespeare drew inspiration from a variety of genres across a range of time periods, including the anonymous comedic play *Timon* (possibly performed in the early years of the seventeenth century for the *cognoscenti* at the Inns of Court), a brief section of the "Life of Marcus Antonius" in Sir Thomas North's translation of Plutarch's *Lives* (1579), in which the story of Timon and Apemantus is described as derived from "Plato and Aristophanes' comedies,"[45] and Shakespeare's own grammar school experiences with Lucian's satiric dialogues by way of Erasmus' Latin translations (Dawson and Minton 18). While these various sources freely mix examples of satire with comedy and tragedy, the two most compelling sources for Shakespeare's play, the Lucianic original and the lost *Timon* comedy, suggest a Timon who is less the deliverer of a satiric vision and more the comically ridiculous target, as the menippean tradition of Lucian would have him, and as The Poet reveals him to be: "It must be a personating of himself; / A satire against the softness of prosperity."

To return once again (briefly) to Bakhtin's formulations of *menippea*, the Timon of Lucian's dialogue is an ideologist, an embodiment of a philosophical position that serves as part of a dialectical project for "seeking and *testing* truth" (*Problems* 111). Structurally, this search for truth involves subjecting the exemplar to radical changes of fortune that

152 *Shakespearean Satire*

land the figure in comically crude circumstances that force him (and the reader) to question the system of belief he embodies, all of which apply fairly well to Shakespeare's Timon, but less so to Apemantus (*Problems* 114–119). As Jody Greene has argued (see note 42), the Timon typology is a useful and safe means for Shakespeare to explore the unscrupulous nature of England's patronage system, among other subjects, but in any case, the point remains that the mercurial Timon figure was conceived as the laughable subject of the satiric lesson, not the preceptor, which is much closer to Apemantus's function in the play. The Timon figure is not a satirist; he is a satiric *exemplum* of effete hypocrisy whose rage against his self-inflicted wounds is wholly different from the Juvenalian *indignatio* that provokes a true satirist to attack discriminately for the benefit of the auditor. As the embodiment of the worst excesses of vanity, hypocrisy, and those social economies that foster them, Timon is ripe for Apemantus' degrading translations; however, whereas Timon spews his rage at all, Apemantus chooses "to vex" Timon specifically, not out of hatred, but out of a desire to reform him, and perhaps society, too, by showing him his own ugly image, as a satirist should (4.3.236).

The dialogic structure between the cynic and the hater of humanity allows Shakespeare's work to expand "the boundaries of Lucianic satire from which it was partially composed" to include a meta-satiric reflection on a question that has interested him from the time of *As You Like It*, if not before: is there any utility in the misanthropic impulse? As the two ideologists develop their individual perspectives on the question, the differences between satiric indignation and misplaced rage against humanity are made evident to the readership, if not to the characters themselves: Timon, a self-described "Misanthropos" (4.3.54), is not *ipso facto* a satirist as he has no purpose. A satirist proper, Shakespeare suggests, is compelled to "rail on society" not to avenge personal slights, but for a broader salutary purpose. Although not discussed in these terms, misanthropy in the play appears indiscriminate and solipsistic, as conservative critics imagined the Juvenalian satirists to be, while satire is activistic, as Apemantus's arguments make clear.[46] Although often cynical, satire must engage with rather than withdraw from the material world in order to fulfill its purpose-driven agenda, even at the risk of being corrupted by that same world: "If I should be brib'd too," states Apemantus, "there would be none left to rail upon thee, and then thou wouldst sin the faster" (2.1.238–240).

In Act One, Timon's mischaracterization of Apemantus' indiscriminate fury, "*ira furor brevis est*" ("anger is a brief madness," 1.2.28), will prove an ironically true depiction of Timon himself once he has fled from the city to the wilderness. Apemantus, motivated by his reformatory satiric purpose, joins Timon's greedy coterie not to obtain gifts from Timon, but to bring him self-awareness: "Let me stay at thine apperil [risk], Timon," Apemantus tells Timon, "I come to observe, I give thee warning on't" (1.2.33–34). The 'warnings' characteristic of satire are best when intended as "counsel" rather than as a weapon, as Shakespeare suggests through Apemantus (1.2.250); however, as Timon's resistance suggests, because of its unpleasant, choleric nature, satiric counsel is often ineffectual because it enrages rather than persuades the vice-ridden target.

Still, much like the structure of the Fool's critical commentary in *King Lear*, the self-reflexive meta-structure grants a dramatic irony to Apemantus' satiric comments so as to make them instructive to the auditors, if not to the exemplar. For example, well before Timon meets him in the woods, The Poet and his celebrated vocation are diminished by Apemantus so as to enlighten both The Poet and Timon, but again, the critique is received as counsel only by the audience, as both the Poet and Timon remain blind to their faults:

APEMANTUS: Art not a poet?
POET: Yes.
APEMANTUS: Then thou liest: look in thy last work, where thou hast feigned him a worthy fellow.
POET: That's not feign'd, he is so.
APEMANTUS: Yes, he is worthy of thee, and to pay thee for thy labor. He that loves to be flatter'd is worthy of the flatterer.

(1.1.220–227)

Furthermore, satire's tendency to represent unorthodox versions of ideological truths are presented in the play as valid only when used to provoke moral introspection, as when Apemantus creates an inverted perspective of the great banquet that opens Act One, scene two. For early modern society, this type of ceremony is obligatory for establishing decorous social and economic relationships, but from the iconoclastic perspective, the ceremony is simply a pretense for sycophancy and metaphorical cannibalism:

O you gods! what a number / of men eats Timon and he sees 'em not! It grieves / me to see so many dip their meat in one man's blood, / and all the madness is, he cheers them up too… those healths will make thee and thy state look ill, Timon.

(39–57)

Similarly, during the masque of Cupid and the Amazons, Apemantus proffers a kind of alternative choral commentary by translating a ceremony normally understood as an intensely political "patriarchal product—richly tapestried expressions of King James's agendas"[47] into a duplicitous disguise for humanity's egotism. However, unlike the Marstonian satirist who recognizes the futility of trying to influence the

154 *Shakespearean Satire*

vicious, Apemantus uses his revised image pointedly to provoke moral caution in the reader:

> What a sweep of vanity comes this way!
> They dance? They are madwomen.
> Like madness is the glory of this life,
> As this pomp shows to a little oil and root.
> We make ourselves fools to disport ourselves...
> I should fear those that dance before me now
> Would one day stamp upon me.
>
> (1.2.132–144)

As mentioned, the consistency of worldview is another distinction between the satirist and the misanthropist suggested by the play's meta-satiric references. The protracted dialogue between Timon and Apemantus in the woods outside Athens' walls (Act Four, scene three) suggests that the satiric impulse is both inherent and immutable, impelled by circumstances, perhaps, but not created by circumstances nor subject to shifts in fortune. The philosophical debate opens with Apemantus' accusation that Timon's misanthropy is nothing more than an unnatural mien, a self-indulgent "likeness" of a true arbiter of social customs that Timon 'uses' but that is not intrinsic: "men report / Thou dost affect my manners and dost use them" (218; 198–199). Apemantus (and Shakespeare) makes a valid point: Timon has not, to this point, ascribed to Cynic or Stoic primitivism and the rejection of all social orthodoxies as the Juvenalian satirist does; in fact, he formerly embraced those same social customs because they were to his benefit. Now, however, Timon's embrace of Cynic asceticism is done "enforcedly" (241), his raging antisocial "*ira*" born not of an honest desire to influence social conditions, but "a nature but affected, / A poor unmanly melancholy sprung / From change of fortune" (202–4). Had Timon "put this sour cold habit on / To castigate thy pride," Apemantus informs him, "'twere well," inferring that Timon's incognizant railing lacks the kind of moral purpose that could improve both himself and society (239–240). To the Juvenalian, Timon is not a fellow iconoclast but a fool deservedly brought low by his own pride ("'Tis most just / That thou turn rascal; hadst thou wealth again, / Rascals should have't. Do not assume my likeness" 216–218), an hypocritical gull who has substituted the mask of the benevolent philanthropist for "the cunning of a carper" (209), a mask he would quickly doff if the opportunity arose to return to his old eminence: "Thou'dst courtier be again," Apemantus tells Timon, "wert thou not beggar" (241–242).

Timon's responses ironically underline the need for consistency and purpose in the satiric worldview. Timon argues that Apemantus is only a railer who despises mankind because his low birth has prevented him from ever knowing the pleasures of life ("Thou art a slave, whom

Fortune's tender arm / With favour never clasp'd, but bred a dog,"; 250–251), as opposed to Timon himself, who once "had the world as my confectionary," and thus deserves to rail against man's ingratitude (260). However, Apemantus' ambiguous rejoinder to Timon's assault, "Art thou proud yet [i.e. still]?" (276), suggests Shakespeare's understanding that Timon's change in fortune is not a sufficient justification for universal outrage because it stems from pride in his former circumstances rather than from a genuinely activistic desire to influence those circumstances. Apemantus' subsequent contention that, "the middle of humanity thou [Timon] never knewst, / but the extremity of both ends" (300–1) invalidates Timon's vitriol as egotism rather than satire as Timon lacks the type of deep understanding of the vices prevalent at all levels of humanity that motivates a true satirist to create negative perceptual translations for a social purpose.

Where Timon comes closest to the activistic nature of satire is his uneasy speculation on the consequences of satire's often radical iconoclastic impulse, a meta-satiric moment much like those in *Troilus and Cressida*. Just as Ulysses expresses concern over the power of the individual will to destabilize sanctioned images of authority, Timon asks the satirist, "What wouldst thou do with the / world, Apemantus, if it lay in thy power?" "Give it the beasts, to be rid of the men," Apemantus replies (4.3.321–323). Timon then argues that should Apemantus overthrow the orthodox world and descend to the level of the beasts, he would inevitably be overcome either by his own viciousness, or by the viciousness of those unfettered by traditional notions of decorum:

> If thou wert the lion, the fox would
> beguile thee; if thou wert the lamb, the fox would eat thee...
> if thou wert the wolf, thy greediness would afflict thee,
> ....
> What beast couldst thou be, that were not
> subject to a beast?
>
> (328–344)

Timon's brief attempt to reform the actions of another through unpleasant perceptual translation (the satirist as various beasts) accords well with the Juvenalian mode, and as such, Apemantus is content: "If thou couldst please me with speaking to / me, thou mightst have hit upon it here. The common- / wealth of Athens is become a forest of beasts" (346–348).

However, Shakespeare quickly returns Timon to his fruitless curses, which seems to provoke Apemantus into a Marstonian awareness of the futility of offering satiric "counsel" to one who is willfully impervious to revised, ridiculing images of his own errors. With no possibility that Timon will achieve the kind of self-awareness that could motivate change, the distinction between the two figures collapses, and both satirist and misanthropist indulge in the most pointless aspects of invective criticism, alternatively hurling base insults such as "Beast!" / "Slave!" / "Toad!" / "Rogue, rogue, rogue!" (371–374). Here, the meta-satire demonstrates the frequent failure of the Juvenalian mode: without purpose to justify the animosity, the mode can (and sometimes does) offer only futile misanthropic abuse, exactly what many objected to during the Poets' War period. Apemantus, and the satiric ideology he embodies, vanish from the play at this point because he has failed his purpose. In order for the activistic element of satire to be effective, the targets must be sensitive to manipulations of their public image, and Timon lacks the capacity for introspection. Timon's scathing assaults late in the play are as self-serving as his munificence was early in the play, just empty "words, words, words" (*Hamlet*, 2.2.192).

Notes

1 All quotes from Shakespeare's plays are taken from the Riverside edition, 2nd edition, edited by G. Blakemore Evans et al., Houghton Mifflin, 1997.
2 Dowden, Edward. *Shakespeare: A Critical Study of His Mind and Art*. 3rd edition, Harper and Brothers, 1875, pp. vi–vii. Uploaded by American Libraries, 19 June 2011, archive.org/details/shaksperecritica00dowd.
3 See Campbell's *Comicall Satyre and Shakespeare's Troilus and Cressida*, p. 186.
4 See Bednarz, James. *Shakespeare and the Poets' War*. Columbia University Press, 2001. See p. 9. The quote from *Satiromastix* is from the prefatory epistle "To the World." See *The Dramatic Works of Thomas Dekker*, edited by Fredson Bowers, Vol. 1, Cambridge University Press, 1953. See lines 6–9.
5 Fleay, Frederick Gard. *A Chronicle History of the Life and Work of William Shakespeare: Player, Poet, and Playmaker*. J. C. Nimmo, 1886. Uploaded by Harvard University, 2008. archive.org/details/achroniclehisto01fleagoog. See pp. 36–37.
6 "Introduction." *Troilus and Cressida*, edited by David Bevington, Arden Three Edition, Thomas Nelson and Sons, 1998, p. 10.
7 See Joseph F. Loewenstein, "Personal Material: Jonson and Book-Burning." *Re-Presenting Ben Jonson: Text, History, Performance*, edited by Martin Butler, Macmillan Press, 1999, pp. 93–113. The quote is on p. 97. See also Clare, Janet. '*Art Made Tongue-Tied by Authority': Elizabethan and Jacobean Dramatic Censorship*, 2nd edition, Manchester University Press, 1999.
8 Frank Kerins concurs with Campbell's position. See Kerins, Frank. "The Crafty Enchaunter: Ironic Satires and Jonson's Every Man Out of His Humour." *Renaissance Drama*, vol. 14, 1983, pp. 125–150.
9 Riggs, David. *Ben Jonson: A Life*. Harvard University Press, 1989. See p. 58.
10 Campbell, Oscar J. *Shakespeare's Satire*. Oxford University Press, 1943.
11 Jonson, Ben. "To the Reader." *Poetaster*. *Ben Jonson*, edited by C. H. Herford and Percy Simpson, vol. 4, Clarendon Press, 1932. See lines 184–186; 102; 85.
12 See Bevington, David. *Tudor Drama and Politics: A Critical Approach to Topical Meaning*. Harvard University Press, 1968; Fleay, Frederick. *A Chronicle History of the London Stage: 1599–1642*. Reeves and Turner,

1890; Honigmann, E. A. J. *John Weever: A Biography of a Literary Associate of Shakespeare and Jonson*. Manchester University Press, 1987, pp. 42–56, and *Shakespeare's Impact on His Contemporaries*. Palgrave-Macmillan, 1982; Steggle, Matthew. *Wars of the Theatres: The Poetics of Personation in the Age of Jonson*. English Literary Studies, University of Victoria, 1998; and James Bednarz, *Shakespeare and the Poets' War*. Columbia University Press, 2001, pp. 133–165 and 278. See also Duncan-Jones, Katherine. *Ungentle Shakespeare*, Arden Shakespeare, 2001; Finkelpearl, Philip J. *John Marston of the Middle Temple*. Harvard University Press, 1969, p. 167; and Steggle, pp. 40–48. For a reading of Jaques as a typical melancholy satirist, see Sujata Chaudhuri. "Shakespeare and the Elizabethan Satire Tradition." *Shakespeare Commemoration Volume*, edited by Taraknath Sen, Presidency College, Calcutta, 1966, cited by Birney, Alice L. *Satiric Catharsis in Shakespeare*. University of California Press, 1973, p. 80. The equation of Malvolio and Jonson is David Riggs' in *Ben Jonson: A Life*. Harvard University Press, 1989, p. 84.

13 Bednarz, pp. 32–33. Bednarz notes that in *The Metamorphosis of Ajax* (1596), John Harrington "encouraged his readers to pronounce the hero's name with a stress on the second syllable ("a jakes"; p. 33), and he notes similar puns in *Ulysses Upon Ajax* and in Thomas Nashe's pamphlet *Have with You to Saffron-Walden* (both 1596).

14 See, for example, Honigmann's suppositions that Weever was personated on stage as Thersites, Slender, and Andrew Aguecheek (*John Weever*, pp. 49–51). The term "Problem Play" applied to *Measure for Measure, All's Well That Ends Well, Timon of Athens*, and *Troilus and Cressida* was coined by F. S. Boas in 1896. See Ure, Peter. *Shakespeare: The Problem Plays*. Longman Group, 1961.

15 See Bevington's Arden Three edition, pp. 3–5; *Troilus and Cressida*. Edited by Anthony Dawson, Cambridge University Press, 2003. See pp. 1–6; Sacharoff, Mark. "The Tradition of the Troy-Story Heroes and the Problem of Satire in *Troilus and Cressida*." *Shakespeare Studies*, vol. 6, no. 1, 1972 for 1970, pp. 125–135; *Timon of Athens*. Edited by Anthony Dawson and Gretchen Minton, Arden Three Edition, Cengage Learning, 2008. See p. 35. See also Kernan, p. 252.

16 Spencer, Luke. *Self and Society in Shakespeare's Troilus and Cressida and Measure for Measure*. Edited by John Jowett and R. K. S. Taylor, University of Leeds Press, 1982, pp. 80–94. See p. 81. The notion that *Troilus and Cressida* demeans ideas of Honor and Chivalry comes from Bevington's Arden edition of the play, pp. 19–33.

17 It should be noted that Bednarz, too, uses the term "meta-satiric" in reference to the Jaques-Touchstone "subplot" of *As You Like It*, but for Bednarz, the meta-satire is limited to advancing Shakespeare's native "festive comedy" over Jonson's neoclassical comical satire. See p. 106.

18 The quotation is from Nathaniel Leonard's essay "Metatheatricality and the Interaction of Representational Layers in *A Midsummer Night's Dream*" delivered at the 2017 SAA seminar, "Meta-Shakespeare." I owe a debt of thanks to all of the participants for offering insights into Shakespeare's metadramatic structures. The final quotation is from Spanos, William V. "What Was Postmodernism?" *Contemporary Literature*, vol. 31, no. 1, 1990, pp. 108–115. JSTOR, www.jstor.org/stable/1208640.

19 Calderwood, James L. *Shakespearean Metadrama: The Argument of the Play in Titus Andronicus, Love's Labour's Lost, Romeo and Juliet, A Midsummer Night's Dream, and Richard II*. University of Minnesota Press, 1971. See p. 4.

20 Steiner, Peter. "Preface." *Russian Formalism: A Metapoetics*. Ithaca: Cornell University Press, 1984, p. 10. www.jstor.org/stable/10.7591/j.ctt1g69xpg.3.
21 Bourdieu, Pierre. *Language and Symbolic Power*. Edited by John B. Thompson, translated by Gino Raymond and Matthew Adamson, Harvard University Press, 1991. See pp. 84–85.
22 The quote is from *The Second Part of the Return from Parnassus*, 4.3.1766, where Kempe argues that Shakespeare and Jonson have bested such university wits as Marston, Dekker, and Thomas Nash.
23 Ramsey, Jarold W. "The Provenance of Troilus and Cressida." *Shakespeare Quarterly*, vol. 21, no. 3, 1970, pp. 223–240. See p. 237.
24 See Campbell, p. 191. Also, see Taylor, Gary. "*Troilus and Cressida*: Bibliography, Performance, and Interpretation." *Shakespeare Studies*, vol. 15, 1982, pp. 99–136; Jensen, Phebe. "The Textual Politics of *Troilus and Cressida*. *Shakespeare Quarterly*, vol. 46, no. 4, 1995, pp. 414–423. Elton, W. R. *Troilus and Cressida and the Inns of Court Revels*. Ashgate, 2000.
25 Dawson, Anthony. Review of *Troilus and Cressida and the Inns of Court Revels*, by W. R. Elton. *Modern Language Review*, vol. 97, no. 2, 2002, p. 391.
26 See Greenfield, Matthew. "Fragments of Nationalism in *Troilus and Cressida*." *Shakespeare Quarterly*, vol. 51, 2000, pp. 181–200. See p. 181.
27 Kaula offers a similar supposition: "As William Empson remarks, Troy, like all large towns in Shakespeare's plays, is analogous to London, and its dilemma reflects the author's uneasy premonition of civil war." Kaula, David "Will and Reason in *Troilus and Cressida*." *Shakespeare Quarterly*, vol. 12, no. 3, 1961, pp. 271–283. See p. 271.
28 Gray's Inn stood in the parish of Portpool (Finkelpearl 40).
29 The first quotation is from Bakhtin's *Problems of Dostoevsky's Poetics* (17) and the second quote is from Bakhtin's *Rabelais and His World*, translated by Helene Iswolsky, Indiana University Press, 1984. See p. 89.
30 Gras, Henk. "*Twelfth Night, Every Man Out of His Humour*, and the Middle Temple Revels of 1597–1598." *Modern Language Review*, vol. 84, no. 3, 1989, pp. 545–564. Quotation is from p. 557. Quotations from *Every Man Out of His Humour* are taken from *The Cambridge Edition of the Works of Ben Jonson*. Edited by David Bevington et al., vol. 1, Cambridge University Press, 2012. Quote is from Randall Martin's introduction, p. 247.
31 Watson, Jackie. "Satirical Expectations: Shakespeare's Inns of Court Audiences." *Actes de Congrès de la Société Française Shakespeare* 33 (2015). http://shakespeare.revues.org/3352. Jonas Barish argues that Jonson "clearly is thinking of the play now as a reading experience rather than a theatrical experience, as a literary entity, with its own rules," as the title page of the First Quarto suggests. See Barish, Jonas. "Jonson and the Loathed Stage." *A Celebration of Ben Jonson*, edited by William Blissett et al., University of Toronto Press, 1973. See p. 33.
32 Martindale, Joanna. "The Best master of Virtue and Wisdom: The Horace of Ben Jonson and his Heirs." *Horace Made New: Horatian Influences on British Writing from the Renaissance to the Twentieth-Century*, edited by Charles Martindale and David Hopkins, Cambridge University Press, 1993, pp. 50–85. Quote is from p. 57.
33 Shuger, Debora, p. 76. See Chapter 1, note 26.
34 See R.C. Horne, Chapter 3, note 53.
35 See Hall's *Virgidemiarim*, Book Five, satire three, line one. The quotes from *Troilus and Cressida* occur at 2.1.21 and 26.
36 The dialogized structure of many verse satires is discussed in Chapter 3.
37 See Weever's *The Whipping of the Saytre*, line 277, for example.

38 Geoffrey Bullough, *Narrative and Dramatic Sources of Shakespeare*. Edited by Geoffrey Bullough, vol. 6, Columbia University Press, 1966, pp. 81–221. Both William Caxton (*The Recuyell of the Histories of Troy*; circa 1474) and John Lydgate (*The History Siege and Destruction of Troy*; 1513) record how Troilus was assaulted and disarmed by Achilles' Myrmidons, and how Achilles then slew him (Bullough, pp. 184; 214).
39 See Charnes, Linda. *Notorious Identity: Materializing the Subject in Shakespeare*. Harvard University Press, 1993.
40 See the concept of the "loser's epic" in Quint, David. *Epic and Empire: Politics and Generic Form from Virgil to Milton*. Princeton University Press, 1993. See p. 9.
41 The quotation, "a cynic and a hater of humanity," is from *Timon of Athens*. Edited by John Jowett, Oxford University Press, 2004, p. 77.
42 For two sources on the "effeminacy" or sodomitry associated with Timon's relationship to his flatterers, see Prendergast, Maria Teresa M. *Railing, Reviling, and Invective in English Literary Culture, 1588–1617: The Anti-Poetics of Theater and Print*. Routledge, 2016 (Ashgate 2012); and Greene, Jody. "'You Must Eat Men': The Sodomitic Economy of Renaissance Patronage." *Gay and Lesbian Quarterly*, vol. 1, 1994, pp. 163–197. Prendergast comments how, "Greene argues that the pathologies of *Timon* result from an economy of patronage in which 'the boundaries of friendship and sodomy collapse'" (186). Prendergast, however, argues that the flatterers' homoerotic desire for Timon transfers to his wealth (see note 57 in Prendergast's introduction).
43 Dawson and Minton provide a full overview of scholarly opinions concerning which scenes in *Timon* were written by Shakespeare alone, or by Middleton alone, and those scenes that seem to have been written collaboratively, although the editors contend that every scene suggests high degrees of "cross-fertilization" (4). Of the scenes under consideration here, Dawson and Minton argue that 1.1 seems to be wholly Shakespearean, 1.2 wholly Middletonian, 2.1 is ambiguous, and 4.3 is primarily by Shakespeare. The paraphrased quote is from Dawson and Minton, p. 4.
44 Painter, William. *The Palace of Pleasure* (1566). Edited by Joseph Jacobs, D. Nutt, 1890. Digitized by Google from an edition held by Harvard University Library, 5 July 2009, archive.org/stream/palacepleasuree00haslgoog/palace pleasuree00haslgoog_djvu.txt, p. 112. For other sources on Shakespeare's sources for *Timon*, see Dawson and Minton's Arden Three edition; Bond, Warwick R. "Lucian and Boiardo in *Timon of Athens*." *The Modern Language Review*, vol. 26, no. 1, 1931, pp. 52–68; and Honigmann, E. A. J. "Timon of Athens." *Shakespeare Quarterly*, vol. 12, no. 1, 1961, pp. 3–20.
45 Skeat, Walter W. *Shakespeare's Plutarch: A Selection from the Lives in North's Plutarch Which Illustrate Shakespeare's Plays*. Macmillan, 1875. See p. 215.
46 See John Weever's *The Whipping of the Satyre* (1601), 334–336, where the conservative speaker rails at the Juvenalians with, "And whom you pleased, did liberally defame. / For shall we his by right a Libel call, / That touched but some? Not yours, that aimed at all?"
47 Barroll, Leeds. "Inventing the Stuart Masque." *The Politics of the Stuart Court Masque*, edited by David Bevington and Peter Holbrook, Cambridge University Press, 1998, pp. 121–143. See p. 121.

Index

Abedin, Huma 98
Abel, Lionel 135
Abu-Ras, Wahiba 12
Achilles (character) 147
1554 Act Concerning the Regal Power 120–1
The Actes of Queen Elizabeth Allegorized (Wodwall) 113
Act in Restraint of Appeals 38
activistic satire 14–18, 22–3, 74–5
Act of Supremacy (1559) 113
Act of Uniformity (1559) 47
Alamanni, Luigi 50
al-Assad, Bashar 6
al-Baghdadi, Abu Bakr 8
The Albasheer Show 8
Albasheer, Ahmed 8
al Bernameg 7
Albright, Madeleine 96
Aldington, Richard 67
Amazon image 100–1
American Idol 6
Anatomy of Criticism (Frye) 5
Anderson, William 37
anti-feminism 30, 66–7; *see also* specific works; satire and the Bishops' Ban 67, 96–122; social regulation and 101–7
anti-ISIS satires 8–9
Apemantus 150–6
appearance and essence 88
Arcadia (Sidney) 90
Aretino, Pietro 71
Aristophanes 101
Ars Poetica (Horace) 43
The Arte of English Poesie (Puttenham) 15, 46
The Art of Satire (Worcester) 4
Ascham, Roger 47
Astrea iconography 113

As You Like It (Shakespeare) 130, 133, 134, 142–3
Augustus 72
authority, centralization of 21–2
Axton, Marie 140

Bakhtin, Mikhail 21, 26–8, 36, 108, 140, 151
Ballaster, Rosalind 103
ban: Bishops' Ban of 1599, 20, 21, 27, 30–1, 38, 64–92, 96–122; on satiric production 27, 29
Bancroft, Richard 67
Banksy's art exhibit 18
Barclay, Alexander 57
Barclay, John 30
Barnfield, Richard 132
Barthes, Roland 4
Bates, Catherine 50
Baumgartner, Jody 20
Baumlin, James 80
Beardsley, Monroe 4
Beauvoir, Simone de 119
Bednarz, James 120, 128, 133
Beeshu (character) 6
Behn, Aphra 103
Bell, Ilona 106
Benedick 127
Betts, Hannah 121
Bevington, David 128, 133, 137
bin Laden, Osama 10
Bishops' Ban of 1599, 20, 21, 27, 30–1, 38, 64–92; anti-feminist satire and 96–122; due to linguistic indecency 67; John Weever's defense of 90–2; libel 68–9; of *Of Marriage and Wiving* 114–22; nature of 66–71; objection to misogyny 114–15; rising influence of Juvenalianism 70–1; stylistics and

accountability 69–70; of *XV Joys of Marriage* 107–14
"Biting Satires" (Halls) 70, 75–8
blasphemy *versus* freedom of expression 10–14
bodily and spiritual imperfection of women 117–18
Bogel, Fredric 3, 5, 71
Boleyn, Anne 121
The Book Named the Governour (Elyot) 47
Book of Common Prayer 47
Bourdieu, Pierre 26, 39, 64–5, 136
Brant, Sebastian 57
Breitenberg, Mark 101, 110
Breton, Nicholas 90
Bryan, Francis 50
Buckridge, Patrick 84
Burrow, Claude 50, 51
Burrow, Colin 43, 45
Burton, Robert 30
Butler, Judith 98–9, 112, 119

Calderwood, James 135
Callaghan, Dympna 103
Caltha Poetarum (Dymoke) 9, 66, 114
Calvinism 85–6
Camden, William 53, 106
Campbell, Oscar 2, 67, 78, 128–30, 132, 138, 150
The Cankered Muse (Kernan) 30
The Canterbury Tales (Chaucer) 57
carnivalization 140–1
Carnival rituals 29, 138–40
Catherine of Aragon 56
Catholics influencing English national affairs 47–9, 56–7
censorship: during Bishops' Ban of 1599, 12–14, 64–92; hermeneutics of 64; influenced by nepotism 71; regulating defamatory language 90; of *South Park* 10–11
centrifugal-centripetal binary 21–2
centripetal-centrifugal binary 21–2
centripetal satire 40–1, 45, 72, 77–88, 98; of Ben Jonson 141–2; of William Shakespeare 142–3
Chapman, George 128
Charbonnier, Stéphane 10
Charles V, king of England 52
Charlie Hebdo 2015 attack on 10, 11
Charnes, Linda 148
Chaucer Geoffrey 57, 108

City of Ladies (Pisan) 103
Clarence House 12
Clegg, Cyndia 68–9, 71, 81, 115
Clinton, Bill 98
Clinton, Hillary Rodham: satire to translate image of 96–8; translations of identity of 97–9
Coldiron 108, 109, 111
Colley, Scott 85
comedy, topical 13
Comedy of Errors (Shakespeare) 138
Comicall Satyre and Shakespeare's Troilus and Cressida (Campbell) 2, 128
Commodus (character) 48–9
conservative revolutionary persona 18, 51
Content, Rob 113
Coriolanus (Shakespeare) 129
Cressida (character) 147–9
cynicism in satire 150–6
"A Cynic Satire" (Marston) 88–90

The Daily Show 7
Dante 35–6
Dasenbrock, Reed 49
Das Narrenschiff (Brant) 57
Davenport, Arnold 71, 73, 90
Davies, John 66, 70, 142
Davis, Joel 52
Davis, Natalie 102
Dawson, Anthony 133, 138
The Defence of Poesy (Sidney) 15, 46
"Defiance to Envy" (Hall) 74
Deighton, Kenneth 127
Dekker, Thomas 128
De Ratione Studii (Erasmus) 44
Derrida, Jacques 4
De Tradendis Disciplinis (Vives) 44
Devereux, Robert 68
dialogic exchange 26
The Dialogic Imagination (Bakhtin) 28
A Discourse of Marriage and Wiving 110
"Dismaland Bemusement Park" 18
distance in satiric imitation 16, 19, 28, 73, 83–4, 136–7, 150
divine right of kings 120–1
Domitian 72
Donne, John 70
Dorp, Martin 44
Dowden, Edward 127
dramatic satire 128–9

Drant, Thomas 14, 38, 45; endorsement of Horatianism 47–9; endorsing stability and coherence of English empire 48–9; translations of Horace's works 45–7
Drayton, Michael 53
Dryden, John 2, 16, 19, 37, 40
Duncan-Jones, Katherine 132
Durling, Robert 35
Dymoke 71, 79–80

Eastwood, Clint 23
Edward VI, king of England 57
Egerton, Thomas 81
Elizabethan image, satiric threat to: in *Of Marriage and Wiving* 114–22; in *XV Joys of Marriage* 107–14
Elizabeth I, queen of England 47–8; gender image of 112–14; refusal to marry 105–6
Elliott, Robert 5, 9, 15
el-Sisi, Abdel Fattah 7
Elthelbert, king of Kent 54
Elton, W. R. 138
Elyot, Thomas 46–7
empire and satire 35–58
enclosure of grazing lands 77–9
England: foreign influence on national affairs 48; influence of Catholicism 47–9, 56–7; nationalistic ideology 49–54; patronage system of 152; regulating satirical media 12–14, 20, 27, 30–1, 38, 64–92; reinforcing national identity of 21, 37–9, 82, 87–8; religion mixed with politics in 67–8; Thomas Wyatt fostering nationalistic ideology 49–54
English Humour play 128
English imitative satires 49–58; *see also* specific works
"Epic and Novel" (Bakhtin) 28
Epic poetry 28
Epigrams (Davies) 66, 70
Epistles (Horace) 43
epistolary satires 50, 55–6
Erasmus 30, 43, 44, 57
Esler, Anthony 87
essence and appearance 88
Essex, Earl of 68–9
Every Man in His Humour (Jonson) 128
Every Man Out of His Humour (Jonson) 127, 140–1, 147

The Faerie Queene (Spenser) 39, 114
Familiarum Rerum Libri (Petrarch) 44
Faunus and Melliflora (Weever) 90
Feichtinger, Barbara 105
female *see* women
Ferzat, Ali 6, 9, 12, 31
Fey, Tina 20
The Fictions of Satire (Paulson) 4
The Field of Cultural Production (Bourdieu) 26, 39
A Fig for Momus (Lodge) 70
Finkelpearl, Philip 87, 139
Fleay, Frederick 127–8, 132
formalism 3–5, 26
formal verse satire 66, 70
Fortescue, John 122
Fowler, Alastair 54
Freccero, Carla 102
freedom: endorsement of in satire 71; of expression *versus* blasphemy 10–14; of speech 10–12; unrestrained 80–2
Freudenburg, Kirk 37, 42, 49
Frye, Northrop 5, 17, 24

Gaddafi, Muammar 6
gender: -based ideologies and satire 96; power and 96–7; power hierarchy 109–11; regulation and anti-feminism satire 105, 116
Gender Trouble (Butler) 98
George I, king of England 2
Gill, R. B. 5
Gleckman, Jason 54
Gorboduc 114
Governance of England (Fortescue) 122
Gras, Henk 141
Greenblatt, Stephen 51
Greene, Jody 152
Greene, Roland 49
Grey, Jane 56
Griffin, Dustin 3, 5, 13, 67
Guilhamet, Leon 5, 17
Guilpin, Everard 20, 66, 68, 70, 90
Guthrie, Alice 9

Habinek, Thomas 37
Hall, Joseph 38, 66, 69–70; "Biting Satires" 75–8; horatian mode of satire 72–5; imitative satire of 71–80; Juvenalian mode of satire 75–7; satire of enclosuring of

Index

grazing lands 77–9; "Toothless Satires" 72–5
Hamlet (Shakespeare) 129, 130
Harvey, Gabriel 66, 70–1
Hasteley, Helen Lewis 13
Haugerud, Angelique 18
Haydn, Hiram 87
Hayward, John 68
Hector (character) 148
Helgerson, Richard 38
Henry IV (Shakespeare) 129
Henry V (Shakespeare) 68
Henry VIII, king of England 38, 50, 111
heteroglossia 30, 41
heteroglot language 28–9
Hic Mulier: or the Man-Woman 102
hijá 9
Historicist-formalist binary 1–5
historicity and temporal specificity of satiric 1–5, 18–19
Histriomastix (Marston) 128
Hobson, Christopher 51
Honigmann, E. A. J. 132
Horace 19, 142; being imitated by Hall 71–5; as a centripetal satirist 40–1, 45, 79–80; having imperialistic ideology 37–8; imitated by Thomas Wyatt 50, 51, 55; juxtaposing negative and positive moral *exempla* 42; as model 43–7; as moral satirist 35–7; paternalistic ideologies of family and nation 42; relationship to fields of power 39–41; translated by Thomas Drant 45–9
Horatianism 36, 37–9, 49, 71; endorsed by Thomas Drant 47–9; in English Renaissance scholarship 45–7; focusing on human potential 43; having little antagonism with the dominant fraction 40; humanism and 42–58; in satires of Thomas Drant and Thomas Wyatt 47–57
Horne, R. C. 85–6, 89
humanism and Horatianism 42–58
An Humorous Daye's Mirth (Chapman) 128
humourous defects in women 117
Hutcheon, Linda 17, 24–5

ideological reorientation 96–7
ideologies of Otherness 101
ideology of satire 14, 18, 20, 22–4

image translation 18
imitative satire 45–7, 49–58
Imperial Britain 38–9; *see also* England
indecency, linguistic in satires 67
Inferno (Dante) 35–6
Inns of Court Revels ceremonies 138–40, 142
intentionality of satirist 16–17, 22, 24, 30, 51, 56
"Invisible [President] Obama" 22–3
Irigary, Luce 99, 119
ironic social performances 18
irony 24–5
Irony's Edge (Hutcheon) 24
ISIS (Islamic State in Iraq and Syria) satires 8–9
Islamic fundamentalism being satirized 8–12

James, Heather 37, 139
James, king of England 150
Jameson, Fredric 101
Jensen, Phebe 138
Jerome 101
Jonson, Ben 20, 30, 82, 90, 127–8, 140–1, 144–5; centripetal satire of 141–2; *Every Man in His Humour* 128; *Every Man Out of His Humour* 127, 140–1, 147; *Poetaster* 82, 128, 131, 142, 144; satirical form of 128–9; Shakespeare using Jonsonian satiric principle 129–30
Juvenal 2, 19, 22, 39–40, 42, 44, 46, 50, 66, 91, 101, 116; being imitated by Hall 71–2, 75–7; imitated by John Marston 80–2
Juvenalianism 150; Horatianist brand of 79; Juvenalian satires being banned 66–7; rise of in philosophical uncertainty 87; rising influence of 70–1; spectrum of 71–90
Jyllands-Posten 10

Keener, Andrew 104
Kent (England) and its political autonomy and nationalist significance 53–4
Kernan, Alvin 15, 17, 30, 38, 51, 57, 71, 85, 87, 108, 150–1
Kett Rebellion of 1549, 77
King John (Shakespeare) 129
Knapp, Jeffrey 49
Knight, Charles 1, 5, 15, 17, 20, 21
Kraidy, Marwan 8, 9

Langland, William 57
Lanyer, Amelia 103
Lawrence, W. W. 127
Law Sports 139
lesbian typology as threat to masculinity 98, 99–100
Levin, Carole 112, 120
Lewinsky, Monica 98
libel and censorship 68–9
The Life and Raigne of Henry IIII (Hayward) 68
linguistic indecency and censorship 67
Lives (Plutarch) 151
Lodge, Thomas 70
Love, Nancy 14
Love's Labour Lost (Shakespeare) 129
Lucilius 40, 42, 81

Mack, Maynard 3–4
Maclean, I. 118
magic and satire 5
male identity reinvigorated by anti-feminism 101–3
Man, Paul de 4
Mandelbaum, Allen 36
marriage: linked to misogynistic images of women's imperfections 105–6; in *XV Joys of Marriage* 107–14
Marston, John 14, 20, 22, 31, 66, 70, 72, 79, 128, 131, 146; "A Cynic Satire" 88–90; authority of individual free will 80–2; criticism of in 16th century 83–4; imitating Juvenal 80–2; John Weever's response to 90–2; populist philosophy of 82–5; rejection of humanistic ideological principles 88–90; religious philosophy of 85–6; satiric orientation to England 82; use of everyday language 82–4
Martin, Randall 141
Martin, Richard 142
Martindale, Charles 37
Martindale, Kathleen 101
Mary I, queen of England 47, 103, 112, 119–20
Mary Tudor 56
Masasit Mati 6, 9
The Masque of Pallas 114
Mattern, Mark 14
McCabe, Richard 65, 71
McCain, John 20
McEachern, Claire 38, 39, 49
McLeod, Bruce 38

McPherson, David 70
Measure for Measure (Shakespeare) 129
Melancthon, Philip 43
menippea 151
menippean satire 29–30, 108–9
Menippus of Gadara 29
The Metamorphosis of Pigmalion's Image and Certain Satires (Marston) 70
metapoetics 135–6
meta-satire 134–43; in *Timon of Athens* (Shakespeare) 149–56; in *Troilus and Cressida* 144–9
metatheatre 135
Metatheatre: A New View of Dramatic Form (Abel) 135
Micro-Cynicon: Six Snarling Satires (Middleton) 70
Middle Eastern satire 6
Middle East sociopolitics 8–10
Middleton, Catherine 12
Middleton, Thomas 66, 70, 150
A Midsummer Night's Dream (Shakespeare) 104
military conflicts and presence of satire 6
Miller, Anthony 50
Milton, John 73
"Mine Own John Poyntz" (Wyatt) 50, 52–5, 79, 103–4
Minton, Gretchen 134
The Mirror of Modestie 110
misanthropy 152
Miscellany (Tottel) 56
The Misfortunes of Arthur 114
misogynistic satire 97–8; in *XV Joys of Marriage* 114–22
monarchial authority 120–2
Monmouth, Duke of 2
Montagu, Mary Wortley 103
Montrose, Louis 72, 107
Moore, Edward 36
More, Thomas 30, 44, 57
Morsi, Mohamed 7
Mother Hubberd's Tale (Spenser) 57
Mubarak, Hosni 6, 7
Muhammad and cartoon representations of 10, 11
Mukherjee, Neel 47–8
Muslim Brotherhood 7
Muslims and prejudice against 12
"Muslims in America, post-9/11" (Abu-Ras) 12
"My Mother's Maids" (Wyatt) 50

166 Index

Nashe, Thomas 66, 70–1
nationalism 38–9, 41; being challenged by philosophical uncertainty 72, 87–8; reinforced by Thomas Wyatt 49–54; satiric 17, 21, 37–8
nepotism influencing censorship 71
nihilism 86–7
nominanza 35
North, Thomas 151
Nott, G. F. 50
No Whipping, nor Tripping: but a Kind Friendly Snipping (Breton) 90
Nussbaum, Felicity 100, 118

Of Marriage and Wiving (Tasso and Tasso) 66, 67; being banned 104–5, 107; satiric threat to Elizabethan image 114–22
Old Arcadia (Sidney) 113
Old Historicist Chicago School of satiric criticism 3
Oliensis, Ellen 37
Oliver, John 13
Orazio satiro 35–6, 40
Outhwaite, R. B. 77
Oxfordshire Enclosure Riots (1596) 77

pagan authors in Christian context 35–6
Page, William 107
Painter, William 150
The Palace of Pleasure (Painter) 150
Palin, Sarah 20
Papal Bull of 1570, 121
Parker, Trey 10–11
parlilamentary procedures not allowed in satirical context 13
Parnassus plays 83–4
parody 2, 6, 8, 17, 49, 145
Parsons, Ben 71
patriarchal regulatory system in satire 99–101
patronage system: in England 152; Roman 41
Patterson, Annabel 64, 66
Paulson, Ronald 4, 15, 17
perceptual translation 8–10, 20–1
performative aesthetic 14–16
Persius 42
Pertinax (character) 48–9
Peter, John 57, 58
Petrarch 44–5
Petrarchism 49
Phiddian, Robert 4, 25

Philip II, king of Spain 75
Phylo (Marston) 84–5
Piers Plowman (Langland) 57
Pisan, Christine de 103
plowman tradition of satire 57–8
Plutarch 151
Poetaster (Jonson) 82, 128, 131, 142, 144
Poetomachia 127–8
Poets' War 127–8, 130
political attacks 20, 22–3
politics with religion in England 67–8
Poly-Olbion (Drayton) 53
Pope, Alexander 101
populism in imitative poetics 80
power and gender 96–7
The Power of Satire: Magic, Ritual, Art (Elliott) 5
The Praise of Folly (Erasmus) 44, 57
Prescott, Anne Lake 29–30
Privy Council of Queen Elizabeth 67–8
Problems of Dostoevsky's Poetics (Bakhtin) 29
public perceptions being changed by satire 8–10
public performative aesthetic 14–16
Purkiss, Diane 102
Puttenham, George 15, 46

Quintero, Ruben 12

Rabelais, François 19
Rabelais and His World (Bakhtin) 29
rack-renting 77
Ramsey, Jarold 137, 139
Rankins, William 70
religion with politics in England 67–8
revolutionary conservative approach to satire 51, 79
Reynolds, Suzanne 36, 43
Richard II (Shakespeare) 104
Riggs, David 129
Roman system of patronage 41
Rome as national authority 43
Romeo and Juliet (Shakespeare) 129
Romney, Mitt 23
Rosenheim, Edward 4
Rudov, Marc 96
The Rules of Art (Bourdieu) 26
ruling class conventions, satire of 140

Sacharoff, Mark 133
Salve Deus Rex Judeorum (Lanyer) 103

Index 167

satire: activistic 14–17, 22–4, 36, 74–5; adapted to the stage 128–9; anti-feminist 96–122; banning of by the Bishops 20, 21, 27, 30–1, 38, 64–92; chronotopic structure of 18–19, 55–6; critique of ruling class conventions 140; defining features of 1; dialogic and socially engaged nature of 10–12; dramatic 128–9; effects of 25–6; empire and 35–58; English imitative 49–58; epistolary 50, 55–6; formal verse 66, 70; ideological threat to authority 14; as imitation of Juvenal 71; impact on ideological perceptions 14, 18, 20, 22–4; magic and 5; menippean 29–30, 108–9; nationalistic 21; native English 57–8; perceptual translation of 8–10; plowman tradition of 57–8; presence in military conflicts 6; reacting to historical forces 2–5; rhetoric of 3–4; Shakespearean 127–56; sociological approach to 27–8; study of 25–31; temporal specificity of historicity 18–19; topical comedy being different than 13; topical referentiality of 2, 4–5; as a weapon 9
Satire 1.5 (Horace) 47
Satire 1.9 (Horace) 40–1
Satire 2.6 (Horace) 50, 75
Satires 2.1.34–41 (Horace) 43
satiric nationalism 17, 37–8
satiric slogans 97–8
satiro 35
Satiromastix (Dekker) 128, 131
Scaliger, Julius Caesar 46
Schaefer, Sara 97
The Schoolmaster (Ascham) 47
The Scourge of Villanie (Marston) 70, 80, 131, 146
Second Act of Succession 121
The Second Part of the Return from Parnassus 83
self-defensive formula in Hall's satire 72–4
Semonides 101
Seven Satyres (Rankins) 70
Shaftesbury, Earl of 2
Shakespeare: A Critical Study of His Mind and Art (Dowden) 127
Shakespeare, William 30, 68, 104; *As You Like It* 130, 133, 134, 142–3; *Comedy of Errors* 138; *Coriolanus* 129; cynicism of 150–6; engaging with satire 133–4; *Hamlet* 129, 130; *Henry IV* 129; *Henry V* 68; *King John* 129; *Love's Labour Lost* 129; *Measure for Measure* 129; meta-satire of 134–43; *A Midsummer Night's Dream* 104; non-partisan satiric intentionality 136–7; reflective approach to satire 150; *Richard II* 104; romantic image of, 127; *Romeo and Juliet* 129; satiric intent of 131–3; *The Taming of the Shrew* 104; *Timon of Athens* 129, 133, 134, 149–56; *Troilus and Cressida* 127, 129, 130, 133, 134, 137–8, 144–9, 155; *Twelfth Night* 130, 138; using Jonsonian satiric principle 129–30
Shakespearean satire 127–56
Shakespeare's Satire (Campbell) 129
Shakespeare's Troilus and Cressida and the Inns of Court Revels (Elton) 138
Shakespeare's Troy (James) 139
Sheerin, Brian 121–2
Shelburne, Steven 51
Shuger, Debora 13, 22, 64, 90, 143
Sidney, Philip 15, 46, 90, 113
Sinclair, John 36
"Sixth Satire" and misogyny 115
Skelton, John 57
Skialetheia (Guilpin) 68, 69, 70
slogans, satiric 97–8
social performances, ironic 18
social regulation and anti-feminism 101–7
sociolinguistic systems 26, 27–8
Songs and Sonnets (Tottel) 50
South Park and censorship 10–11
Spacks, Patricia 16
Spencer, Diana 18
"A Spending Hand" (Wyatt) 50
Spenser, Edmund 39, 57, 114
statement of intent 22, 24
State of Myths 8
Stationers Company 65
status quo, ideological stance against 18
Steggle, Matthew 132
Steinem, Gloria 96
Steiner, Peter 136
Stewart, Potter 1
Stone, Matt 10–11
structural subordination 26
Stubbs 106, 112
Swift, Jonathan 2, 14, 101

Index

The Taming of the Shrew (Shakespeare) 104
Tasso, Hercole 66, 67, 104, 114–22
Tasso, Torquato 66, 67, 104, 114–15
Taylor, Gary 138
Templin, Charlotte 98
temporal specificity of satiric historicity 18–19
Tertullian 101
Thersites (character) 146, 147, 148
Thirsk, Joan 77
Thompson, I. A. A. 87
Tilney, Edmund 104
Timon (character) 149, 151–6
Timon of Athens (Shakespeare) 129, 133, 134, 149–56
Tofte, Robert 115
"Toothless" satires of Hall 72–5
"Top Goon: Diaries of a Little Dictator" 6
topicality in satiric literature 2, 4–5, 13
Tottel, Richard 50, 56
translatio imperii 37, 38
Treasons Act (1534) 50, 51
Troilus (character) 147–8
Troilus and Cressida (Shakespeare) 127, 129, 130, 133, 134, 137, 155; Inns of Court Revels ceremonies and 138; meta-satire in 144–9
Troy legend 139, 144, 148
Trump, Donald 97
Twelfth Night (Shakespeare) 130, 138

Ulysses (character) 134, 144–7, 155
Utopia (More) 57

vestiarian controversy 47–8
Villeponteaux, Mary 100
Virgidemiarum (Hall) 69–70, 71, 74
Virgil 35, 142
Vives, Juan Luis 43, 44

Watson, Jackie 141
Weever, John 20–2, 30, 31, 38, 72, 104, 147; response to Marston 90–2
Wentworth, Peter 105, 107, 112
What You Will (Marston) 128
Wheeler, Angela 36

The Whipper of the Satyre (Guilpin) 90
The Whipper Pamphlets 90
The Whipping of the Satyre (Weever) 20, 90
White, Hayden 20
Whitgift, John 65, 67, 69
Who Wants to Be a Millionaire? 6
William, prince of England 12
Wimsatt, Willlam 4
Wittig, Monique 119
Wodwall, William 113
women: being oppressed 31; bodily and spiritual imperfection of 117–18; deficiencies of in satires 96–7, 101; as excluded participants 103; humourous defects in 117; misogyny in *Of Marriage and Wiving* 114–22; misogyny in *XV Joys of Marriage* 107–14; natural excesses being prevented by men 99–102; portrayed as nonexistence 119–20; in power 96–7; as President and satire to sway voters 96–7; submission to patriarchy 102
Woodward, William 43
Worcester, David 4
Wyatt, Thomas 30, 38, 70, 79, 103–4; adapting horatian satire 50, 51, 55; "A Spending Hand" 50; classification of his satires 49–50; fostering nationalistic ideology of England 49–54; "Mine Own John Poyntz" 50, 52–5; "My Mother's Maids" 50
Wyatt, Thomas the Younger 56

The XV Joys of Marriage 66, 67; being banned 104–5, 107–14; bodily and spiritual imperfection of 117–18; Heroic Couplet style of 108; monarch's inseparable material and immaterial bodies 120–1; violations of chastity in 109–10; women as nonexistent 119–20

Yale Formalist School 3
Yates, Frances 113
Youssef, Bassem 6–8, 9, 12